Hear th
Ancient
Wisdom

Hear the
Ancient
Wisdom

Daily readings from the
Early Church to the Reformation

CHARLES R. RINGMA

Originally published in North America by Cascade Books,
199 West 8th Ave, Suite 3, Eugene, OR 97401

First published in Great Britain in 2013

Society for Promoting Christian Knowledge
36 Causton Street
London SW1P 4ST
www.spckpublishing.co.uk

British Library Cataloguing-in-Publication Data
A catalogue record for this book is available from the British Library

ISBN 978-0-281-07112-8

Printed in Great Britain by 4edge Limited

Produced on paper from sustainable forests

For
Adam Duncan Gresley East
and
Hendrika Roelofina Grada East-Aangeenbrug
and
Jordan Hendrik Gresley East
Ruben Derrick Gresley East

and in memoriam for
Daniel Benjamin Gresley East
Toby Adam Gresley East
who died tragically on 12 December 2006

"For since death came through a human being, the resurrection of the
dead has also come through a human being; for as all die in
Adam, so all will be made alive in Christ."
—1 Corinthians 15:21–22

"If tears are still shed in heaven, then carry my tears to the feet of God."
—Giuseppe Verdi in *Don Carlos*

Contents

Preface

This book is but a small offering in that the reader will only gain a limited taste of the wisdom of the early church fathers, the desert fathers, the monastic tradition, the leaders of the church throughout the Middle Ages, leaders of renewal movements, the medieval mystics, and the pre-Reformation reformers.

The reader will meet Justin Martyr, St. Ambrose, St. Augustine, Gregory of Nyssa, St. Basil, St. Jerome, Thomas Aquinas, St. Francis, Bonaventure, Meister Eckhart, Hildegard of Bingen, Julian of Norwich, and John Hus, amongst many other leading figures over these fourteen centuries.

A wonderful outcome in engaging this book would be that the reader, having tasted, might gain a hunger for more. The extensive reference material listed in the endnotes would be a place to start.

The question, however, needs to be posed: why engage Christians who lived such a long time ago? As they sought to live in fidelity to the gospel, were they not simply relevant for their time and not for ours?

The most basic answer to these questions is that these witnesses are part of our tradition. They have left us a legacy and we would do well to afford them a respectful hearing. Moreover, some of them—martyrs, monks, mystics, prophets, healers, theologians, revivalists—are the most exemplary Christians who have ever lived. We do ourselves a disservice not to be challenged by their lives, their writings, and their service. But finally, it could well be that our present-day Christianity, so shaped by the values of modernity, could learn from this ancient wisdom. It is possible that our Christianity could become revitalized and more robust by hearing the ancient wisdom.

Some major qualifiers are in order at this point. Just because I quote Maximus the Confessor or Gertrude the Great or Origen or St. Catherine of Genoa or St. Ephraem of Syrus, I am not, therefore, advocating everything they have written. This book is not a systematic treatment of any of the over seventy authors quoted. Moreover, I am also not entering the scholarly debate about contested dates and authorship of certain documents. The brief historical material I have provided in the index is from standard sources. Finally, this book is not pining for the "good old days." It does not suggest we should go back to the past. It simply suggests we can learn from the wisdom of the past.

This book reflects almost a lifetime of reading. It has been written over a very long period of time and in various countries including Australia, the Philippines, Canada, Myanmar, and The Netherlands.

There are some special places where parts of this book were penned that I particularly wish to acknowledge: the Benedictine Monastery near Mission, British Columbia; the Myoora Retreat Centre of Chris and Marilyn Brown, Currimundi Lake, Queensland; the holiday home of Dr. and Mrs. Paul and Gail Stevens, Ruxton Island, British Columbia; the holiday home of Drs. Terry and Rosie Gatfield, Mt. Tamborine, Queensland; The Winner Inn, Yangon; The Community of Rivendell, Bowen Island, British Columbia; Mt. Archer Christian Community, Woodford, Queensland; the retreat centre of the Sisters of the Cenacle, Metro Manila; the home of Russell and Kay Brothers, Noosa Heads, Queensland; the Bamboo House, Mindoro, Philippines; the home of John Robertson and Dr. Marguerite Robertson, Sunshine Beach, Queensland; the Servants Retreat Centre, Metro Manila; the Thamada Hotel, Yangon; Kathi Bentall's Hermitage, Bowen Island, British Columbia; the home of Rita Petersen, Peregian, Queensland; the S.I.L. Guesthouse, Manila; The Tulip Inn, Franeker, The Netherlands; and the home of Dr. Neil and Sue Paulsen, Indooroopilly, Brisbane.

There are a number of people who have contributed to this book: Bill Reimer from Regent Bookstore gave me valuable information about relevant books; Pieter Kwant, my ever positive literary agent; the staff of Wipf and Stock, who believed in this book, even when the publishing market is deeply in trouble; Ms. Annette Ganter who once again magically turned my handwritten pages into typescript; and Ms. Teresa Jordan who added life to this book with her illustrations. To each I am deeply grateful.

The reader will note that this book does not freeze the voices of the past in the past. Rather, this book seeks to bring them into the present. The voices of the past are meant to enrich and challenge us. May that indeed be the case!

Charles R. Ringma
Brisbane, Australia
2012

Introduction

To write a meaningful historical and theological introduction to a meditational reader that spans some fourteen hundred years of the history, thinking, and praxis of the church, would take much more than the whole of this book. If this is what the reader is wanting, then other sources will need to be consulted.

The introduction, therefore, will need to be much more limited. The focus then will be on what one could possibly gain from a book like this.

This book is meant to be a companion for a year. It is meant to assist you in building into your normal day some time for reflection, meditation, and prayer. This is a reminder that as humans we are to be more than only workers and achievers. We are also meant to be contemplatives.

Life is not only about the busy round of activities and relationships; it is also about withdrawal and the practices of solitude. And it is in these practices we can find insight, renewal, and inspiration. In these spiritual routines we can also gain a better equilibrium as well as health and wellbeing.

But there is more. In spiritual practices we want to grow not only in self-insight, but also in our love for others and in our concern for the world. Meditation is not to feed one's narcissism but one's growth and wholeness that is both self-nurturing and other-regarding.

And while reflective practices may remain at the horizontal level, this reader includes the importance of the transcendental dimensions of human existence. And it does it particularly within the wider Christian tradition. As such, this book acknowledges the importance and value of a faith relationship with God the Creator and Redeemer who, in the face of Christ, has written us the clearest letter of his love and purposes.

In drawing on the wider Christian tradition, this book has specifically focused on what is often the most neglected phase of the tradition—the period from the early church fathers up to the pre-Reformation reformers. But interestingly, some key figures in this period are enjoying a present-day comeback. One is St. Benedict. The other is St. Francis. But so are medieval mystics such as Hildegard of Bingen and Julian of Norwich. And of course, Celtic spirituality is enjoying contemporary interest.

So, what may we gain from reflecting on key sayings of these and many other writers from this period?

The first thing is the sense that all of life is sacred. There is no such thing as a secular sphere and a spiritual sphere. *All* of life is to reflect the goodness and glory of God. All of life is a prayer. St. Benedict's voice is important on this point.

The second thing is the importance of a sacramental view of life. This means normal things may carry and mediate to us a deeper spiritual reality. The world reflects something of the glory of God. Friendship is a symbol of the Trinity. Brotherhood and sisterhood demonstrate the friendship of Christ. Hospitality is a glimpse of the welcome of God. Bread and wine, the presence of Christ. Anointing oil, God's healing presence. Thus, all of life is charged with grandeur of God and is impregnated with the holy. St. Augustine is but one important voice regarding these matters.

Thirdly, while the writers of the ancient wisdom stress the mystery of God, they celebrate God's knowability. They speak of the traces of God in pagan philosophies, the beauty of God in nature, the revelation of God in Scripture, the voice of God in human affairs, the unveiling of God in our dreams, and the presence of God in the sacraments. While for us the knowability of God is such a problem, for them it was a matter of becoming attentive to the many signs already given. Thus, they stressed contemplative practices in order to hear God's voice more clearly. John Cassian has much to teach us here.

Fourthly, the culture of these many centuries was fundamentally hierarchical and patriarchal, and while this was reflected in the church's art and theology, the martyrs, theologians, monks, and mystics in this book speak of an amazing intimacy with God. God for them was like a father and mother. And for some, their intimacy with Christ was of such dimensions that they received the stigmata. St. Anselm speaks much of the motherly compassion of God and St. Francis is a witness to a form of intimacy that resulted in his bearing the marks of Christ.

Fifthly, while the writers of the ancient wisdom celebrated both the knowability and intimacy with God, they nevertheless practiced a committed discipleship. Their passion was to be like Jesus, to obey him, to reflect him in the world, and to do the works of the kingdom of God. Unlike our half-hearted discipleship in the modern world, our ancient forebears knew a lot about the cost of discipleship and clearly challenge us in this regard. One key voice amongst many others on this theme is that of Thomas à Kempis.

Sixthly, the final outworking of a committed discipleship for some of our witnesses in this reflective reader is the embrace of a martyr's death. Baptized into Christ and into the faith community, and baptized in the Spirit, they embraced a baptism of blood. In this they became true witnesses in fidelity to the gospel of the Christ they acknowledged, even in the face of death. There are many of their voices in these pages, including that of Justin Martyr.

Seventhly, while there are voices in these pages that reflect a more intellectual and rational understanding of faith, there are other voices in the Christian mystical tradition that highlight more the mystery of God, the grace of unknowability, and the desert and darkness in the Christian's journey. That such voices are part of the ancient wisdom is an encouragement for us today as we seek to live a spirituality beyond the modernity paradigm. Here the voice of Meister Eckhart is a challenging guide.

Eighthly, living in a present-day setting where many Christians have a most tenuous relationship with the institutional church and where the church itself has lost much of its social standing, the voices of the past point us in a new direction. In their time the church also had its problems. But instead of abandoning the church our forebears took on the shame and weakness of the church and were willing to suffer it into recovery and renewal. St. Catherine of Siena and Hildegard of Bingen are but two of many witnesses.

Finally, the list could go on and on, as there is much we can gain from these voices from the past. There is much in these pages about prayer, meditation, and contemplation. These pages speak about Christian witness and service to the world. There are voices who speak about both the motherhood and fatherhood of God. There are reflections that speak about justice and nation building. And there are voices who speak of the hope of God's final future in new heavens and a new earth.

Fourteen hundred years is no sprint in the park. But many contemporary Christians are sprinters. They almost think Christianity came into being with their faith awakening and so have little sense of the rich tradition that is theirs. This book, in a small way, is an invitation to discover this rich heritage—to hear the ancient wisdom.

ST BENEDICT

1

Psalm 103:1–5

January 1

The God Who is for Us

The God of the biblical story is both wholly other and wholly concerned. This God is both veiled in mystery and made himself known in the nakedness of Golgotha's cross.

The grand song of the biblical narrative is that God, the creator of the world, is especially attentive to humanity. And this attentiveness is not like critical parents frustrated with their teenage son or daughter.

Even though God is before all things and above all things, God has chosen to enter the human fray. And we can know God not only in the otherness of God's mystery, but in the presence of God's caring love.

St. Augustine gets to the heart of all of this. He writes, "I [have] always believed that Thou art and that Thou hast a care for us."[1]

The mere knowledge of God is not the heartbeat of the biblical story. The center of the narrative is that this God draws near. This God cares. This God comes to redeem and make us whole.

And it is in Christ that we can most fully see the way in which God has drawn near to us. Fully amongst us. Full of compassion. Full of grace. Full of healing power.

The God who is for us is not the God who seeks to control, but is the God who seeks to make us whole. God's care is one of self-giving love.

Reflection

The safest place in all the world is to be sheltered in the love of God.

Psalm 42:1

January 2

The Longing Heart

While the God of the biblical story is the God who is there, God can be found when we come in humility and faith. Thus we are to be the seekers of God even when we have already been found.

The life of faith is characterized by a strange dialectic, where two seeming opposites are in creative tension. What this looks like is that we have been given grace, but need to ask for it; we have been forgiven in Christ, but need to seek forgiveness; we have been found by the seeking God, but need to find the God who has already embraced us.

St. Anselm understands this. He prays this prayer to Christ: "My Lord and my Creator, you bear with me and nourish me—be my helper. I thirst for you, I hunger for you, I desire you, I sigh for you, I covet you."[2] This prayer expresses the further longing of someone who has already come home to the heart of God. Homecoming is only a beginning. Growth in relationship and intimacy is the great desire, for enough is never enough in the intimacy of love.

The life of faith, therefore, is a life of response and longing. We respond in love, worship, and service to the God who has first reached out to us. And we long to know more fully the God who already knows us and has called us into the wide spaces of his presence. In the art of longing we lean into what may yet be and what we may yet become.

Thought

The longing heart is the heart already gently touched by the Great Lover.

1 John 3:18

January 3

The Mark of the Christian

First and foremost we do not bear the mark of our church or our denomination, but we bear the grace and presence of Christ whose death on our behalf and whose welcome and empowerment issue in a life of love and service.

In our modern world being a Christian can mean far too many things: being a Westerner, holding a belief in God's existence, being a political conservative, being committed to justice issues, being an emotional Pentecostal, being an activist Evangelical, being a highbrow church person. The list could go on and on.

But all of these attempts to typify miss the mark. The heart of Christianity is about knowing God the creator and redeemer who brings us to fullness of life in Christ through the Spirit.

The heart of being a Christian is to bear the mark of Christ. That mark symbolized in baptism means to come to new life and to be graced by the Holy Spirit and the Spirit's gifts. And it is the Spirit's pleasure to ground us in Christ and to make us more Christlike.

The Christian life, therefore, does not first and foremost move us towards something, but issues *out* of something: God's indwelling presence. From this presence comes the desire for worship and obedience and the longing to love and serve. It is the indwelling presence of God rather than the external law of God that truly empowers us.

St. Ignatius of Antioch is, therefore, right: "we have not only to be called Christians, but to *be* Christians."[3] And to be Christians means that Christ must ever more take shape in us.

Thought

The more we are like Christ, the more fruitful our lives will be.

Psalm 69:16–17

January 4

Walking by Faith

While we love to bask in the light of God's presence with us, we also have to learn to walk in the seeming darkness of God's strange absence. Streams of living water and the desert are part of the Christian experience.

There is not one color to the Christian life. There is no single pattern to Christian spirituality and there is no singular theological theme that captures God's wisdom. But there is complexity. There is revelation. There is growth. There is mystery.

Living the Christian life is full of color. And there are also times of darkness.

There are many contours in the road of faith and we often move between indifference and fervor, despair and hope, faithlessness and obedience.

In the midst of this ever changing landscape of the journey of faith, Meister Eckhart poses an important question for us: "When you are in low condition, and feel forsaken, see if you are just as true to him [God] as when your sense of him is most vivid and if you act the same when you think all help and comfort [is] far removed as you do when God seems nearest."[4]

This penetrating question lays bare our motivations in the spiritual life. The answer is that by ourselves we would probably waver in the dark place. But God can firmly hold us even by his seemingly absent presence. Even in the darkest of places we can grow in faith.

Reflection

God reveals and hides himself. When the latter occurs we are called to great trust, attentiveness, and faith in the God who will draw us back in time to the open spaces of light.

Romans 5:3–5

January 5

The Struggle of Faith

To know God is to know him as the God of love who enters suffering in order to redeem it. When we enter into the love of God we also enter into God's suffering for our world.

It is simply not true that because God in Christ has suffered to redeem us, therefore, we will never need to suffer. In Christ, the Christian has become identified with the suffering God who continues in his love for the world to suffer its alienation and waywardness.

In various ways the Christian is called to suffering, particularly in suffering what God suffers.

Thomas à Kempis speaks of a suffering that leads to growth and maturity: "You cannot win your crown of patience without some struggle. If you refuse suffering, you also refuse the crown."[5]

There are also other forms of suffering. Christians suffer the indifference of others. Christians suffer in their witness and service. But Christians most profoundly suffer the pain in the heart of God that has to do with the world's lack of shalom and wholeness.

As parents suffer the pain of wayward children, God suffers a wayward humanity despite the offer of Christ as the way, the truth, the life. In prayer we are called to be with God in this suffering as we associate with our family, friends, and neighbors who are still far away from the ever open welcome of God.

Thought

Identification with God involves identification with God's pain for our world.

Matthew 6:33

January 6

First Things First

While Christian discipleship has to do with living all of life to the glory of God and the well-being of others, there are some central impulses from which everything else flows. One of these key springs of life is the desire to do God's will.

It is important to be attentive to and protect the various tributaries of a river system. But it is most important to safeguard the headwaters of such a system. The place where the river has its source is critical to its far-reaching, life-sustaining ability.

So it is in the Christian life. Everything we say and do has to do with seeking to live in the way of Christ. But the desire for this has a central impulse and this is the grace and blessing God has poured into lives through the Holy Spirit.

What follows from this central source of inspiration is the desire to live in and for the purposes of God. To seek his kingdom ways. To do his will.

The founder of the Brethren of the Common Life, Geert de Groote, expressed this most clearly: "let me first seek the kingdom [of God] and then I shall so much the better be able to serve my neighbour."[6]

Neither our church, nor our mission, nor our own needs are to be central to living the Christian life. God and God's way and purposes are to be the source from which all good comes. And it is there that we can find our inspiration and our greatest happiness.

Reflection

The greatest challenge is not first of all to do much, but to do first things first. In the long journey of life we need to be sustained in our doing and service.

Isaiah 57:18–19

January 7

God's Healing Presence

To know God and to live in God's presence is not only to live in truth and light, but also to live in wholeness and well-being. This is what we grow into through God's enabling, our participation in the community of faith and the practice of the spiritual disciplines.

When we live only in and for ourselves we do damage to the very fabric of our being. We were never meant to be the center of life. *God* is at the center and we are invited to live life to the full with all our powers and energies to the glory of God.

But since we have placed ourselves at the center and are selfish and wayward, we need to be healed and restored. In fact, first and foremost, we need to be turned around. This is the call to conversion.

This restorative work is the genius of God. God knows not only how to create well, but how to *re*-create well when things have gone wrong. God can make all things new.

St. Augustine speaks about this. He writes: "[God] has prepared for us the medicines of faith and applied them to the maladies of the whole world."[7]

Through God's presence, his word, and his creative Spirit, God renews all things. In Christ there is healing, not only for all people, but also for every dimension of life, and the whole creation.

Healing can come to my inner being, but also to my relationships, to my family, even to the place I work, and in a small way to the nation as a whole. One day, the whole world will know this healing and restoration.

Reflection

Where does the healing presence of God need to come into my life and in our world?

Exodus 20:18–21

January 8

Trials and Testing

Growth in the Christian life does not happen only in fair weather. The testing of our faith more readily occurs in times of uncertainty and difficulty.

Throughout the long history of the Christian church there have been those who have given their lives for their faith. They faced the great test: faithfulness at the threat of death. They found grace in martyrdom.

Most of us on the journey of faith face other tests and trials. These may be coping with life's difficulties, broken relationships, financial or health issues. But it may also include various forms of relinquishment, including voluntary downward mobility.

Whatever may come our way on life's journey, St. Cyprian is convinced that "God wills us to be sifted and proved, as He has always proved His people, and yet in His trials help has never at any time been wanting."[8]

Invited to live this strange dialectic of the wounding-healing hand of God, we are called to trust God's strange way with us. Blessing and testing. Support and challenge. Growth and pruning. Presence and absence.

While we would like only to know God's hand of blessing, we also need to know God's hand of correction and guidance. While we would like the smooth path, we need to know the God who faithfully accompanies us on the rocky road.

Thought

In wounding us, God's purpose is to bring us to greater wholeness and to deepen our understanding that God's ways with us are different than our expectations.

Romans 5:8

January 9

New Life for All

The greatness of the work of Christ in his life, suffering, and death is that it had all of humanity in view. Christ's was no sectarian love, but a boundless redemptive love for the world, so that all things may come to fullness and wholeness.

While we are so limited in our affections, so parochial in our attitudes, and so tribal in our commitments, the towering-yet-humble figure of Christ points us in a very different direction.

His was the way for all. No one, whether great or small, was excluded from the generous love of Christ who made a way for the healing of all of humanity. St. Anselm understood this. He prayed: "Jesus Christ, my dear and gracious Lord, you have shown a love greater than that of any man and which no one can equal, for you in no way deserved to die, yet you laid down your dear life for those who served you and sinned against you."[9]

The grace of Christ is both for the religiously faithful and the unfaithful. It is for the irreligious and the pious. It is extended to betrayer and friend; to priest and prostitute; to rabbi and rebel. Both the oppressed and the oppressor need the healing grace of Christ. There is no one who does not need this grace. There is no one who is not welcome.

The wideness of Christ's love is expressed in the wideness of his mercy. And there is room for all.

Prayer

So dear Lord, may all turn to you and pray, whether saint or sinner, profligate or virtuous, seeker or skeptic. Amen.

Isaiah 48:17–18

January 10

Grateful Faithfulness

The grace and blessing of God are given freely. They don't come with strings attached. But they do call us to community, worship, faithfulness, responsibility, and service.

God is not first and foremost there for us, as if we are the center of things. We are there for God. And God is no Father Christmas.

God is a covenant-making God, calling us into his grace and goodness and into a relationship where our greatest desire becomes the vision to glorify God and to do his will. St. Clement is clear about this. He writes, "Take care, my friends, that his [God's] many blessings do not turn out to be our condemnation, which will be the case if we fail to live worthily of him . . . and to do what is good and pleasing . . ."[10]

Grace issues in gratefulness and obedience and this forms the ethical shape of our lives. This is living life in God, in the Spirit. And this will always be a cruciform life.

Graced by the love of God in Christ Jesus through the Holy Spirit, we will seek to conform our ways to God's ways and will. This both honors God and replicates the way of God in our world. Thus godliness shapes all we are and do.

Our activism, therefore, should spring from grace. And it is to be marked by joy and gratefulness.

Thought

A God pleaser will do more for the well-being of humanity than a people pleaser.

1 Corinthians 7:29–31

January 11

Pilgrims

Christians are pilgrims in that they are on a journey of faith leading to on-going growth in Christ. But there are also other journeys that they are called to make in the service to others.

Traditionally, the pilgrim status of the Christian has been cast in terms similar to that articulated by Thomas à Kempis. He writes, "Live as a *pilgrim and a stranger on earth*, unconcerned about the world's cares, and keep your heart free and raised to God, for this earth of ours *is no lasting city.*"[11] Here pilgrimage has to do with our journey towards heaven.

There are also other pilgrim journeys we are called to make. One is the literal one where Christians go on a faith and prayer pilgrimage to a spiritual site. Another is when Christians take time out of their regular routines in order to deepen their prayer life. Thus, a retreat is a form of pilgrimage.

Furthermore, women and men of faith in relocating for the sake of mission and ministry practice a form of pilgrimage. They have heard the call to leave and go into service for the kingdom of God. They become pilgrims in another culture.

But finally and most profoundly, the call to be a pilgrim is to live in Christ through the Spirit in counter-cultural ways. In step with the kingdom of God one is out of step with the dominant values of our world. Thus, one is always a pilgrim, even though one remains right where one lives and works.

Thought

The life of a pilgrim marks one for conversion, movement, resistance, and suffering.

1 Corinthians 7:17

January 12

The One Life of Faith

There are not two significantly different ways of living the Christian life: as a monk or as a "lay" person, for example. We may have different vocations and callings, but we are all called to live the one Christian life.

St. John Chrysostom once made the observation that "those who live in the world, even though married, ought to resemble the monks in everything else."[12] This helpful reminder points to the fact that there are not two forms of spirituality with one being higher than the other. Monks by virtue of their vocation are not superior to a Christian artist or business person seeking to live in fidelity to the gospel.

All Christians—whether monk or business person, whether clergy or artist, whether a member of a religious order or a farmer—are called to love God and serve their neighbor. All are called to worship and prayer. All are called to community and participation in the sacraments.

Love is to characterize all. Obedience to the way of Christ is the call to all. To live in the power of the Spirit is the invitation to all.

But we have different gifts, different vocations, and different settings in which we are to live the Christian life in all its textured richness. As Christian's live their differing vocations this allows for the gospel to shine in all its varied colors and allows for Christians to be salt, light, and leaven in our world.

Thought

There is one Lord, one faith, one baptism. There is one Christian life lived out in the diversity of our world. And whether one is a monk or a Christian politician, all are called to the service of God and to love of neighbor.

1 Samuel 20:17

January 13

Friendship

Relationships lie at the very heart of what it means to be human. And to have companions on the journey is the extra gift that makes life rich and meaningful.

That our Western emphasis on autonomous individualism has left many people isolated and bewildered should not surprise us. Despite this, the hunger for relationships, friendships, and community continues unabated.

To have friends, therefore, is a great gift. And while God can be one's most special friend and one's spouse can fill that role, other friends are also needed.

Friendship can't be demanded, it can only grow. Friendship can't be manufactured, it can only come as a gift. Thus, friendship is so often the great surprise. But this surprising gift needs careful nurture through presence, attentiveness, availability, and care. Friendship can die as easily as it can spring into being.

St. Aelred of Rievaulx, drawing on St. Augustine, writes that friendship means "to converse and jest together, with good-will to honor one another, to read together, to discuss matters together, together to trifle and together to be in earnest; to differ at times without ill-humour."[13]

Such a friendship, which includes fun as well as sharing the journey of faith, can be a sacrament of the friendship of God with us and can be a sign of what a good world should be like—a world of companionship rather than one of isolation and competition.

Reflection

Those with companions on the journey can be the builders of a newer tomorrow, for in the gift of solidarity lies the hope of creating a better world.

Romans 8:12–13

January 14

God the Source of Life

It is one thing to acknowledge our need of God's grace in the radicality of our sin and brokenness; it is another to see our need for God when we think we are doing well.

At the time of one's initial conversion one is often gifted with profound insight. Things are seen much more clearly, both in terms of who God is and who we are. God is seen as blinding light. We are seen in the rags of our sinfulness. Over time this sharper vision begins to blur. We often begin to see God less clearly and begin to think too much of ourselves, our piety, and our service.

St. Augustine puts all of this in a much clearer perspective. He writes, "For when I am wicked, to confess to thee means nothing less than to be dissatisfied with myself; but when I am truly devout, it means nothing less than not to attribute my virtue to myself."[14]

This way of seeing things need not be an unhealthy self-deprecation. Virtue in the sight of God is not self-produced but grace-induced. It is the Holy Spirit doing his renewing and beautifying work in us. We live and act graced by the goodness of God.

While we are called to cooperate with the Spirit, we are not the source of goodness. Goodness is the fruit that the Spirit grows within us. Thus, God is to be praised rather than we should lapse into self-congratulation.

Thought

God alone is the life-giver who makes me whole. Therefore, God's grace is the source of goodness rather than mere human self-effort.

2 Timothy 4:7

January 15

The Long Journey of Faith

The beginning of the Christian journey needs to be deeply rooted in the grace of Christ. Its long continuance needs a similar source. The Holy Spirit needs to sustain us.

Living the Christian life well is not to be a solo hero. Instead, it is all about being sustained by the goodness of God. And it is all about companions on the journey.

St. Ignatius writes, "I am only beginning to be a disciple [of Christ], so I address you as my fellow students. I needed your coaching in the faith, encouragement, endurance, and patience."[15]

This is a surprising call in the midst of a hierarchical culture where the bishop or the teacher was above the need of others. This humility in this early church father follows the humility of Christ. Christ called companions to be with him. They were with him in his earthly mission. He needed their prayers in the dark garden of Gethsemane.

We need to be marked by the same humility. We need others to accompany us; others to teach us; others to nurture and encourage us; and others to be patient with us. The Christian life is lived in community. It is a common journey with brothers and sisters in the faith.

The Christian life is, therefore, so much more than merely attending church. It is building a life together with family and friends for a common journey of faith.

Thought

Let me thank God this day for the companions he has given me for my faith journey. Let me be thankful for those who teach, nurture, challenge, and encourage me in the way of faith and in living life well.

Galatians 6:14

January 16

A Different Way

Christ's way was out of step with both the religious leaders and politicians of his day. The follower of Christ should share a similar fate. In step with Christ means to be out of step with the world's agenda and priorities.

In his *Rule*, St. Benedict writes: "Your way of acting should be different from the world's way; the love of Christ must come before all else."[16]

The challenge of this church father is that when we live and serve in and through the love of Christ our way of being and acting in the world will have qualities that should make us different from the dominant values of contemporary culture. Christ's way disconnects us from what is, but reconnects us to the world as prophet and healer.

A number of things stand out as to what that may look like when we seek to go Christ's way.

The first is that Jesus was not driven by a self-seeking agenda. He sought only to do the will of God. Second, Jesus was not driven by a societal agenda but a reformist one. He sought to bring in the reign of God. Third, Jesus was not committed to the rule of law but the power of love. Restoration, healing, and the renewal of persons and communities was his great mission.

Finally, Jesus was willing to pay the price for the outworking of his vision and love. He gave himself to voluntary suffering. Clearly, if we seek to live Christ's way in the world these are the challenges we also need to face.

Reflection

The way of Christ in the world is different than the way of religion. The latter has often sought to dominate, but Christ came to serve and renew.

1 Corinthians 13:13

January 17

The Power of Love

When compared with various forms of power—political, institutional, or ideological—love seems to be so weak. But love's power lies in its ability to create a different way of being that leads to goodness and wholeness.

While some wish to contrast love and power—making love powerless and power powerful—love is a form of power. Love has an effect. Love does make an impact. Love does have the power to do, to achieve, to create, to move people forward. And while negative forms of power may also move people, but at a great cost in terms of goodness and well-being, love has its own way. It has its own unique form of power that moves others to well-being.

William of St. Thierry reminds us that: "The art of arts is the art of love."[17] Love, therefore, is the greatest creativity.

Put differently, the greatest wisdom one can achieve is the wisdom of love. The greatest skill one can develop is the ability to love well—that brings empowerment and wholeness to others. And the greatest quality one can have is to be a loving person.

While we may want to celebrate a person's position, role, possessions, and popularity, these things are never the most important. Lacking in love, all that we are and do becomes hollow, and at the end of the day results in a descent into fruitlessness. Love, on the other hand, can move people to great well-being and to do the noblest acts and the greatest deeds.

Thought

Love fructifies. It brings life to desert places and hope to despair.

Isaiah 44:22

January 18

The Return

Much of our contemporary language in church and society is about moving forward. But the secret of life is also about moving backward to the places of failure and need. The very places we seek to run away from may well be the places to which we need to return.

That humans want to move forward is a part of their existential longing for fullness and completion. This is an important dimension of human existence: reaching towards the future.

But there is more to the human story. We are also people in flight and as such we are moving away from where we ought to be and where we need to remain. This is so often true in our relationships, commitments, and priorities. It is also true in our relationship to God.

St. Anselm exhorts us: "Hope in him whom you fear, flee to him from whom you have fled."[18]

Thus there is the call to return. And what a difficult call it is. We would rather forget and move on. To return often means to face the difficult and neglected places.

Much grace is needed to return to the places of neglect, hurt, and disobedience. The return invites us to linger at these places in order to face them and to work things through in the journey of forgiveness, reconciliation, and healing.

The greatest return is not only to the places of pain, but also to the places of our willfulness, our disobedience, and our flight from the loving heart of God.

Thought

To return in order to receive much-needed reconciliation and healing makes us candidates for truly moving forward.

Acts 2:44–46

January 19

Christian Community

Throughout much of the history of the Christian church, Christians have sought to live their faith with a great level of intentionality. As such, they have created communities along-side of and in relation to the parish church.

The Didache, a first or second century early church teaching manual, states: "Do not turn your back on the needy, but share everything with your brother and call nothing your own. For if you have what is eternal in common, how much more should you have [in common] what is transient."[19]

This articulation of a life of common sharing goes back to the common purse community of Jesus and his disciples, the example of the Jerusalem church, and the emphasis in the Pauline house churches of the call to care for one another in practical ways.

This vision of a common life in Christ has been lived out throughout the ages and poses a particular challenge to the contemporary Western church with its consumer Christianity where little commitment is made to have and share a life together.

The church and intentional communities are to reflect the life of the Trinity and as such call Christians, not only into participating in worship, teaching, and sacraments, but also in sharing time, resources, and possessions.

A shared common life in Christ is key to both our personal formation in the way of Christ and in our witness to the world. And such a life may well help us minimize our exploitation of the earth's fragile resources.

Reflection

Community in and through Christ, which practices hospitality, can become a window for others into the heart of the gospel.

Psalm 65:9–13

January 20

God the Sustainer

While we have made a dichotomy between the natural world, as the world of science, and the spiritual world of faith, our Christian forebears made no such distinctions. God is above, but also in all things.

Sadly, we moderns have become terribly reductionistic. Things of God and of faith have largely been relegated to the private sphere of life and to the sanctuary. All else has been relegated to the secular sphere of life.

Neither the biblical story nor our Christian foremothers and forefathers support such a view. In fact, the opposite is the case. God as the creator and sustainer of the universe and of our world is involved in all things. No sphere of life is outside of God's love and concern.

St. Patrick, reflecting an Irish spirituality of God in the midst of all the daily activities of life, writes: "He inspires all things, he quickens all things, he is over all things, he supports all things."[20]

This is a wonderful vision of life. God's Spirit at work in nature. God's Spirit renewing our inner life. God's Spirit sustaining and empowering the church. The Spirit at work in families and social institutions. God's presence everywhere working unseen and mysteriously to sustain, renew, and bring goodness and love.

We will need new eyes of faith to see such things. But the biblical story and the inspiration of the Spirit can give us such a new vision. And such a vision can provide a new impetus to the contemporary church in its witness to the world.

Thought

If God is not nowhere, then God is everywhere.

Matthew 6:9–10

January 21

Kingdom and Spirituality

*When the church and the kingdom of God have been confused
with each other then the church has received too much power
and the church has been tempted to bring in the kingdom by
human means. But the kingdom or reign of God is always first
and foremost the presence and action of God in the world.*

Florentius Radewijns, one of the key leaders of the Brethren of the
Common Life, stated: "Our aim and final destination is the Kingdom of
God. The road which leads to that goal is purity of heart."[21]

In this statement, the connection is made between personal and
communal spirituality and the in-breaking kingdom of God. While *our*
spirituality is not the ground of the kingdom, it is the fruit of the reign of
God. And such fruit brings goodness wherever it is manifested.

An inner life devoted to prayer and the presence of God is a life
marked by the kingdom and as such is a life that opens the door for being
a servant of the kingdom that expresses the way of Christ rather than the
way of the world.

Purity of heart opens the way for God's love and justice to be
manifested in life-giving and empowering ways rather than the processes
of manipulation. Such a purity of heart is to will *one* thing, that God may
be manifested and glorified amongst us.

Reflection

To force the kingdom of God undoes the very nature of the reign of God.
To pray for the kingdom is the way of peace. And to serve the kingdom is
to follow Christ's way in the world. This way brings forgiveness, healing,
and justice.

James 3:17–18

January 22

The Praxis of Knowledge

Knowledge is never something neutral. Knowledge has consequences. It calls us to responsibility and action. It calls us to be what we know and to do what we must.

In the West we have a tendency to separate things. Theory and practice often are not held together. Knowing and doing are frequently separated. Even emotion, passion, and wisdom are placed in separate boxes.

In the biblical story, it is all quite different. We learn, not so much about a God who thinks, but about a God who *acts*. In fact, we know the thoughts of God in and through the acts of God. God's being is seen in his redemptive love and actions. We know God best through what he does.

And so it must be with us. The important theme in the biblical story is about a love that issues in action: care, support, mercy, and justice. The love of heart becomes the love of the hand in action.

The church Father Diadochus understood these things. He wrote: "Woe to the knowledge that does not turn to loving."[22]

Knowledge can be used and misused in many ways. It can be misused as a form of power that excludes others. But it can be a positive force when it issues in care for the other. To truly know is to care and this leads to love in action.

Thought

When I really know I will also love. And what I truly love I will shelter, care for, and support.

Psalm 27:4

January 23

The Beauty of God

If we think about God at all, it is usually in terms of God's helpfulness. And while we may also think of God's greatness, we hardly ever think of God's beauty.

St. Augustine makes a helpful connection between nature and the being of God. He writes: "Now all the things that thou hast made are fair, and yet, lo, thou who didst make all things art inexpressibly fairer."[23]

God has left us with a variety of traces and symbols that may help us understand who God is. All of these point back to the nature of God.

There is the book of nature. There is the book of books: Holy Scripture. There is the Word made flesh: Jesus Christ. There is the work and witness of the church. There is the book of life in which we may also see the traces of God. And there is our own personal journey marked by God's generous sustenance and interventions.

With the eyes of faith and with a prayerful heart we may see the signs of God in each of these ways. While Jesus Christ will always be the greater sign than the book of life, and Scripture is clearer about who God is than nature, we can see God is not only forgiving and loving, but also beautiful.

God's beauty is in his creative power, redeeming grace, the fructifying work of the Spirit, the beauty of nature, human creativity, and in all the ways goodness and wholeness come to us and to our world.

Thought

Beauty and justice do belong together. A just world where goodness is for all, and not merely for some, is where shalom reigns. This is an expression of beauty.

Acts 17:28

January 24

God Our Being

Living the Christian life does have to do with participating in a range of spiritual practices and disciplines. And so we pray, partake of the sacraments, read Scripture, and so on. But more fundamental to all of these activities is the joy of God's presence within us and in our world.

At the very heart of Christian experience lies a profoundly mystical reality: God at work within us through the Holy Spirit. And to put that more strongly: God makes himself at home within us. This is the swan song of Immanuel—God with us.

This has two important dimensions. The first, God makes himself at home in making us in God's own image. And this creative initiative is complemented by the redemption in Christ where the Trinity abides with us and in us.

Gregory of Nazianzus, in the light of the above, reminds us that "we ought to think of God even more often than we draw our breath."[24]

This is possible not so much because we are so hard at work in remembering, but because God is constantly at work within us. Our awareness comes from God's presence.

Like a fountain bubbling upward from deep and sometimes seeming desert places, the Spirit is mysteriously sustaining us and calling us to greater spiritual attentiveness so that the life of God may spring up within us and amongst us.

Reflection

When God is at the depths of our being, all we do has the flavor of the Spirit. This is living a graced life.

1 Corinthians 13:3

January 25

Generosity

Christ has given his very life for the world. We are invited to receive the benefits that flow from this generous self-giving. But we are also invited to give our all for God's purposes.

Christ's great act of self-giving love invites us to give of ourselves as well. As we have generously received, so we also give. We do this in gratitude and love.

It is one thing to do this in the joy and enthusiasm of a new found faith. It is another to continue to live a life of *generosity* in the long journey of discipleship. Since this road is long and may be hard, fervor can easily weaken or dissipate altogether. And in the latter stages of life, we can so easily close in on ourselves.

But it is one thing to give and quite another thing to become free from avarice.

The ancient monk John Cassian notes that there are people "who have given away worldly wealth in gold or silver or lands [who] are afterwards agitated about a knife, a pencil, a pin, or a pen."[25] We can so easily major on minors.

Giving, therefore, must come from a place of inner freedom and not from compulsion or mere necessity. Thus giving needs to come from a place of grace. This can only be the fruit of the renewing work of the Holy Spirit. And this freedom is living in joy in the goodness of God rather than in the quest to secure our own future and our own security.

Giving is more than an act of the hand. It is a grace that springs from the heart.

Thought

Giving becomes a grace when it blesses the receiver and transforms the giver.

John 12:26

January 26

The *Imitatio Christi*

The Christian life has to do with beliefs, worship, prayers, community, and service. But the very heart of a life of faith is following Christ's way in the world. The way Christ lived and acted is the example that we are called to follow.

Christians have not always followed Christ's way in the world. There has been violence instead of peacemaking; controversy instead of reconciliation; division instead of cooperation; legalism instead of grace; condemnation rather than welcome. The list goes on.

What this highlights, however, is that Christ will always continue to challenge us in the way we think, live, and act. To live the way Christ lived will be a lifelong challenge and process for us.

Gregory of Nyssa reminds us that "those who have an equal zeal for the good must thoroughly imitate and follow the pioneer of our salvation, and must put into practice what he has shown them."[26]

Christian zeal must be patterned on Christ. We must not live our own agenda seeking God's blessing. Instead, we must humbly seek to do only God's will and way.

This calls us to ongoing conversion and repentance, for the way of Christ is a way that is so different to our natural inclinations. Thus, the *imitatio Christi* is grace we must receive through the Spirit, so we can live this grace in joy and faithfulness.

Reflection

The way of Christ calls us to the way of peace-making, self-giving, and suffering.

John 10:27–29

January 27

Holding and Being Held

No matter how great we are, we still have the need for love and care. And at times, when strength fails us, we need to be held and carried. This is all the more true in the spiritual journey. No matter how mature we may think we are, we will always be spiritual babes.

The Christian life is a life lived towards God. In reflection and prayer we seek to be attentive to the God who is with us and who calls us forward.

At times, and particularly in difficulty, we need to cling to this God, seeking God's presence and help. And in times of vulnerability and need we need to be held in God's love and in the care of others who need to nurture us.

Thomas à Kempis reminds us: "Hold fast to Jesus both in life and in death and commit yourself to His steadfast love, for He alone can help you when all others fail."[27]

Here a double movement is identified: holding and being held. Clearly, the former flows out of the latter. God holds us and we cling to God. We call out to God but God is drawing us by his love and power.

Thus, it is never a matter of hanging on for grim death, but being secure in the great love of the Father through Christ. In that love lies our final security and safety. Finally, we are more held than we will ever realize.

Thought

Being held is no affront to our ability, just as being loved is no negation of our personhood.

Isaiah 55:6

January 28

A God Seeker

One cannot seek for what one does not know at all. One seeks for what one already knows. We thus seek the God we already know in some way.

Meister Eckhart makes the helpful point that having once tasted the goodness of God our appetite for God increases. He writes: with people seeking God "if they get no taste of divine sweetness, they drag; but if a man lies in wait until he does catch the taste of the divine, ever afterwards he is a glad seeker of God."[28]

What needs to be noted is Eckhart's emphasis on waiting and seeking. This is insightful because we cannot orchestrate or demand the appearance of God. God is not at our beck and call. God comes in his own way and time.

Waiting and seeking not only point us in the direction of humility, but invite us on the pathways of contemplation. It is a walk of faith. It is prayer in darkness. It is seeing in anticipation. It is living in hope.

When the seeking heart finds, the seeking does not end. In fact, the opposite is the case. The search increases just as love may deepen when the beloved has been embraced. Once having tasted, the longing for more may become insatiable.

As a consequence, there is a certain restlessness about the Christian life. Having come home to the heart of God we seek to enter more fully into the purposes of God. Thus longing and journey are the hallmarks of the Christian way rather than rest and fulfillment.

Reflection

Having found we still seek. Such is the Christian journey.

Hosea 6:1

January 29

The God who Wounds and Heals

God is no favorite teddy bear or Father Christmas. God is the sovereign Lord of the universe whose ways with us, bathed in both mystery and revelation, will always challenge us.

One wonders whether the God of contemporary Western Christianity has anything very much to do with the God of the biblical story. It seems we have made God into a benign and convenient figure who is there to support us in our needs. Instead of God as Lord, we have made God the divine butler simply there for our own wants.

Gone is the sense that God is sovereign and that we are invited into both the joy and journey of a life of worship, prayer and obedience. When God is seen as central, rather than ourselves, then the focus of our lives is not how we can "use" God, but how we can be drawn more fully into God's purposes. These purposes are not according to our agenda. They may be strange and difficult.

The desert father Abbot Apollo speaks of a God who "makes the sore and bindeth up: . . . woundeth and His hands make whole . . . bringeth low and lifteth up . . ."[29]

The way of God with us is one of correction and blessing. It is the way of the cross and the resurrection. But one can't have one without the other. So with us—sorrow and blessing are part of the tapestry of the Christian life. We are, after all, the cruciform people of God. The purposes of God to bring shalom to the world will call us into both suffering and service and our own ongoing purgation will invite us into confession and healing.

Thought

We are healed through wounding and in a little dying lies the gateway to life.

Mark 10:45

January 30

For the Other

Ours has become such a self-preoccupied and pragmatic age that the call to serve the other sounds most strange, even alienating. Yet, it is at the heart of Christianity.

While our contemporary world still knows something of those who are lesser serving those who are more powerful, generally speaking the language of serving others has fallen from view. We don't serve, we just do our job and for this we are paid.

But the Christian story knows much about serving. Christ came as the Servant-King to give his life for the world. We are called into the footsteps of Christ and are called to serve others.

What is remarkable in the Christian story, however, is that the stronger serve the weaker, not the other way round. This is a call to downward mobility for the sake of blessing the other. This is following the movement of Christ so clearly expressed in the great hymn of Philippians 2.

St. Benedict in writing about the role of an Abbot in a monastic community knows about this movement. He elaborates: "Let him recognize that his goal must be profit for the monks, not preeminence for himself."[30]

So often those in positions of leadership and prominence think it is all about them. But it is all about *others*. It is not about the pastor but the community of faith. It is not about the teacher but the students. And so it goes on. This is the Christian way.

Reflection

To be prominent and yet to serve is a great grace.

Psalm 19:1

January 31

In Praise of Seeing

There are three books in the Christian tradition: the book of nature, the Word made flesh, Jesus Christ, and the Word of God—Holy Scripture. All need to be read. And all point in the one direction.

Life is about being, seeing and acting. What we see flows from who we are and this shapes our engagement with others and the world.

There are many ways of seeing and there is much to see. Seeing can be internal and reflective and external and evaluative. But amongst the many ways of seeing there is also *appreciative* seeing. It is seeing as feasting. Seeing as celebration. Seeing with the eyes of faith and love.

The theologian Bonaventure, reflecting a Franciscan spirituality, writes "open your eyes, alert the ears of your spirit, open your lips and apply your heart so that in all creatures you may see, hear, praise, love and worship, glorify and honor your God."[31]

To see beauty in nature is to see the generous hand of God, is to see the great heart of God, is to see God as artist as well as sustainer. And seeing thus we are to bestow dignity and care on all that has been made, for in all we see the traces of God's hand of love.

And in seeing Christ we see the source of our healing and purpose, while in Scripture we discover the heart of God, and God's way for us to live life to his glory and the blessing of others.

These many ways of seeing can give us a life of joy, a heart of purpose, and a way of being in the world that makes for forgiveness, healing, and shalom.

Reflection

With a contemplative spirit we can see and celebrate and act in healing ways.

MEISTER ECKHART

Romans 8:35–39

February 1

A Bond of Love

There are many things that can bind a person to another. Convention and fear are two such things. But love and friendship is the life-giving bond.

Peter Abelard wrote: "So we, through his grace, are joined to him [God] as closely as to our neighbor by an indissoluble bond of affection."[32]

This beautiful vision of friendship and connectedness does not mean God is like a "buddy." God is the sovereign Lord. But our relationship with God, while marked by awe and mystery, is also one of friendship. Ultimately within the framework of grace, the true bond is one of love. Such a bond is life-giving and life-sustaining.

This love is God-initiated. It is God's love shed abroad in our hearts that moves us to wait and long for the fuller presence of the living God. This love is grounded in Christ's self-giving love for humanity. And this love is painted into the fabric of our lives by the beautifying Spirit. Thus we are birthed in love, we are woven in love, and love sustains us. Love marks our identity and our way of life.

Possibly, we could turn Abelard's phrase around: because of the grace and love of God in Christ we are loved into a love for neighbor, stranger, and even our enemy. Hence, true service becomes a place of deep gratitude and empowerment to do for others what has so graciously been given to us.

Thought

To be a friend of God is an act of grace and calls for great humility. And the bond of friendship moves us to extend this kind of friendship to others. Friendship making thus becomes a way of life.

Ephesians 3:1–6

February 2

A Way to Christ

One may know about Christ, but to know Christ by way of revelation and encounter can occur in strange and wonderful ways, both in the sanctuary and in the street. In the final analysis, we need an existential encounter with Christ.

To experience the presence of Christ in the Spirit can occur anywhere and at any time. Both in the place of prayer and at work Christ may make himself known. This encounter may confront us in our sin or in our goodness, but is always an invitation to forgiveness and homecoming.

This revelatory experience or encounter can come in a flash. It can also come through long seeking and searching. It may come at the end of one's life.

Clement of Alexandria believed that things in the ordinary world can point us to Christ. He writes: "philosophy was a 'schoolmaster' to bring the Greek mind to Christ, as the Law brought the Hebrews."[33]

To this we may add that the grappling scientist, the inspired artist, the searching philosopher, and the committed medical specialist in the midst of their work may be led stumblingly to Christ. So may the farmer and the factory worker. In the midst of the ordinary the light of Christ may break in. Christ dances in many ways to draw us into relationship with him.

Anything in the world of human experience and endeavor and dreams and aspirations may be a trigger to a spiritual search that leads to an encounter with the Christ of the gospel.

Reflection

While the church seeks to mediate Christ in particular ways, Christ may throw open doors and windows and come in any way to the seeking heart.

Psalm 119:81–82

February 3

Longing

Having come home to the love and grace of God in Christ does not mean that the journey has ended. In fact, it has merely begun. And while previously we may have been longing for all sorts of other things, we now long for the living God.

The heart of Christian spirituality is the longing and seeking heart. This longing never ends. Never in this life is it fully satisfied.

St. Anselm has expressed this well: "My consoler, for whom I wait, when will you come? O that I might seek the joy that I desire; that I might be satisfied with the appearing of your glory for which I hunger; that I might be satisfied with the riches of your house for which I sigh."[34]

The longing heart for the presence of God, the seeking heart for the purposes of God, the praying heart for the will of God, is the heart throbbing with the life of the Spirit.

Having come home, we seek to be more deeply grounded. Having been forgiven, we seek to bring goodness to our world. Having been inspired, we long to see more clearly. Having been befriended, we seek to grow in love. Having been well loved, we long to see others come into the goodness of God.

The longing heart is not the ungrateful heart, it is the hungry heart for a greater vision of the God who has made himself known to us. This is the heart that leans into the future.

Thought

Longing is the human being leaning towards eternity. In the act of longing we transcend the present and open windows to a future yet to be unveiled.

Ephesians 4:25–27

February 4

Discerning the Enemy

The world is shaped by goodness but pocketed by evil. Grace abounds but evil lies close at hand. God is present but the enemy of our souls waits in the wings.

We have seen amazing scientific progress during this past century. But this has also been a time of terrible wars and atrocities. Goodness and evil are clearly part of the human condition. To think otherwise is to live in unreality.

This double movement is also evident in the spiritual realm. The Holy Spirit ever brooding and life-giving brings peace and hope into our world. Evil spirits bring fear and chaos.

One of the desert fathers made this observation: "Whatsoever things are from God, have their spring in humbleness; but such things as spring from authority and anger and strife, these are from the Enemy."[35] Sadly, both forces impact us and both bring forth very different fruit.

Thus we are invited into the art of careful discernment. Understanding the ways of God, we are called to discern the work of the Enemy who sows discord and fear.

The testimony of the desert fathers and mothers is clear: the greater the awareness of God, the greater the watchfulness for the ways of the Evil one.

Reflection

True seeing involves seeing that which negates and destroys and seeing what brings life and hope.

Ephesians 1:22–23

February 5

The Joy of Wholeness

Well-being is never simply determined by health strategies alone. It also has to do with what I believe and what sustains me inwardly. Exercise brings well-being. But so does prayer.

There is a great emphasis in our contemporary world regarding the quest for wellness. This is partly due to the fact that in our world of economic rationalism and consumerism we are living toxic lives. Our driven and self-preoccupied lifestyle is barely sustainable and so we look for ways to cope.

That this search for well-being requires more than good eating and recreational habits is rather obvious. Well-being also has to do with our inner being. Wholeness is never merely circumstantial; it is also inward and spiritual.

St. Augustine understood well the ultimate source of wellness: "[It] is that I may serve and worship thee to the end that I may have my well-being from thee, from whom comes my capacity for well-being."[36] This church father saw wellness as a gift of grace from the God of life.

God as the source for my well-being is not the demanding and judgmental God of our own making, but the God of love and companionship and nurture in Christ. This is not the far away God, but the God who through the Spirit lives within me. This God is the One who upholds me and showers the gifts of love and peace upon me. This God calls me beloved and nurtures me in the paths and ways of life. This God is the healing and sustaining God.

Reflection

With the Creator carefully and artfully reshaping my inner being with love, the core of who I am is nurtured.

Matthew 19:12

February 6

A Holy Calling

Throughout the history of the Christian church there have been those who have lived the Christian life with great intensity and commitment. These persons are to be seen as a challenge to all of us to live the Christian life with greater fidelity.

St. Francis of Assisi in his Rule of 1223 writes, the Christian way of life is "to observe the holy gospel of our Lord Jesus Christ, living in obedience without personal possessions, and in chastity."[37]

This calling, lived out fully amongst those who have been called to this activist religious order, is a calling that has implications for all of us. Their way of life and service, while the way of greater intentionality, is also in some sense to be our way.

Whether married or single, in secular work or holy orders, with riches or in poverty, we are called to live in the power of the gospel. The gospel is to indwell us and we are called to be in Christ and to live for Christ. All of us, no matter what our life circumstances are, are called to live in obedience to the way of Christ and all of us are called to great generosity because God has been generous towards us in Christ.

The heartbeat of the monk or that of a member of a religious order to live one's whole life for Christ is a calling for the *whole* people of God, even though they may need to outwork that calling in different ways.

Reflection

The *imitatio Christi* lies at the heart of Christianity. We are all called to follow Christ's love for the Father in heaven. We are all called to community. We are all called to purity of heart and to a life of service.

John 2:23–25

February 7

Silence

Jesus both spoke and acted and was silent. He healed people in the public square and went to desert places to pray alone. He made himself known and he asked people to be silent about him.

Living the Christian life is not simply an outpouring of love and service to others. It also has to do with the growth of an inner life. And it is from these interior resources of prayer and reflection that a life of service can come and be sustained. Interiority is not a withdrawal but a spring from which flowing waters can come.

St. Ignatius once made the seemingly enigmatic remark: "He [or she] who has really grasped what Jesus said can appreciate his silence."[38] This can mean many things, but it does make an important connection between one's interiority and one's externalization. Put differently, behind the words or deeds of a person lies an inner reality that also needs to be understood and appreciated and needs to be nurtured. In fact, it is only when the latter is understood that the former can be appreciated.

In the case of Jesus, his words and deeds invite us to an intimacy of the Spirit. And being drawn to the inner person of Jesus—and into his silence—is an invitation into the very presence of a love that knows no bounds, is willing to suffer and to give its all.

The invitation for the Christian is not only to imitate the deeds of Christ, but to become like him in our inner being and in prayer and silence. From such an inner life good fruit can come.

Thought

Entering into the silence of Christ opens a new world. This silence needs to become our own silence for which all goodness springs.

John 15:15

February 8

Friendship with God

We must never reduce our relationship with God to a glib familiarity or an estranged distance. God is sovereign and Lord of our lives. But God can also be the great friend.

It is possible to think of God in images of distance. This is particularly so when we use the language of distance: omnipotent, sovereign, all powerful. But there is also another language that we are invited to use. This speaks of intimacy and closeness: lover, healer, redeemer, friend.

Clearly both forms of language are appropriate. It usually depends on the way and the circumstances in which we seek to approach God. Being in a certain phase in our spiritual journey means that we will think of God in certain ways and use language accordingly.

St. Thomas Aquinas points out that "Charity signifies not only the love of God, but also a certain friendship with him."[39] And so it is. For if the love of God is in us, then the Great Lover is hauntingly close. If grace is given, then the Great Giver is at hand. If healing comes our way, then the healing presence of God is within and around us. The presence of love in the relationship of friendship with this awesome God means that we may call God "Father" and "Friend."

The worship of God, while recognizing God as wholly Other, is also worship in the joy of friendship. The God of the Bible is hauntingly close, is the unceasing lover and the faithful friend.

Thought

God is so close. God is within us through the Spirit. God is always closer than we think or feel.

1 John 1:9

February 9

A Deeper Confession

There are sources of human goodness out of which I act that may not be immediately apparent to me. There may also be fault lines and ungoodness in my life of which I am not fully aware. A deeper self-reflection is, therefore, called for.

St. Augustine makes a seemingly strange confession: "I would therefore confess what I know about myself; I will also confess what I do not know about myself."[40] This is both a revealing and an appropriate statement. Revealing in that this ancient church father knows something of the psychology of the human person. Appropriate, in that since part of what we do lies below the surface, such a confession is always called for.

Confession should occur not only at the level of awareness of wrongs done. It lies much deeper. It also lies at the level of my intentions and motivations. Actions of the hand find their source in both the goodness and dysfunctionality of the heart. But there is more to this story. Confession also has to do with what I am, not only with what I do. It has to do with my essential being. It has to do with ontology.

To acknowledge that I have committed a particular sin is one thing. To confess that I am a sinner is something that goes much deeper. The one has to do with an act; the other with who I am. And it is also at this deeper level that the grace and healing presence of Christ in the Spirit needs to be embraced.

Reflection

It is not only what I do, it is also what I am that matters. And the renewing work of the Spirit in making me a new person builds on the forgiveness that is found in Christ.

Psalm 61:5–6

February 10

Reflection

Ours is a world of busyness and we live with many distractions. Our inner world is, therefore, restless and preoccupied. In the midst of this, we are invited into the practice of solitude and reflection.

Inwardly restless and outwardly preoccupied, ours is the journey of flight—away from ourselves and away from God. And thus away from an inner peace and centeredness. We are, therefore, both distracted and fractured.

God's invitation however is one of homecoming—coming home to God's grace and healing and coming home to accept God's gifts and calling. This calls us to stop running and to turn in the right direction. This also means that we come home to ourselves.

The spiritual discipline of silence, solitude, and reflection is an important part of this homecoming. It helps us to see who we are, where we are, and where we need to be. Thomas à Kempis challenges us regarding these matters. He writes, "Set aside an opportune time for deep personal reflection and think often about God's many benefits to you."[41]

This simple advice poses a challenge for us. On the run, we are invited to stop. Ever planning, we are invited to reflect. Wanting to do things, we are called to pray. Ever restless, we are invited into the place of surrender.

As we reflect on ourselves and our world we are called to cling to the God who alone can make us whole and bring our world to peace. Thus, reflection will always call us to prayer.

Thought

Publicly, we are known by what we do. But God also knows us in the quiet places of the heart. These latter places should be the places where we are most truly at home.

John 10:10

February 11

Generativity

While some think that Christianity is all about doctrines, rituals, and ceremonies, they miss the heart of the biblical story. The heartbeat is God's creative and sustaining presence in our lives and communities.

The fourteenth-century Christian mystic Meister Eckhart sees God not as some remote and static being, but as close and dynamic. He writes: "God in things is activity, reality, and power, but in the soul he is procreative."[42]

God's Spirit—personal, creative, life-giving, healing, forward moving—is no lover of dull conformity and repetitive ceremony. Instead, the Spirit is ever animating and revitalizing. Through the Spirit the tired places are renewed, the broken places are healed, and the places of despair are filled with hope. The work of the Spirit is ever to renew.

Through inspiration and illumination, the Spirit brings not only new insight and wisdom, but also new energy and vitality. Thus, we do not only see more clearly, but we are carried forward by the breath of the Spirit. The Spirit blows us to new places. This is important. It is never simply a matter of new ideas. It is much more a matter of a new inspiration and motivation, and the will to do and the passion to move forward.

Thus the work of God in us is life-giving and generative. And this generativity is one that blesses others and seeks to cooperate with God's renewing work in our world.

Thought

Like a mother, God brings the new into being. And in being and doing the new we are nourished.

Ephesians 1:7–10

February 12

Union with God

The great longing of Christians throughout the ages has not so much been a longing for heaven, but to be more fully united to God. The great love of the Christian is to be lost in the love of the Father, the Son, and the Holy Spirit.

In our world of pragmatism and activism driven by the economic dream of much-having—a dream that has also impacted the vision of the church—we need to be careful that we do not lose the central thrust of the biblical story.

That central thrust, while it includes the call to serve God in our world in the ministry of evangelization and the work for justice, is the invitation to know God and to enjoy him forever. The first call is always to spiritual intimacy before we hear the call to loving service. Homecoming to the embrace of God is always the first move before being scattered to be salt, light, and leaven in our world.

While we need to be immersed in the world, we first need to be enamored with God. While there is the call to serve, there is also the call to love and friendship.

The medieval mystic Jan van Ruysbroeck reminds us how important it is to become friends with God and to enter into a fuller communion with God. He writes, "All our powers then fail us and we fall down in open contemplation. All become one and one becomes all in the loving embrace of the threefold Unity. When we experience this Unity, we become one being, one life, and one blessedness with God."[43]

Reflection

To enter more deeply into the love of God in Christ through the Spirit is to find our true home and our true purpose.

Acts 1:4–5

February 13

The Life-giving Spirit

It is not so difficult to keep Jesus in view, but the Holy Spirit can so easily fall out of sight. The Spirit, the most mysterious member of the Trinity, the go-between God, the Silent One, is the One who most deeply and profoundly emanates our lives.

St. Bernard has captured well something of the Spirit's gracious work. He writes, "The revelation which is made by the Holy Spirit gives light so that we may understand and fire so that we might love."[44] This highlights the way our minds are opened and our passions are enlivened by the Spirit. The Spirit thus gives insight and empowerment.

This is one part of the story of the Spirit. There is more. The Spirit renews the face of the earth and revitalizes the people of God. Thus both the created order and the body of Christ are under the energizing work of the Spirit. This says a lot about the amazing diversity of the Spirit's interests and concerns.

The Spirit is at work in the church. The Spirit accompanies the proclamation of the gospel and the reading of Scripture. The Spirit is present in the sacraments. The Spirit is with us in fellowship, prayer, and service. The Spirit thus energizes the gathered and scattered people of God. The Spirit is in the midst of the community of faith. But the Spirit is also at work in the world. The Spirit prepares hearts for openness to the gospel. The Spirit generates movements of goodness and liberation. The Spirit inspires creativity and beauty. Where there is hope, creativity, and goodness the Spirit is at work.

Reflection

Hidden yet ever present, the Spirit is the source of all wisdom, renewal, and beauty.

Hebrews 12:1

February 14

Hold Fast

The greater the revelation of Christ in our hearts and minds, the greater is the desire to cling to Christ. The more our response to Christ has been one of social convention or psychological need, the easier we may let Christ slip out of our lives because our circumstances may have changed.

Becoming a Christian is premised on a revelatory event. Christ reveals himself to us by Word and Spirit and we are captivated by his love and grace. And thus we respond in faith and surrender. In Christ we have come home to the heart of God in the power of the Spirit.

St. Ambrose understands this. He writes, "you received Him into the dwelling of your mind; you saw Him in spirit; you saw with inner eyes. Hold fast your new Guest, long awaited, but lately received."[45]

Becoming a Christian is not primarily a social activity, but a spiritual one. It is Christ through the Spirit meeting the seeking and longing heart. It is, therefore, an encounter that is profoundly mystical, even though it may be a response to the gospel or the witness of another person. This is no simple rational experience. It is profoundly spiritual and life changing.

The more profound this experience the more joyfully we will cling to Christ in the long, and at times torturous, journey of faith. And because Christ is deeply embedded within us and is the faithful guest, he will hold us fast. And in both light and darkness we will cling to him. Having been captivated by Christ's love, we will not let him go.

Reflection

Holding on to Christ, while being held, is the journey of faith.

Jeremiah 23:3-4

February 15

Making Others Whole

The journey towards wholeness is one of grace and one of often painful transitions. But wholeness cannot only be the fruit of a personal focus, wholeness is communal. It's the fruit of open receiving and gracious giving.

Anthony, one of the desert fathers, pointed out that, "The Fathers of old went forth into the desert and when [they] themselves were made whole, they became physicians, and returning again they made others whole."[46]

Clearly, the journey towards wholeness for the desert fathers and mothers was one of withdrawal, prayer, purgation, and suffering. Lost in the love of God they endured difficulty. But it was love that transformed them. And this love moved them to deeds of love that brought blessing and healing to others. Their withdrawal from the world, therefore, was not an end in itself. They withdrew to lay a foundation for a new world.

Their journey was one of union with God, moving ever closer into the heart and purposes of God. But this movement in and towards God drew them ever more deeply into seeking to be God's healing hands towards others.

This is what true wholeness is all about. Living more fully in God and more truly at home with ourselves, we become agents of goodness towards others. Blessing, therefore, is never only for ourselves. It is for all. It is for the world.

Thought

Wholeness is the fruit of holiness, which issues in giving gifts of healing and hospitality. This builds the new humanity of which Christ was the New Adam and the pioneer.

2 Corinthians 13:4

February 16

Mere Servants

Whatever our position in the world or in the church, this does not finally define us. What does define us is who we are in Christ and that the way of Christ becomes our way in the world.

The way of Christ was that of a humble servant of the Father. Christ's joy was to do the Father's will. His purpose was to make the Father known. His mission was to bring into being the healing and restoring reign of God.

Christ did all of this in the power of the Spirit and with his Father's blessing and benediction. Thus Christ's work was Trinitarian work, not a solo effort.

We too are invited to participate in the same mission as Christ. But we do so from a much more fragile position. We are not Christ, only his followers. We are more mixed in our motives, while Christ was singular in his commitment. We are hesitant in our love, while Christ loved fully.

St. Anselm's prayer is therefore appropriate. He prays: "by your powerful kindness complete what in my powerless weakness I attempt."[47] In our weakness God produces his strength.

In being the mere servants of Christ, we need the grace and sustaining presence of God. In and of ourselves we cannot be what God calls us to be. Therefore, we are always called to rely on God. We are called to live in faith. We are invited to prayer.

Thought

No matter how far we are into the journey of faith and love that issues in service, we will always need the Spirit to carry us along.

Romans 5:1–2

February 17

The Movement of Grace

Grace is God extending his love, forgiveness, and goodness to us, not because we deserve this but because of God's generous heart is towards all of his creatures.

Being a Christian and living the Christian life is to be in and to live in the sphere of grace, which is God's undeserved favor. Grace is the realm in which we live, move, and dance. Being the grateful recipients of God's grace is what marks us and shapes our identity as much as our genetic inheritance and our socialization.

Meister Eckhart understood well the significance and power of this grace. He writes, "Grace is not a stationary thing; it is always found in a Becoming."[48] Grace moves us from where we are to where we need to be. Grace radically reorients us.

Grace, therefore, is not a gift we put in our backpack. Grace is an intrusion into the basic fabric of our lives. It is a powerful intervention. Grace is what radically reorients and renews us. And this is because grace and forgiveness are welcoming and interpersonal dynamics. Grace links us to Christ the giver of grace.

Grace moves us from enmity or neglect of God to a place of embrace and friendship. Grace frees us from the destructive forces within our own being. Grace makes us gracious towards others. The grace of God in Christ makes us more Christlike.

Eckhart is, therefore, correct. Grace is dynamic. It moves us. It reorients us. It makes us more truly human. It makes us more Godlike.

Reflection

The power of forgiving grace transforms us and makes us open to extend love and goodness to others.

Psalm 84:1–2

February 18

The Heart of the Matter

While a generous person is known for his or her generosity, such a person should be primarily appreciated for who he or she is, and not only for what one does and gives. So it is with God. The great Life-giver is to be loved even in times of darkness and difficulty.

There is little doubt that life in the modern world is very pragmatic and utilitarian. It is all about progress and benefits for me. As a consequence, little attention has been given to the true meaning and purpose of life. But life is more than security and material much-having. It is also about love and beauty. It has to do with relationships, with care, with giving and receiving, with forgiveness.

A vibrant spirituality at the heart of life cannot be one of mere benefits and blessings. This follows too much the contours of our present age. Instead, such a spirituality should focus on the source of all things. Thus the focus is on the Giver, and not only on the gifts.

Thomas à Kempis points us in the right direction. He notes, "A wise lover considers not so much the lover's gift as the giver's love. He attends more to the giver's affection than to the gift's value."[49]

And so it is. The source of all things is the loving heart of God who called all things into being and who recreates us in love to be whole, full of goodness, and in service and care to the neighbor and stranger.

Thought

The heart of the matter is the loving heart of God and not only the blessings that God gives.

Psalm 69:1–3

February 19

God's Strange Way

There is a strange contradiction in the way we so often live the Christian life. We so easily take God for granted. And we so often get upset when God does not respond to our cry for help in the way we want.

One of the flaws of the Christianity of the modern world, particularly in the West, is that Christians have the idea God is there just for them. They are the center and God is there just to bless them.

There is little idea that things should be the other way round. God is the center and we should live our lives for the glory and purposes of God.

This flawed way of living the Christian life means we have expectations regarding the way God should act towards us and on our behalf. Usually, we have the idea that God should jump to our attention. Some have the idea that God is their butler.

That things are different is a lesson we need to learn, however confronting and painful that may be. St. John Chrysostom begins to point us in the right direction. He writes, God "does not cut calamities short at the outset, but averts them only as they approach their climax when almost all have abandoned hope."[50] Thus, God does not wrap us up in cotton wool. But God does come to our aid.

And God is not at our beck and call. God has his own sovereign way with us. God's way with us is one of love and care, but so often God works differently than our expectations. Thus in faith we have to embrace God's strange way with us.

Prayer

I will with difficulty bend my will to yours, O God, and embrace your mysterious way with me. Amen.

James 2:1–5

February 20

Equality

It is stating the obvious to say our world is deeply divided: the first world and the two-thirds world; rich and poor; the powerful and the oppressed; majority groups and minorities. In the community of faith it can and should all be very different.

Throughout the entire Bible there is a consistent message that God has a heart for the poor and powerless and such persons should be treated with love, care, and justice.

That message is in the Pentateuch, the Prophets, the Psalms, the Gospels, and the Epistles. If there is anything that is clear in the biblical story, it is this message: love of God involves love of neighbor and in particular the poor, the fatherless, the widow, those in distress, those oppressed, and those in need. Thus to have a Christian heart is to have a heart for the poor.

The place where this great generosity of heart should begin is in the community of faith. But often this is not the case, hence the challenge of St. Augustine. He writes, "But it ought never to be that in thy Tabernacle the persons of the rich should be welcome before the poor, or the nobly born before the rest."[51]

The great vision of Scripture is a new humanity in Christ. This is a humanity in which the way of Christ is embodied and where the old ethnic, economic, and gender barriers are broken down. When the church lives this vision, its witness will be revolutionary. Living this vision could change our world.

Reflection

"There is no longer Jew or Greek, there is no longer slave or free, there is no longer male and female, for all of you are one in Christ Jesus" (Gal 3:28).

Psalm 119:124–25

February 21

Love of Knowledge

The Christian life is all about faith, love, and prayer. But it is also about the knowledge of God and in that light our knowledge of ourselves and of our world.

Sometimes in certain circles of Western Christianity things are played off against each other. Work is played off against prayer. Spirituality is played off against daily duties and responsibilities.

But the Christian life can only be lived well as an integrated whole. Head, heart, and hand; knowledge, spirituality, and service, belong together. The one dimension impregnates the other.

St. Bernard points us towards a further integration, the inter-connectedness between love and understanding. He writes, the one "who understands truth without living it, or loves without understanding, possesses neither the one nor the other."[52]

To love God also means knowing God and this knowing is both informational *and* existential. In other words, we know things about God *and* we know God experientially.

This is equally true of the neighbor and our world. To love the neighbor well involves knowing our neighbor. And to know the neighbor in love is to truly know him or her.

Equally we are invited, not simply to know things about our world, but to love our world—to love our world for the sake of Christ. This means to love our world redemptively and transformationally.

Thought

To know and see in love is to see truly.

Hebrews 12:3

February 22

Strong and Gentle

To be marked by love does not mean one is weak. Rather, it means one's strength is used, not to exploit, harm, or dominate, but to build up, nurture, and care.

Because there is such stress in the biblical story on love and humility, one can easily misread this to mean Christians are to be gullible, exploitable, and weak. This is a serious misreading of Scripture.

Moses was called the meekest or humblest man in all the earth. But he was the great prophet-leader of Israel, used by Yahweh to lead the Israelites out of Egyptian captivity and oppression. Thus one can be strong and gentle at the same time.

St. Ambrose makes this point more generally. He writes that the "man who is both severe and gentle is blessed: his severity, by striking terror maintains discipline; his gentleness does not crush innocence."[53]

While we may want to word this somewhat differently, the point is clear: strength and love can go together. In fact, love is a particular form of strength. It is strength expressing itself in caring ways.

And to put all of this differently, there is nothing weak about love and humility. To love is to be strong and to be humble is simply to recognize that the sources of a strong love lie in the goodness of God in our lives.

Thought

To be strong without love can lead to domination. To be strong in love is true freedom.

1 Corinthians 3:11

February 23

Forerunners for Jesus

The Christian life is to live in Christ and to live for Christ. Living for Christ is to live in such a way, in the power of the Spirit, that people will be attracted to Christ, will consider Christ, and will embrace him. Thus we are to be a sign pointing to Christ.

The desert fathers lived their lives to point to Christ. They believed certain qualities would assist them in this witness to Christ. "Humility," they said, "is the forerunner of love, as John was the forerunner of Christ; . . . humility draws to love, that is to God Himself, for God is love."[54]

There are also other qualities that reflect the way of Christ and therefore point to him. To go the way of peace, to be a peacemaker, is also a reflection of Christ and a pointer towards Christ.

And so we may speak of faith, hope, and love. We may point to gifts of healing and reconciliation. We also may note the blessing of hospitality freely extended to others. These are all signs and indicators of the way of Christ and therefore are ways to bring Christ into focus.

But while we may be forerunners or signposts it is only when Christ "appears" to a person that eyes are opened and hearts are changed. We may prepare the way, but only Christ himself is the way, the truth, the life. Thus we play our part as a witness, but Christ is the one who captures a person's heart.

Reflection

In pointing to Christ we are not first and foremost pointing to the church or to ourselves, but to the Christ in the Gospels who makes himself known in the encounter of faith.

Ephesians 4:26–27

February 24

Dealing with the Small Issues

We are ever busy and always preoccupied. In this state we easily overlook things. And we are not too discerning and thus leave things undone that should not be left unattended.

There are many good reasons for learning to slow down, no matter what this may cost us in terms of a life reorientation. To do less and think more is a good idea. To create space for reflection is valuable for one's way of life. To practice solitude is not only good for prayer, but also good for one's health.

But Thomas à Kempis helpfully reminds us that, "If you do absolutely nothing about your small faults, you will, little by little, fall into greater ones."[55] This is true regarding our faults. It is also true regarding most other matters. If we don't attend to things that need to be dealt with, then soon we will find ourselves in more difficult circumstances or we become overwhelmed.

The matter of attentiveness is key. And so is taking appropriate action. Surprisingly, this does not come from doing more but from doing less and from creating space. Time to be still. Time to listen. Time to discern.

To live this way inevitably means changing our lifestyle. It is, in our daily affairs, becoming more like monks. It is becoming a contemplative in the midst of life.

Reflection

At the heart of contemplation is attentiveness. And this is both a gift and a work.

Deuteronomy 5:15

February 25

Memory

While we are to live the present and to anticipate the future,
the past is still very much with us. It lives on in our memory
and continues to shape us for good or ill.

It is true there is much we forget. With the passage of time things simply drop away. They fall into forgetfulness. But it is also true there are
things we actively remember. These things are part of our conscious
life. There are also things that come to memory at certain times and in
certain circumstances. We thought we had forgotten some things, but
suddenly the memories are back with a vengeance.

St. Augustine understood this. He writes, "My childhood, for
instance, which is no longer, still exists in time past. . . . But when I call to
mind its image and speak of it, I see it in the present because it is still in
my memory."[56]

It is good to remember both the good and bad times. The latter
we need to grieve, the former calls us to ongoing thankfulness. And in
remembering we can often see more clearly the traces of God's loving
fingers and the footprints of God's grace.

To remember the faithfulness of God in our past is a way of
reminding ourselves of our journey and of the One who has so amazingly
accompanied us. And while much of this accompaniment may have gone
unnoticed, God's goodness has left its traces.

Thought

To remember is to embrace all of who we are and to see the signs of God
as a reminder of God's presence.

Job 1:18–19

February 26

When Things Suddenly Change

While we may wish we could be safely cocooned in life, this is not the case. Unfortunate and even terrible things can happen to all of us. Trials, therefore, are also the important transition points in life.

There are those, of course, who have a sunshine theology. Only bright days ever come their way and only good things ever happen. They seek to live a fair-weather gospel. Bad things only happen to bad people, never to those who are good.

Such a simplistic vision of life has nothing to do with the biblical story. In that story even God's only and beloved Son is cruelly put to death.

Therefore, to reframe the above, we must say that all sorts of things can happen to all kinds of people. Loss, ill health, and suffering also come to the good. And Christians are not immune to the pain and difficulties of life. They too face the whole gamut of weakness, life's difficulties, and the pain and brokenness of our world.

Meister Eckhart, regarding these matters, points out, "A man who has been well-off for many years, loses it all. He ought then to reflect wisely and thank God for his misfortune and loss, for only then will he realize how well off he was before."[57]

The point Eckhart is making is clear. There are lessons to be learned in goodness and in times of difficulty. It is both joy and difficulty that shape our lives for the glory of God. And difficulty in particular can help us make transitions and can make us more thankful for what we have been given, even when these are taken away.

Thought

Loss invites us into reflection, and reflection can lead to transformation.

Psalm 91:4

February 27

Healing

Healing has many dimensions. While there may be need for physical healing, there may also be need for emotional restoration. And full restoration is always relational.

St. Anselm in his writings on prayer, pens one of great tenderness. He writes, "run under the wings of Jesus your Mother and lament your grief under his feathers. Ask that your wounds may be healed and that, comforted, you may live again."[58]

This prayer recognizes the importance of shelter, nurture, and home-coming in the healing process. The language in this prayer is significantly feminine, relational, and profoundly healing.

Unwellness can come from many sources, but it can also come from a sense of lostness, alienation, and fragmentation. It is often the sad result of relationship breakdown. We don't live well when we are isolated and alone.

Christ is the great healer and restorer and one of the key dimensions of the healing process is to find comfort through closeness, through acceptance, through embrace. In this embrace we are invited to cry out our hurts, sorrows, and pain. We are invited to speak our doubts and to express our hopes.

In being heard and embraced we are healed. Therefore, the community of faith needs to be a place of welcome and honesty. It needs to be a place where we are accepted with all our hurts and needs. It must be a place where masks can be dropped and where our true self, rather than our social self, is in the forefront.

Thought

Healing is being comforted into wholeness.

Philippians 2:22

February 28

The Caring Friend

Great friendships come from great hearts tempered by love and suffering who have come to the place where the well-being of the other is more important than their own concerns.

The twenty-first-century Western world is not rich in deep friendships. Our individualism and self-preoccupation have left us so self-focused and self-concerned that we are imploding. We have little sense that we are well loved and cared for.

St. Bernard, writing to the parents of a new monk, assures them: "I will be for him both a mother and a father, both a brother and a sister. I will make the crooked path straight. . . . I will temper and arrange all things that his soul may advance and his body not suffer."[59]

Here we have a very different vision of friendship. It is one of deep care and nurture. This is a level of care that we feel we could never promise or deliver. Yet St. Bernard could do this within the framework of a monastic community.

The challenge, therefore, for us, is not to try to become the heroic, caring individual, but to create communities of care and friendship in the midst of which great friendships can emerge and grow. Nothing great comes from isolation. Only in relationship do we become who we can be, and from common nurturing much goodness can emerge.

Thought

Friendship is possibly the greatest gift we can give to another.

ST CATHERINE OF SIENA

MARCH

Galatians 2:19–20

March 1

Christ in Us

Living the Christian life is not simply believing Jesus is Savior and Lord. It is also that Christ is found in us and grows in us and that our lives resemble that of Christ.

While the important theme of justification by faith was already emphasized by the early church father, St. Clement, the church fathers also focused on the centrality of a Christo-mysticism. Here the theme is that Christ is being formed in us. Thus we take on Christlike gestalt.

St. Simeon the New Theologian, in the eleventh century, wrote "The ineffable birth of the Word in the flesh from his mother is one thing, his spiritual birth in us [is] another."[60]

This clearly is the work of the Holy Spirit weaving the presence of Christ into the very fabric of our being. It is also us taking on the gentle yoke of Christ. This results in us becoming more Christlike.

In this dynamic process we are invited to place the sanctuary of our being open to this inner spiritual formation. Thus we too have to become like Mary. We too need to say, be it to me according to your purpose and word of promise. We too need to allow the Spirit to have her way with us in this creative work of inner rehabilitation.

And throughout the entirety of our Christian life, we need to welcome this renewing work of the Spirit so that the person and the pattern of the life of Christ become embedded in us. This is the heart of Christian formation.

Prayer

Lord Jesus, Son of the Father, may you grow in me and may I become more and more conformed to your likeness. Amen.

Ephesians 3:16–19

March 2

The Nurturing Christ

Being a Christian is not only having come to faith in Christ and living a life of discipleship. It also has to do with being sustained and nurtured by Christ.

Sadly, for many Christians their sense of the life of faith is primarily one of demand. The Christian life is living with intensity the expectations God has of us. And since God demanded a lot of Jesus, God's faithful Son, God will also demand much of us, his often unfaithful followers. The demand of God rather than the grace of God is thus the main theme.

But the life of faith is first and foremost not one of demand but one of welcome, grace, and blessing. It is living in the joy of reconciliation, the goodness of forgiveness and the wonder of God's presence.

The church father Theophilus understood well this uplifting movement of God's grace. He writes, "Today Christ feasts us; today Christ serves us; Christ, the lover of mankind, refreshes us."[61]

This clearly reflects the movement of the gospel. Christ came to forgive. He came to heal. He came to serve. He came to give us life as a blessing for all. Here generosity is the main theme.

Christ loves us into a fullness of life. He sustains us in our faithfulness. He nurtures us into obedience. He empowers us for service. He shapes us into God-likeness.

Thought

The word of demand constrains us. The acts of love free us. The presence of God lifts us up.

Isaiah 40:10–11

March 3

God's All-Encompassing Love

What we think of God often has more to do with what we think of our parents, other authority figures, and of ourselves. But Scripture invites us into the open spaces of God's all embracing love.

God gets a lot of blame in our contemporary world. God is the cause of religious conflict and bigotry. God causes wars in our world. God is self-interested in the call to worship. God causes people to become dependent. God fails to solve the world's ongoing problems. The list could go on.

But the Bible gives us quite a different picture of God. This God has made a beautiful world. This God calls unlikely people to do acts of wisdom and goodness. This God cares about the oppressed. This God blesses an unlikely people to become a light to the world.

And in Jesus Christ this God shows himself to be the God who identifies with us, enters our struggles and sorrows, and gives his life for the world. This God seeks to make all things well.

Lady Julian of Norwich, the English mystic, talks about the wideness of God's love. "God is the power and goodness of fatherhood; God is the wisdom and loving kindness of motherhood."[62]

This God, beyond human gender, is a God of sovereignty and power and a God of nurture and care. All children and women and men can find a place of safety and refreshment in the love of this God.

Reflection

Embrace God as true mother and father. Be directed by this God. Be nurtured by this God known in the face of Christ.

Proverbs 8:30–31

March 4

The Joy of the Trinity

The thought that there is great joy in the relationship between the Father, the Son, and the Holy Spirit means that joy rather than chaos or despair lies at the heart of the universe. The dancing God rather than the vengeful God is revealed in the biblical narrative.

When in alarm and dismay we see the way in which war, poverty, injustice, and environmental degradation continue to mar our world, then it is hardly surprising that some would embrace the politics of despair. There does not seem to be a lot of good news in our world.

And when one thinks of the bleakness of the crucifixion of Christ, one can easily think that the weight of the world's madness dominates the heart of God. But this is not so. Love and joy are at the heart of the Trinity. The mission of God, while a painful one, comes from the generosity of God's love.

The German mystic Meister Eckhart writes "When the Father laughs to the Son and the Son laughs back to the Father, that laughter gives pleasure, that pleasure gives joy, that joy gives love."[63]

To see God merely as one who is burdened by the world's realities and difficulties is to miss something fundamental about the nature of God. God is first and foremost a community of mutual love and care marked by joy. And it is out of this inner joy and love that God loves our world. Thus love—not chaos and craziness—is our central impulse.

Thought

If we were also marked by joy maybe our loving would have a greater depth and endurance, and our exploitation and warmongering would diminish and finally cease.

70

1 Timothy 3:16

March 5

A Vision of the Christ

Jesus Christ, Son of God and Son of Man, is central to the Christian faith. Truly God, he is also truly one of us and took upon himself the sin and suffering of all humanity.

The mystery of God is not cleared up or resolved in the person of Jesus Christ. It is only deepened. For he too is bathed in mystery as the eternal Son of the Father, who in time becomes one of us and shows us the love of the Father in his life, death, and resurrection.

The early church father St. Ignatius puts this mystery in dialectical terms. He writes, "There is only one physician, who is both flesh and spirit, born and unborn, God in man, true life in death, both from Mary and God, first subject to suffering and then beyond it, Jesus Christ our Lord."[64] To talk about Christ in this way only deepens the mystery of the Savior of the world.

While in our modern world we may be enamored with rational clarity and precision, the Christian faith is as much an invitation to mystery as it is a passion for a faith seeking understanding.

Jesus of Nazareth so clearly portrayed in the Gospel narratives, and further revealed in the Pauline and Johannine reflections, is a man of mystery as much as he is the healer and redeemer of humanity. Thus we are invited to embrace him in faith in his radical otherness as well as in our supposed familiarity.

Thought

Jesus is the God-man. This is already profoundly paradoxical. Thus Christ is both other and one of us.

1 Chronicles 28:9

March 6

The Ever-Seeking God

The good news of the biblical story is not that we find God through our own efforts, but that God seeks us out and wins us over to seek his face. The welcoming God has drawn us into his presence.

God created the world and humanity out of love and joy and for the purpose of relationship and friendship. And it is clear from the biblical story that this God seeks us with passion and persistence. God is ever the Hound of Heaven.

St. Augustine made this confession, "I sighed, and thou didst hear me. I vacillated, and thou guided me. I roamed the broad way of the world, and thou didst not desert me."[65] Thus even in Augustine's waywardness God was already at work.

All of this was true before this church father came to faith in the living God. Augustine knew God was already with him and was already somehow present in his life. How much more then is this true when one has surrendered in faith to this seeking God. All the more, this God will then sustain us and draw us into his presence.

God the Father seeks us out and calls us by name. God the Son goes looking for us and brings us home to his healing arms. God the Spirit broods over us and with renewing breath wings us on our way into the welcoming presence of God and into service in our world.

Reflection

The God who seeks me out truly identifies me, marks me for God's purposes, and shapes my very identity.

Mark 1:32–39

March 7

Contemplation and Action

There are two extremes in the Christian life that should be avoided. The one is to work and serve but not to pray. The other is to pray but not be willing to immerse oneself in the suffering and needs of our world.

Whenever the church in the past has thought in dualistic terms it has emphasized the personal over the social, the soul over the body, the spiritual over the material, celibacy over marriage, and contemplation over action. This has led to a one-sided Christianity.

But the church has also thought in much more integrated ways, recognizing that life is a whole and things belong together. The inner and outer worlds should not be separated and all dualisms should be transcended.

The Desert Father Abbot Silvanus from Mt. Sinai commented to a brother monk, "So Martha is necessary to Mary, for because of Martha is Mary praised."[66] Thus it is important to sit at the feet of Jesus and learn. It is also important to prepare food. It is important to pray. But it is equally important to engage in the work of justice.

Now it is one thing to say that some Christians have the gift to pray and meditate, while others have the gift to work and serve. But to live the Christian life in an integrated way all of us are called to both pray and serve.

Reflection

We pray in order to be with God. We pray to be nurtured. We pray to hear God's voice. We pray in order to serve. And in the very midst of our serving we also pray.

James 1:13–15

March 8

Temptation

Temptation comes to all of us. Most often it comes in unexpected ways. Its movement is towards death rather than life. But good can come out of it, for grace can follow close on the heels of every temptation.

To be tempted presupposes there is a God from whom one can deviate. And it presupposes one can compromise one's own values. It also assumes the Christian has an enemy who is the great Tempter and this personage has some power and influence.

But what is clear from the biblical story is that the great Tempter has limited power and the Christian is safe in the sheltering presence of Christ. Thus, we need not be afraid. But we do need to be aware and vigilant.

The early church father Origen however, believed that the movement of temptation is not wholly negative. Good can come out of it. He writes, "Temptations . . . serve the purpose of showing us who we really are."[67]

Since we are usually tempted in the area of our own foolishness, pride, vulnerability, or weakness, temptation has a way of drawing our attention to those areas of our lives where we are blind or out of kilter. Thus temptation is a wake-up call, inviting us to attentiveness in those areas of our lives where we take things for granted and where problems exist. Temptation can remind us, therefore, what we need to change to and become.

Reflection

In the hands of the enemy of our soul, temptation is the blunt instrument of death. In the purposes of God, it is a gentle blessing unto life.

2 Corinthians 5:18–19

March 9

All of God in the Grace of Salvation

While we tend to speak of God the Father as the Creator, God the Son as the Savior, and the Holy Spirit as the Sanctifier, in the great mutuality of the community of God each of the persons of the Trinity is involved in the work of the other.

In the references in Scripture to worship, baptism, and benediction, we see the beginnings of the later church's formulation of the doctrine of the Trinity. Clearly, here are the foundational references to God the Father, God the Son, and God the Holy Spirit.

This doctrine was never meant to be an arid formulation of mystery. Instead, it was meant to safeguard the divinity of each of the "persons" in the Godhead and to highlight the great love, mutuality, and cooperation between Father, Son, and Holy Spirit.

Julian of Norwich highlights this theme of cooperation. She writes, "The whole Trinity was involved in the passion of Christ, giving us an abundance of virtue and grace by him, though only the maiden's Son suffered."[68]

This mutuality and cooperation, without blurring distinctions, says much about the wonderful nature of God. The members of the Trinity are wholly there for each other. What a picture of unity and diversity.

This mirrors what could be possible amongst us. The church as icon of the Trinity means a church in communion with people being there for each other in love and service. And so should our world be. Communities of cooperation and love, rather than communities and societies based on exclusion and distrust, could swim into view.

Thought

Maybe the Trinity can point us to a whole new world.

Isaiah 55:6–7

March 10

The Seeking Heart

That our hearts are restless is stating the obvious. That restlessness leads to seeking is a basic truism. That we often don't know what we are looking for is the human tragedy.

The human quest for meaning and fulfillment is fundamental to the human condition. But what is worth longing for and seeking after is mainly sculpted by the dominant values of one's society and culture. Society has a good way of inculcating us into the politics of much-having.

But in the Western world we are also influenced in the quest for self-fulfillment shaped by individualism and the myth of the autonomous self. Thus the movement of our being is towards an isolating inwardness.

The ancient writer St. Anselm suggests that such a quest is doomed to failure. He writes, "I sought for peace within myself, and in the depths of my heart I found trouble and sorrow."[69]

He seems to suggest that the inward journey in and of itself will not renew us. We will only find our dark side and our failures. We will only find a greater emptiness.

Instead, we need to find the Other. The welcoming Other. The Great Other who surprisingly does not overwhelm and does not condemn us, but welcomes us to a healing homecoming.

Self-redemption is an illusion. It is only more of the same. God's redemption renews us at the very core of our being.

Thought

Do seek. But don't seek the self. Seek the Loving Other.

2 Timothy 1:13–14

March 11

A Spiritual Companion

Living the Christian life is a calling each individual person must embrace and outwork. But such a life is not a solo journey. There should be companions on the journey, guides along the way, mentors to encourage us.

The biblical story is clear. We need no one else except Christ to bring us to salvation. But we do need others to sustain us in our fidelity to the gospel and to encourage us in our growth towards wholeness and maturity. And we do need others in the joy of witness and service.

The early church father St. Basil talks about the importance of finding a person "who may serve you as a very sure guide in the work of leading a holy life." He goes on to say that such a person must know "the straight road to God."[70]

To be part of the community of faith is an important element in our Christian growth. So is having Christian friends. But to have a mentor or soul friend or spiritual director is a wonderful gift. Such a person can more specifically aid us in the deepening of our life in Christ. And such a person may help us in the important transition points of life.

But such a person must be characterized by humility and wisdom. He or she must know the ways of God and understand the workings of the Holy Spirit. And such a companion must understand psychological and social development as much as the path to spiritual maturity.

Prayer

Lord, grant that I may find such a companion in the journey of faith. Amen.

Luke 22:19–20

March 12

Healing in the Eucharist

Embedded in the biblical concept of salvation is not only the idea of reconciliation and forgiveness, but also the power of healing. Faith in Christ brings grace and restoration. Christ also seeks to make us whole.

Within the life and praxis of the Christian community there are many avenues for healing. The most basic healing is healing for our estrangement from God. This healing occurs when through teaching or speaking or witness one comes to faith in Christ.

Through participation in the life of the church and in small groups various forms of relational healing may take place. And most churches provide healing through their counseling services and pastoral ministry.

But the fathers of early Christianity also understood the healing power of the Eucharist. Theophilus of Alexandria encourages believers, "Eat the bread which purges away the old bitterness, and drink the wine which eases the pain of the wound."[71]

This vision of healing in the Lord's Supper is a recognition that this sacrament is much more than a feast of remembrance. It is a sacramental participation by faith in the Christ who continues to be the life-giver and healer.

Holy Communion is sharing in Christ present with us under the elements of bread and wine. And as such, Christ is truly our spiritual food and drink.

Reflection

Only speak the Word, Lord, and I will be healed.

Romans 8:5–6

March 13

Nature and Grace

The movement of what is natural in us leads only to the self. The dynamic of grace invites us to reach out in love to the other. What is natural to us turns in on itself. Grace is always expansive in its generosity.

To suggest that there is only a singular movement in us is to deny both the witness of the biblical story and the reality of the human condition. We are capable of great good and disastrous evil.

What is clear is that the human being, far from being centered and whole, is instead a conflicted creature. There are contrary forces in the human heart.

Thomas à Kempis understood this well through his own reflections on the biblical story, his own life, and his formation of novices in the religious life. He writes, "nature accomplishes everything for its own gain and profit [and] does nothing without receiving recompense. . . . Grace, however, seeks nothing temporal, asks for no reward other than God Himself."[72]

All of this is not to say that naturally we can't do good. We can and we do. But we are also still on about ourselves. Grace brings a new dimension, however. This is living life out of a deep gratitude because we have been loved into a new existence and have been redeemed by the Christ who gave his life to gain our freedom and healing.

Prayer

Lord, may my life be marked by your grace and my gratitude, and may I live for your glory and the blessing of others. Amen.

Psalm 61:4

March 14

God's Protection

The Christian life is lived not simply by worship and obedience, but also by God's sustaining goodness and protection. And, therefore, think of Christ as a shield before and behind you.

The life of spirituality begins in faith birthed by grace. Grace is the life-giving action of God's goodness in our lives. The impact of this goodness is the movement toward relationship, renewal, and healing.

Living the Christian life also has to do with participation in the Christian community and in practicing the spiritual disciplines. This empowers us for the journey of growth and for the challenges of witness and service.

But there is also more to the Christian life. An underlying theme is not what *we* are and do, but what *God* does in holding us safe.

St. Augustine understood this. He writes, "But see, O Lord, we are thy little flock. Possess us, stretch thy wings above us, and let us take refuge under them. Be thou our glory; let us be loved for thy sake."[73]

This is a prayer. It is a prayer we are invited to pray all of our lives. And it is a prayer we pray not only for ourselves but for the church both local and universal. It is a prayer that recognizes our vulnerability and our need of God's protection and care.

Prayer

Lord, you are the giver of life. Grant us the power of your Spirit to sustain us in the journey of faith. May you hold us, even when we have no sense that we are being held. Amen.

John 17:15–16

March 15

In the World; Not of the World

Christians are fully a part of the world. They too work and play, make things and rest. They too are born and die. But they are also strangers and pilgrims, for they have set their face towards the heavenly city.

Just as a person who has lived cross-culturally no longer fully belongs to his or her homeland nor to the host country, so Christians do not belong wholly to this world nor have they as yet entered heaven. They are in-between, or more correctly, in-both. They have already tasted something of the age to come while they are called to live in and serve the world for the sake of the kingdom of heaven.

The early Christians knew something about this strange status. The author of the *Epistle of Diognetus* writes, "They share their food, but not their wives. They are in the flesh, but do not live according to the flesh. They live on earth, but their citizenship is in heaven."[74]

This in-between and in-both status means Christians can never fully give their full support to a particular political or economic ideology. It also means Christians are able to relinquish things rather than cling to wealth or power, as if these are the whole meaning of life. Further, it means Christians are out of step with the dominant values of a society. Therefore, they are the true subversives, for they see a different world—the world to come—beckoning and groaning towards fulfillment.

And they are to live in the present, anticipating and praying and waiting for what is yet to come.

Thought

To be out of step with the world's agenda is not the place of security. It is a place of insecurity. But it is a step towards a new world.

Ephesians 4:25–28
March 16

Works and Virtues

One cannot truly be great if one's life is based on pride. One cannot truly be generous if generosity is based on self-aggrandizement. One cannot truly be loving if love is some form of manipulation.

There are the things we say and there is the way we truly are. There are the things we do and at the back of those lie the values and motivations that move us.

This highlights that we are complex creatures. It also recognizes that what moves us is as important, if not more important, than what we say or do.

The desert father Abbot Agatho once said, "If an angry man were to raise the dead, because of his anger he would not please God."[75] Such a person would, of course, please others. They would think he was a saint. They would think he was like Jesus and a man of power and virtue. But there is more to the story of a person than simply his or her achievements or abilities, for God looks at the heart.

Thus what moves us is of great importance. Are we motivated by love, even if we are not perfect? Are we moved to bless the other person, even though not everything we say or do is helpful? Are we energized to follow Jesus, even if there are detours in the road?

The mark of a person of maturity, wisdom, and integrity is that what he or she seeks to do harmonizes with one's deepest intentions to live to the glory of God and the well-being of others.

Reflection

When the movement of head, heart, and hand are one, a person is truly integrated.

Psalm 139:1–3
March 17

A Deeper Knowing

We are often only too aware that we really don't understand ourselves and we really don't know what it is we are hoping or looking for.

There is a basic theme in the biblical story that, if understood well, is a source of great joy and comfort. Simply put, the theme is that the God who has created us, redeems us in Christ, and beautifies us through the Spirit, is the God who knows us better than we know ourselves.

St. Anselm knew this well. He writes in a prayer for enemies, "Hear me always with your favor, not according as my heart wills or as my mouth asks, but as you know and will that I ought to wish and ask."[76] In other words, this father of scholasticism and Archbishop of Canterbury in the eleventh century asks that God will know him beyond his own praying and thinking. And so it is. Better to be known well by another and so come to greater self-knowledge.

This is an invitation to self-knowledge and great humility. This means God knows better what I need than what I ask for. God knows more clearly the direction for my life than the choices I make. And God knows more fully what motivates me than my own self-awareness.

As a consequence, I should feel more comfortable in entrusting myself to God rather than to my own abilities. This is truly living God's lordship in our lives.

Thought

To be fully known and yet to be greatly loved is a blessing indeed! It is the great surprise that can nurture us.

John 6:35

March 18

The Living Bread

The Christian life is one of discipleship, obedience, and service. It is also a life of being sustained and nurtured. And in the most unlikely places and ways, God provides bread and wine for the often uneven journey of faith.

We are nurtured by God's providential care through the gifts of creation. These bounteous gifts should be shared equally by all.

We are also invited to share fully in the gift of God's salvation in Christ. He is the true life for the world. He is the living bread. In Christ we find life's joy, meaning, and purpose.

But we all are also invited to open our lives to the renewing, empowering, and life-giving action of the Holy Spirit, who works tirelessly and mysteriously to sustain our lives, to beautify us, and to gift and empower us for meaningful service.

And there are many other ways God seeks to nurture us: in the gift of family, the blessing of friends, and the care of the faith community. Even neighbors and colleagues can be, and often are, a source of encouragement for us. Thus God can use anyone to be a blessing to us. In the Ambrosian Acclamations we read, "O bread eternal, you feed the hunger of your people in desert places."[77] This is a hunger for God, a hunger for wholeness, a hunger for relationship, a hunger for knowledge, and a hunger for justice. And God can meet this hunger in surprising ways.

Reflection

What we hunger for is an indication of what we want to live for. The Living Bread feeds our hunger.

1 Timothy 2:1–3

March 19

Concerned for All

Christianity is sometimes cast as a world-denying religion with little relevance for the issues of our time. The fact that Christians are called to pray for government and for those in authority already suggests an engagement with society that could have great consequences.

One of the great martyrs of the post-apostolic church, Polycarp, called Christians to pray for all. He writes, "Pray for all the saints. Pray also for kings and magistrates and rulers, and for those who persecute and hate you, and for the enemies of the cross, so that your fruit may be evident among all people."[78]

Thus, as an absolute minority in the hostile world at that time, Christians were challenged not simply to be concerned about themselves and their heavenly reward. They were called to pray for the very people who sought to do them harm. Their suffering was to be the seed for a new world.

What is particularly noticeable about Polycarp's call to prayer was that he believed this would have an effect. He believed good fruit would come from the suffering community that was willing to forgive and pray for their very tormentors.

This poses a significant challenge for us in the contemporary world where so often we no longer see God at work, where we doubt the efficacy of prayer and where we tend to see the political realm as self-contained and therefore beyond the reach of our prayers. Polycarp's vision calls us to be a faithful and intercessory people.

Thought

A Christian recovery of prayer may yet revolutionize our world.

Hebrews 12:2–3

March 20

The Strident Christ

There are many ways by which we can typify and imagine Christ: the Innocent Child, the Suffering Servant, the Obedient Son of the Father, the Reformist Rabbi, and the Challenging Prophet. However, the Son of God is always beyond all of our images of him.

How we imagine Jesus often says more about ourselves than it does about the Savior of the world. We try to make Jesus fit into our ideas and values. Often the Christ we supposedly worship is the Christ of our own making.

That we have cast Jesus in soft pastel hues in the modern world says more about the kind of world we have and the kind of savior we want. As a consequence, Jesus is more a loving buddy or friend than a fearless and strong leader. This is because we don't want Jesus to lead us. We only want him to help us. We don't want to obey him.

William of St. Thierry, the abbot of a Benedictine monastery in the twelfth century, casts Jesus in very different terms. He writes, "our most powerful athlete, having entered as it were the stadium of the world, was anointed with the oil of the Holy Spirit for the match and rejoiced as a first to run the course of human dispensation."[79]

It may well help us overcome our soft Christianity by thinking about Jesus as the *fearless* leader, the *valiant* Son of the Father, the *brave* as well as the obedient Son of God. This picture of Christ may challenge us to become the fearless followers of Christ rather than the consumer Christians we are at present.

Thought

If we want to remake ourselves, we may need to remake our image of Christ. Or more particularly, we may need to let Christ confront us in his otherness.

Luke 15:3–7

March 21

Lost and Found

There are two interrelated themes in the biblical story—our flight from God and God's search to find us. In the triumph of grace it is the latter that wins the day.

The ancient church father St. Augustine said it well: "I would not find myself, much less thee."[80]

This is so in a number of ways: we do not so much find God, it is God who finds us. Salvation is not the human climb up to the divine. It is the divine stooping down to embrace a wayward humanity. The great theme of the biblical story is the incarnation.

This, of course, does not mean the human is simply factored out. No. In our seeking God is already drawing us. And in our response of faith grace has already been given us. And in homecoming there is already having been found.

But the church father also reminds us that finding God and finding ourselves are intimately related. This is because God is not only our salvation, but also our true home. We are truly human in relationship with God and others. We are less than what we can be in flight, in isolation, and without an abiding center.

Thus coming to God does not take us away from ourselves, as if we do violence to ourselves in the act of faith. The opposite is true. We come home to ourselves in committing ourselves to God's embrace. And in the face of the God of grace we can more clearly see ourselves.

Reflection

Being found is not simply a return to a previously known place. It is entering a new reality.

1 Thessalonians 5:21

March 22

Discernment

It is important to give ourselves to the wisdom of others. The church in its long journey has produced many saints, teachers, prophets, pastors, and activists. From these we can learn much. But we must practice discernment, for these too must be subject to the wisdom of the gospel.

There are two extremes that must be avoided. The first is to live the Christian life without tradition and assume Christianity can be wholly reinvented. The second, at the other extreme of the continuum, is to live the whole of one's Christian life simply bounded by Christian tradition.

There are much more creative ways to live. These are: to be fully aware of the Spirit's renewing and creative energy; to be deeply immersed in the biblical story; to respect the church's long march in history; and to respond to the issues of our day. To integrate these various dimensions makes the Christian life sustainable, exiting, relevant, and orthodox.

St. Basil, in giving Christian advice, points out that it is important to listen to the wisdom of the past. But he goes on to say, "Do not surrender your mind as if it were a ship's rudder answering to control. No; take what suits you, and learn to discard the rest."[81] Thus, he points us to a creative reappropriation of the past and not to a dull conformity.

Here is the call to discernment for which we need the Spirit's guidance to gain humility and courage. And courage is always needed when one seeks to be relevant.

Thought

Eat the fish but leave the bones. Hold fast to the good of the past and daringly embrace the new.

John 20:23

March 23

Sin Bearer

Jesus is the great sin bearer who in his own body took to himself the sin and suffering of the world. Such a task is beyond us. But we can carry the burdens of another person.

There are burdens a person should bring only to the foot of the cross. Only Christ can take up these burdens, concerns, failures, and sins. And in the very act of laying these things down there can be release and forgiveness. The great exchange Martin Luther so often wrote about can take place. God takes our sin, but gives us his forgiveness.

But there are some burdens one may take up on another person's behalf. It is possible to believe for another when his or her faith wavers. It is possible to intercede for another when her or his prayer life is all but abandoned. It is appropriate to comfort when the other is grief stricken. It is possible to be there for another.

St. Catherine of Siena used to say to sinners who came to her, "Have no fear, I will take the burden of your sins."[82]

This does not mean she saw herself in the place of Jesus the Savior. Rather, it was that the person coming for help could not see the Savior's forgiveness and embrace. St. Catherine then in faith, prayer, and suffering "carried" that person to Jesus.

This is the power of intercessory prayer. It is the power of radical identification. It is being willing to stand in another person's place.

Prayer

Lord, help me and give me the grace to be there for others, and to carry others to you. Amen.

Mark 10:21

March 24

The Challenge of Relinquishment

The Christian's life is gaining a new life in Christ. It is also about leaving behind an old way of life. And it also has to do with the art of relinquishment.

The English medieval Christian mystic Richard Rolle made this challenge: "Take heed also: to seek more than enough is foul covetousness; to keep back necessaries is frailty; but to forsake all things is perfectness."[83]

All of this is a challenge for us Christians in the twenty-first century. We think we never have enough. We believe what is ours is for us alone. And we have the idea that God is supposed to give us things, not us giving anything to God.

It is true the Christian life is about receiving much: salvation, the gift of eternal life, the gift of the Spirit. But it is also about giving. Living the Christian life has to do with giving ourselves to God and to the purposes of God's kingdom and to the love and service of the neighbor.

In giving ourselves to God and the neighbor we learn the art of relinquishment. For some this is being generous with financial resources. For others it is being hospitable. For others again it is mentoring or helping others. For some it is not marrying. For others it is relinquishing a career trajectory. For some it is giving all of one's possessions.

There is no formula here, only acts of love and generosity and self-giving. Here the manifold promptings of the Spirit come to startling clarity in the various ways in which we can honor God.

Thought

In self-giving we follow the way of Christ.

Luke 12:31

March 25

The Seeking Heart

Living the Christian life is receiving the grace of God in Christ. It is living a life of faith, discipleship, and service. It is participating in the Christian church and it is living in the hope of a new heaven and a new earth. But it also has to do with the seeking heart.

In the modern world it does not take much for us to become bored and disinterested. This can be in our love life, our jobs, our interests, our relationships, and even in our life of faith.

At this point in the twenty-first century there are many Christians, in the West at least, who are quite bored with the church, hardly ever read Scripture, and have no interest in theological reflection. They are only interested in God being the magical extra in their lives.

To live the Christian life beyond boredom poses some interesting challenges. St. Augustine suggests we need to be people of passion who continue to seek. He writes, "Give me a man [or woman] in love; he [or she] knows what I mean. Give me one who yearns; give me one who is hungry; give me one far away in this desert who is thirsty and sighs for the spring of the Eternal Country."[84]

This passion of the seeking heart is the fruit of the Spirit. It is the Spirit who renews us. But the seeking heart is also a commitment we make in looking to God in the hard times and the dry places. Thus in the practice of the spiritual disciplines we look to God to give us life and renew us. In these practices we continue to seek for what may yet happen.

Thought

The seeking heart is often the empty heart. It can become the full heart.

Romans 12:3

March 26

Inhabiting Oneself

Many people are uneasy in their own body. Cosmetic surgery offers one solution. Many others are uneasy with their inner life: their soul, their conscience, their hidden thoughts, and their inner story. Various forms of denial offer an unhelpful way forward.

That we somehow want to be different than the way we are is virtually intrinsic to the human condition. The ways to become different are many and varied and range from denial and escape to transformation and transcendence.

While the language about change in Christianity is the language of conversion, renewal, and healing, this is not to suggest that in our essential being and personality we somehow become radically different. The cynic comes to faith, but this does not mean an extrovert becomes an introvert. There is much about us that may well remain the same.

Meister Eckhart's statement—"With every creature according to the nobility of its nature, the more it indwells itself, the more it gives itself out"[85]—is, therefore, insightful. Despite the changes that conversion brings, I still need to embrace my biology, my history, my personality, and my giftedness. And in living fully into who I am, I can more fully bring that to the worship of God, participation in the community of faith, and in service to the neighbor.

In becoming a Christian I do not become an inauthentic person or a religious clone, instead I become more truly who I am meant to be.

Reflection

Faith does not undermine our humanity. It only deepens it.

Deuteronomy 6:5

March 27

Offering Oneself

There is a world of difference between giving something of one's possessions and giving oneself. The latter will always be more difficult and challenging than the former.

The unknown English mystical author of *The Cloud of Unknowing* and *The Book of Privy Counseling* offers this insight: "Now it is enough to worship God perfectly with your substance, that is, with the offering of your naked being."[86] This suggests that God does not so much want our things, but wants *us*.

Because we live in such a materialistic and consumeristic age, aspects of contemporary Christianity have been affected by these values. The most crass version of this is the idea that if we give financially to God (by giving to the church or to a Christian cause) then God will reciprocate by blessing us materially.

But our mystical author points us in a very different direction. The heart of Christianity is worship. And what we bring first and foremost is not our gifts but our very life, our heart, and our passions and commitments. The reference to offering our *naked* selves is significant.

In giving oneself to God one gives to the God who has given everything. In giving only something of what we possess we give partially and we withhold what God asks of us. God asks that we give him our all, our very being.

Thought

To give oneself is to lay down one's life. It is the great act of worship and obedience. This makes God central to our lives.

Galatians 3:28

March 28

All One in Christ Jesus

The history of the church has been blighted with hierarchy, paternalism, and patriarchy. But there have always been voices that have championed a radical egalitarianism in the community of faith through Christ.

To a very significant degree the story of the New Testament is clear enough. All, irrespective of race, gender, or social class, are candidates for the love of God in Christ Jesus. All receive the Holy Spirit. All have gifts. All have a contribution to make in the home, the church, and society. Christ has forged into being a new humanity of equality.

St. John Chrysostom sees this vision of common faith and common participation in the things of God most clearly in the Eucharist. He writes, "There is no difference at all between the priest and the layperson, as for example, when we are to partake of the awesome mysteries, for we are all alike counted worthy of the same things."[87]

The grace of God in Christ places all on the same level. The blessing of God's forgiveness and welcome makes us all one. The commonality of the one Spirit binds us all together. And the call of God places us all in the service of God, even though that may be outworked in different ways. This communion of saints is the bond that makes us one.

And in the Eucharist we confess a common need for Christ, for spiritual sustenance and empowerment. To this feast we all come as those in need of Christ's life.

Reflection

In the Eucharist we confess we are one body, one spiritual family, one community.

Deuteronomy 15:12–15

March 29

A Passion for Justice

Whatever complex factors have been the impulses towards an esoteric and world-denying form of Christianity, this emphasis is not reflected in the biblical story. Nor is it supported by the early church fathers.

The apostolic church father Clement writes with singular clarity about the practical outworking of living the Christian life. He writes, "Put an end to your wickedness; learn to do good, seek out justice; deliver the one who is wronged; give judgment on behalf of the orphan, and grant justice to the widow."[88]

Here once again we are reminded that the grace of God towards us is the grace that has a ripple effect. It is a grace that moves us to forgive. It is a grace that sustains us in the often long work for justice. It is a grace that cares for the vulnerable and the often-neglected members of our society. It is a grace that graces others.

Put more strongly, this is a grace that moves us to build a new world order. This grace is not simply about fostering an inward piety or a church enclave or a "bless me" club. Rather, it is an inner work of the Spirit that moves us to compassion and service.

But to live this way is no picnic. It is the costly side of grace. Grace that comes from the One who gave his life for us is a grace that moves us to live our life for God's kingdom purposes. And this involves costly service to the poor and marginalized. Such a service may cost us our very life.

Thought

If your life of faith costs you nothing and calls for no sacrifices, then you may be following a home-made messiah. Following the Messiah of the Gospels calls you to give your all.

Acts 8:18–19

March 30

The Misuse of Holy Things

It is entirely appropriate for those who serve in churches and religious organizations to be paid appropriately. What is not appropriate is when we use our spiritual gifts and abilities for selfish gain, for power over others, and for the many possible forms of manipulation.

From Gehazi (2 Kgs 5:20–27) through to Simon (Acts 8:18–19) there have been those in the biblical story who have sought spiritual power for financial gain. Sadly, this has also occurred in the history of the church. Spirituality gives us power. And this power can be misused for selfish gain.

The great church reformer John Hus was so concerned about this form of abuse in the church of his day that he wrote a treatise on it. He writes, "all those who buy or sell the gifts of God, either for money or for some other consideration . . . are called Simoniacs."[89]

This also poses a great challenge for our day when consumer values have so penetrated the life of the church and where the misuse of spiritual authority and power has become such a problem. Consumerism has not been changed by the church, rather it has changed the church.

The solution to this temptation is radically simple: spiritual blessings and gifts have been freely received from God's good hand; they should be freely given.

So if a gift of healing from God leads to a ministry of healing for others, then such a ministry must be exercised in humility, thankfulness, and generosity of heart. It should never be exercised merely to gain financial benefits.

Thought

Avarice will destroy us. Generosity is life-giving.

John 3:34
March 31

The Winsome Spirit

At the heart of the Christian life is not simply a set of beliefs, but the presence of the indwelling Holy Spirit. The gentle Spirit renews and fructifies.

Faith is important. Commitment to a life of fellowship in the community of faith is important. Witness and service are important dimensions to living the Christian life.

But all of this is premised on the work of God in Christ in redemption and in the ever present breath of the Holy Spirit. The Holy Spirit within one's very being sustains us in the life and way of Christ. The Spirit renews and revitalizes. The Spirit directs and guides. And the Spirit empowers us for service in the community of faith and in society.

St. Cyprian, bishop of Carthage, writes about the Spirit in endearing terms, "the Holy Spirit came as a dove, an innocent and happy creature . . . [who] loves human company and knows the fellowship of a single home."[90]

What this early church father is touching on is the Spirit's work in bringing about fellowship and unity. The Gentle Dove makes us gentle. And one of the signs of the Spirit's working is harmony and unity.

Divisiveness is the fruit of pride. Fellowship is the fruit of the Spirit. And homecoming to the heart of God and the community of faith is a blessing of the Spirit. Thus the Spirit's work is one of breaking down barriers and creating bonds of friendship and love.

Thought

Stop wandering. Allow the Spirit to bring you home and to make us one.

ST PATRICK

Matthew 23:23

April 1

What We Have Not Done

It is easy to get our priorities wrong in living the Christian life. Head knowledge can overtake heart knowledge. Ceremonies can overtake piety. And churchianity can overtake our call to love the neighbor and the stranger.

The revered abbot St. Maximus the Confessor wrote, "We shall be judged for the evil we have done, but especially for the good we have neglected and for the fact that we have not loved our neighbor."[91]

The good we neglect often springs from the fact that our frame of reference is too narrow. We are comfortable and know what we should do in our family setting. We are familiar with what is required of us in church. But in the affairs of the wider world we are often uncomfortable and insecure and we don't know what is required of us. We are also unclear regarding our role in the marketplace and in the world of politics. As a result, we tend to hold back and not do anything.

But some things are clear and we need the faith and courage to carry them out. We are always called to forgive those who hurt us. We are always called to love irrespective of whether we are loved in return. And we are always called to serve. And we are called to see the increase of the reign of God and see shalom flourish in all the places of our world.

But there are also times where we need to stand up for what is right and serve the cause of justice. This may well be the most costly thing that is asked of us.

Prayer

Lord, grant me the grace to do what I need to do, and not do only what I am comfortable with. Amen.

Hebrews 13:17

April 2

Obedience

This word has become a great problem for us in the contemporary world. We are basically on about mutual decision-making and self-determination. But the Christian life can't be lived without obedience. God is Lord whether we like it or not.

St. Benedict in his *Rule* expressed the idea that obedience is an important characteristic in the Christian life. This is especially so for the monk.

But St. Benedict sees obedience as a great act of humility and believes this particularly characterized the life of Jesus who was obedient to the Father in all things, even in his surrender to the cross. Obedience, therefore, is Christlikeness.

It follows then that we, who name Christ and are baptized into him, should also bear the mantle of obedience. In this we show we are disciples of Christ.

Where all of this becomes difficult for us is not so much in obeying Scripture or the leading of the Holy Spirit—although that too is difficult—but obeying a spiritual leader (priest, pastor, or mentor).

Yet St. Benedict called his monks to live in this Christlike way. He points out the need for sincerity. "If a disciple obeys grudgingly and grumbles, not only aloud but also in his heart, then, even though he carries out the order, his action will not be accepted with favor by God."[92]

Clearly, this heart attitude is something we will need to learn in the dynamics of Christian formation, community, and service. It will greatly challenge our sense of independence and self-determination.

Prayer

Lord, form my heart into the shape that loves to do your will. Amen.

Matthew 22:37–39
April 3

A Beautiful Balance

There is a lot of evidence that life in the modern world is out of balance. We work hard and play hard and then rest. But in our resting we are not renewed. Somehow we are out of joint. We are not centered. We are not at peace.

The unknown mystical writer of *The Cloud of Unknowing* and the smaller book *The Book of Privy Counseling* writes, "That which I am and the way that I am, with all my gifts of nature and grace, you have given to me, O Lord, and you are all of this. I offer it all to you principally to praise you and to help my fellow Christians and myself."[93]

This prayer reflects a wonderful integration. It recognizes the gifts of one's biology, family history, and socialization. It also recognizes the spiritual gifts of salvation, the Holy Spirit, and the various charisms and qualities that grow in our lives.

The prayer makes clear that all these gifts, both natural and spiritual, are the gifts of God. And these gifts—including my personality, education, and training—are first of all gifts that lead to gratitude and to worship.

But these gifts, while they are also for my growth and development, are meant to serve the wider community. In this way the life of God and the goodness of God are shared. It's a life that flows from God, impacts us, and reverberates in the life of others.

What is striking is that the unknown author sees service to others as also being a personal blessing. We give, but we also receive.

Prayer

Lord, help me to live this prayer in the grace of Christ and the power of the Spirit. Amen.

Galatians 6:15

April 4

The Reshaping of a Life

We are both flawed creatures and people who do damage to ourselves in the way we think and act. A reshaping is therefore called for and a healing of what we are and have done becomes a great necessity.

At the heart of Christianity is the incredible message that newness and healing are possible because God is the renewing and restoring God. Thus, the heart of the biblical story is good news indeed.

St. Anselm, the great church father of the eleventh century, fully understood this double movement of God's restorative activity. He writes, "Refashion the face that I have spoiled, restore the innocence that I have violated."[94]

In this statement St. Anselm recognizes that I not only have to be redeemed from my sinning and wrongdoing. I also have to be restored back to a primal innocence. Here my shame and brokenness are dealt with.

This is indeed a great healing, for it means that I can, through the grace of God, live in the realm of love and joy without inner recriminations and without shame. This is inner freedom indeed!

This is a picture, not simply of having my marred coat replaced, but the joy of gaining a new heart and spirit. I have donned on a coat of many colors.

The grace of God thus restores a simplicity of heart and a transparency of being that makes us new creatures in Christ.

Reflection

In what areas of my life do I need this restoration?

2 Thessalonians 2:13

April 5

Life with the Trinity

The Christian life is life in relation to the Father, the Son, and the Holy Spirit. God as Trinity is deeply involved in the sustaining and growth of our life in Christ.

St. Ignatius believed the Christian life was lived in the fellowship of the Trinity. He writes, "you are stones of a temple, prepared beforehand for the building of God the Father, hoisted up to the heights by the crane of Jesus Christ, which is the cross, using as a rope the Holy Spirit; your faith is what lifts you up and love is the way that leads up to God."[95]

While we may find this kind of language somewhat curious, there is an interesting emphasis on relational cooperation. The Holy Spirit lifts us up, but so does our faith. Clearly, this envisages an interpenetration of the work of God with our volition and response.

So God builds us into a spiritual house or community, but through a love that leads us back to God. The Father is at work, this work is through the Son in the power of the cross, and the Holy Spirit is the One who makes it all happen in our experience. And we respond in faith and love to receive what God is doing and what God has given.

The Father as creator, the Son as redeemer, and the Holy Spirit as empowerer, draw us into a fellowship with all that God is and does. What a joy to be part of this Trinitarian community!

Thought

The Christian life is living in the joy of the fellowship of the Father, Son, and Holy Spirit. This is the ultimate homecoming.

Mark 8:34–35

April 6

The Christ of Convenience and the Christ of the Cross

Some want to follow only a fair-weather Christ; others only a Christ who dispenses benefits. But the suffering Christ calls us to share in the suffering of the world.

The salvation Christ brings is a gift that draws us into Christlikeness and into conformity with his plan and desires for our world. This means the benefits of Christ's death and resurrection play out in our lives in such a way that the purposes of Christ and the way of Christ are repeated in us. And this includes the power of the cross in our lives and ministry.

Thomas à Kempis understood this. He laments, "Jesus today has many lovers of His heavenly Kingdom, but few of them carry His cross."[96]

It is hardly different in our day. Our consumer Christianity looks for blessings and benefits that augment and enrich *our* lives. But it knows little of a Christianity that calls us to self-denial and sacrifice. It hardly understands that the Christian life is cruciform in that we bear the mark of the cross.

This does not mean all is gloomy and dark. Rather, it means we live in the challenge and excitement of God's purposes, while at the same time recognizing relinquishment is a key part of this journey. One can hardly follow the call of God if one is not willing to let go of one's own way.

Prayer

All to you, O Lord, I surrender. Keep me safe in this challenging commitment. Amen.

Philippians 4:8
April 7

Growth in Self Love

Because we want to do full justice to the biblical notion of humanity's fall into sin and human on-going wrongdoing, we can wrongly give the impression that Christianity is only about the dark side of life. There is another side. And this is about goodness, growth, and love.

Ramon Lull, the medieval Franciscan mystic and missionary, in his book about the lover and the Beloved wrote this reflection: "The Lover asked his Beloved if there remained in Him anything still to be loved. And the Beloved answered that he had still to love that by which his own love could be increased."[97]

This is both a profoundly spiritual as well as psychological insight. In loving the other, in this case God, the movement of love is not simply to see or to discover what is loveable in the other. It is also a matter of tapping into the depths of one's own being and identifying one's inner longings, hopes, and dreams. Once these are identified one can then love the other with these longings.

What is implicit in this movement is a healthy love of self. It shows an ability to embrace what is good in us who are made in God's image and are marked by his grace.

This movement of love invites us to accept and work with what is embryonic in us, what is small and what is fragile. It invites us not to reject what we are, but to place it in the service of love.

Prayer

Help me Lord, to see what in my life can be placed in the service of love. Amen.

Ephesians 1:17–19

April 8

The Inner and the Outer Life

Ours is an age that focuses on the outer dimensions of life. Beauty, achievements, and productivity are regarded as the signs of life. But the wisdom of the ancients is that the inner life is what determines everything else.

In the early stages of the twenty-first century there are increasing voices that are questioning the dominant logic of the twentieth century with its emphasis on rationality, productivity, and progress. Much of this is now seen as undermining the integrity of a wholesome life, the nature of community, and the sustenance of a very delicate and fragile world.

In this rethinking there is a growing awareness of the importance of imagination, intuition, relationships, care for the earth, and the value of spirituality. And it could well be that the rest of this century may see a growth in these dimensions of life.

The English mystic Julian of Norwich helps us to move in this direction. She writes, "the inward should by grace draw the outward."[98] The outward has to do with our mortal physical nature and all we do. The inward has to do with being united to Jesus and his heavenly kingdom.

So in the light of this the challenge for us is to be deeply related to Jesus, to be prayerful and contemplative. And this inner life is to animate our life of love, service, and work in the world.

Thought

It should not be such that our work determines our prayer. Instead, our prayer should determine our work.

Genesis 1:28–30

April 9

Shaping a World

Whether it is the world of nature, an urban community, or a place of work, we are called to care for and nurture and shape our environment and social settings. In this way we outwork the creation mandate.

Humans made in the image of God are invited to shape their world. They are called to bring order out of chaos and to draw out the earth's potential. They are to build families, institutions, and societies.

This calling is never an invitation to exploitation but to nurturing care. Stewardship is the challenge, not wanton recklessness. We are to build well and with justice for all.

William of Malmesbury, speaking of the work of monks turning unused land to fruitful cultivation, writes, "In the middle of wild swampland . . . [now cultivated] . . . is an image of Paradise."

For the monks, raw nature became sculpted by human hand, not for the purpose of exploitation, but to make a place of life, sustenance, solitude, and spirituality. William goes on to write that such a place became "the school of those who love Divine Wisdom."[99] Here links are made between nature, a place, human habitation, and spirituality.

The power and beauty of this vision is that all of life becomes charged with the grandeur of God. All is sacred. Spirituality encompasses everything. And nature becomes not simply a place for toil and extraction, but it becomes a sanctuary.

Thought

The earth and our social locations are to be places of safety and nurture.

2 Timothy 1:5–6

April 10

A Soul Friend

In the West we think that becoming a Christian and growing in the Christian life is purely an individual affair. All of this is simply about God and me. But neither the biblical story nor the witness of the church in previous centuries holds such a view.

The fourteenth-century English mystic and Augustinian canon Walter Hilton had this to say about Christian formation: "If not even the least of the arts can be learned without some teacher and instructor, how much more difficult it is to acquire the Art of Arts, the perfect service of God in the spiritual life, without a guide."[100]

In the light of this good advice it is imperative we find sisters and brothers in the faith who can play such a formative role in our lives. We should not journey alone in the pathway of faith.

Clearly, instruction in the faith and participation in the faith community are important resources. So is the encouragement of Christian family and friends. But Hilton assumes more is called for.

As a consequence, we need to open ourselves to being mentored and having a spiritual companion or director help us in our discernment of the ways of God with us. This calls us to humility and openness.

While God can and does work directly with us and in us, God is also pleased to use others. Hence relationships, friendships, and community are important in shaping one's life of faith.

Thought

A spiritual companion is only ever a guide. But guides are valuable, especially in difficult terrain.

Psalm 84:1–2

April 11

Living for a Higher Good

Self-transcendence means going through a fiery furnace where we discover that living only for ourselves and our own concerns is not life-giving but death-dealing.

In the modern world, reinforced by our persuasive culture, we are fed the idea that true happiness is found only in self-fulfillment. But at the end of the day this leads to a narrowing of the inner impulses of the heart, a restriction of vision, and an unhealthy social isolation.

There is a sense of health and well-being in the person who has been able to transcend his or her narrow preoccupations and has moved from the shallows into the wide ocean of human experience and concern.

For the Christian there is also the need to move into the wide spaces of God's love and concern for humanity. This means we are to inhabit two horizons: that of the vision of the Bible and the beauty and challenges of our world.

St. Augustine speaks about a transformation where one moves to "taking pleasure in thy [God's] good things as if they were . . . [one's] own."[101] This is quite a revolution for it means that we relate to God not simply for the blessings we may receive, but because we want to share in God's concerns for our world.

This is a true expression of what it means that God is Lord and that we love God enough to do his will. When God's good becomes the focus of our good and the good we wish to do to others, a new world will surely come into being.

Prayer

Lord, give us the vision and hunger for your good. Amen.

John 17:20–21

April 12

Oneness in Christ

There are deep divisions in Christendom, and Reformation Christianity has now splintered into thousands of pieces. And as if this is not enough, there are continued ethnic, gender, and social status differences in many faith communities.

Jesus' prayer that the faith community may be one and united in a common fellowship with the Father and the Son in the power of the Spirit is a prayer that urgently needs to be realized in our day. It is a prayer waiting fulfillment.

The church of the modern world is still deeply divided, even though many Christians no longer hold to the old denominational allegiances. Local churches are divided through a lack of formation into a common faith. People are still marginalized in the church because of gender issues. And the churches themselves are organized along ethnic or economic lines.

St. John Chrysostom has a very different vision—one of commonality and unity. He writes, "One table is set for all, one Father begot us, we are all born of the same birth pangs."[102]

And to this we could add further perspectives. We are all saved through the cross of Christ. We are all blessed with the same Spirit. We all participate in one baptism. And we are all called to the worship of God and the service of the neighbor. Thus, commonality is key to our spiritual DNA and as such needs to come to fuller practical expression.

Prayer

Lord, do truly make us one. Purge all bigotry from our hearts. Help us to overcome all barriers. Amen.

Psalm 138:7–12

April 13

Even in the Depths

In the smooth or the difficult times of life we may not sense God's presence. The biblical witness is that even in the darkest of our places God is there for us.

Sadly, the modern world has not helped us to be spiritually attuned and to be aware of God's presence. In fact, the opposite has happened. Our noisy and preoccupied world has crowded God out of our lives.

The challenge this brings us is that we need to develop a whole new spiritual sensitivity. And the place to start this is in the ordinary flow of our day where we can increasingly stop for a few moments to reflect and pray.

The other arena in which to develop this new sensitivity is in the places of difficulty and darkness where we are so easily tempted to think that God has forgotten us.

St. Anselm understood this. He makes this confession, "Where I now am, you are not absent, for when I descend into hell you are there. And therefore if in my wickedness I flee from you and hide myself in my abyss as one who is damned, even there you behold me."[103]

And so we could make a similar confession. In the places of my fear and failure, you are there, O Lord. In the places of anguish and disappointment, you are there, O Lord. In the places of emptiness and indifference, you draw close to me, O Lord.

Thought

Tell God where you are at, rather than fall into a sullen silence.

Galatians 6:17

April 14

Martyrdom

Throughout the history of the Christian church men and women have believed so deeply and fully in the salvation of Christ that they have been willing to die a martyr's death for the faith.

St. Paul speaks of carrying the marks of Jesus in his body. St. Ignatius uses similar language. He writes, "My chains, which I carry for the sake of Jesus Christ . . ."[104]

History has it that Ignatius was thrown to the lions in the Colosseum in Rome. Paul probably also met a martyr's death in the same city.

In the latter part of the twentieth century in the non-Western world there have been many martyrs for the Christian faith. And this poses a profound challenge for us, in that the Christian faith in the West seems to lack depth and commitment. Ours is a faith of convenience, not a martyr's faith.

This level of commitment on the part of martyrs is not an absurdity. It is a matter of faithfulness and of following of Christ who also went to a terrible death. It is, therefore, the ultimate *imitatio Christi.*

In the history of theological reflection this constitutes a fourth baptism. At conversion there is a baptism into Christ. There is also a baptism into the faith community. And this is accompanied by Spirit baptism. But there is also the baptism of blood, martyrdom for the faith. This martyrdom was meted out to a person of peace being punished for a life of faith and service in Christ.

Reflection

How deep or shallow is my faith? What can deepen my spiritual commitment?

Exodus 33:19

April 15

Mercy and Grace

Many have distorted images of God. God is seen by some as powerful and demanding. Others see God as remote and unconcerned. But God is wholly concerned and wholly for us.

That God is wholly for us does not mean God is for us on *our* terms. This would leave us where we are. And this would be our undoing.

God is for us in a very different way. God is for us for our betterment. God is for us for our healing and transformation.

Julian of Norwich helps us understand what that may look like. She writes, "Mercy works to sustain, to suffer, to vitalize, to heal; and all in tenderest love. Grace works to uplift, to reward, and ever to surpass all we desire or deserve."[105]

This is a helpful picture of God's movement towards us. It is a movement of love and tenderness. It is a movement of healing. But it is also a movement of transformation that takes us beyond where we are to where we could be in the realm of God's future for us. This is, therefore, the gracious movement of hope which takes us beyond the present.

To be taken beyond our present selves into further wholeness is a journey of trust and surrender. It means God knows better than we do what we need and who we are to become. This will always be a challenge for us when we are so often committed to a singular self-determination.

Reflection

God's way is better than our own way. This is a revolutionary confession.

2 Timothy 2:12

April 16

The Charism of Stability

We live in a highly mobile world and we are ever restless to see and experience new things. This mobility for vocational, educational, or recreational reasons has had a huge impact on our Christian formation, the nature of the church, and the shape of the church's mission. An impact that has not necessarily been for the better.

One of the key concepts of Benedictine spirituality is the commitment to stability. That means a monk will remain in a particular community till he dies. But this had earlier roots in the desert fathers. One such father once said, "Even as a tree cannot bear fruit if it is often transplanted, no more can a monk that is often removing from one place to another."[106]

This poses a challenge for us. Are we willing, for the sake of the community of faith, to stay where we are and to outwork our calling and ministry in a particular place? Are we willing to be so committed and grounded?

This, of course, does not mean people should not be sent from the community for mission and witness. But it does mean we are willing for the sake of the gospel to curb our restless spirit and commit ourselves to the long haul of formation and service in a particular setting.

This commitment to the long haul rather than to distant excitement will far more fully shape us in Christian maturity than the restless flight for new places or the hope for quick fixes.

Thought

Maturity can only come in community. And community involves a commitment to relationships and to place.

1 Corinthians 12:4–6

April 17

Different Callings

The Christian church should be incapable of creating a dull uniformity because the colorful Holy Spirit has poured out so many different gifts on the people of God. This calls for sharing, cooperation, and the challenge of unity in the midst of diversity.

Florentius Radewijns, one of the leaders of the Brethren of the Common Life, wrote, "There is one thing which we must all adhere to and observe: our status as Brethren of the Common Life: for although the monastic state is preferable in the opinion of the church, nevertheless he who lives a saintly life outside of the monastery will receive the reward of saintliness."[107]

Monk or married, priest or business person, missionary or motor mechanic, mystic or politician, in Christ these do not constitute the most fundamental differences in the life of faith. In fact, the opposite is the case. In Christ through the Spirit there is a basic commonality between different people, for Christ has made them one in a common faith, baptism, and life in Christian community.

But this oneness can be outworked in a kaleidoscope of colors. This is no place for a grey uniformity with the Spirit giving different gifts and calling people into every sphere of life and activity.

A different sphere of activity distinguishes the Christian priest from the Christian medical practitioner, but both are called to a life of worship, communion, prayer, and service.

Reflection

All in the service of Christ to the glory of God.

Psalm 16:1-2

April 18

A Prayer for God's Protection

The Christian lives the life of faith recognizing there are many dangers: the pull of the world, the snares of Satan, inner temptations, and human frailty. Therefore, prayers for protection are important prayers.

Tradition has it that St. Patrick was responsible for the composition of a beautiful Lorica, breastplate, prayer. Part of it reads as follows, "I arise today through God's strength to pilot me: God's might to uphold me, God's wisdom to guide me . . ."[108]

To bind such a prayer upon one's heart and to have such a prayer in one's mind throughout the day is a wonderful way in which to acknowledge our need of God's protection and care. This is a way of God being with us.

And whether our words are poetic or simply a cry from the heart what matters is that our eyes are towards God and our hearts are attentive to God's presence. These are matters of the heart, a heart that is towards God.

To live life like this, even in the most difficult circumstances, is to invite the possibility of an inner peace forged out of companionship. It is the peace of God with us. And it is the peace of God with us to help and guide us.

The sheltering protection of God and the helpfulness of God are key to living the Christian life in faith and hope. It is God sustaining us.

The great vision is God holds us rather than we hold onto God.

Prayer

Lord, hold me today even in my fear and brokenness. And hold me all the more in my foolish self-sufficiency and indifference. Amen.

Hebrews 13:15–16

April 19

Heart Worship

Major elements of the Western intellectual tradition have to do with the separation of theory from practice and the dominance of rationality and the scientific method over intuition and imagination. The biblical tradition, however, has integration as its main theme. We worship God with our heart and our mind.

Living the Christian life does have to do with asking the hard questions about God, life, and our role in the world. The Christian should never throw his or her mind away in living the faith.

However, we do need to realize we don't come far when we are forever involved in tireless speculation. Speculation at the end of the day will leave us suspended in the middle of nowhere.

The unknown writer of *The Cloud of Unknowing* rightly notes, "go beyond your intellect's endless and involved investigations and worship the Lord your God with your whole being."[109]

The worship of God with our whole being includes our mind and will. But it also involves our inner creativity. And it includes our body and our resources. Moreover, service is also an act of worship. Thus the worship of God is not limited to the sanctuary or to inner piety.

We worship God with all we are and all we have. And we worship God with our hopes and dreams.

Thought

Worship is giving God the rightful place. It is also recognizing that we are not God.

Psalm 119:105

April 20

The Power of the Word

Holy Scripture is much more than a historical record of the acts of God. It is a living testimony of who God is and what God has done. And when accompanied by the Holy Spirit it is a word that can strike deep into the human heart. It is a word that can radically turn us around.

One of the abiding disciplines of the Christian life is the careful listening to Scripture. This listening becomes all the more potent when it is accompanied by prayer and a listening heart.

The great church father St. Augustine of Hippo knew the power of God's word. He writes, "I do not know any other such pure words that so persuade me to confession and make my neck submissive to thy yoke, and invite me to serve thee for nothing else than thy own sake."[110]

What is clear from these words is that the reading of Scripture is not a mere speculative exercise. It is reading that leads to new life. It is reading for transformation.

Confession, surrender, and service are key responses to hearing this living word. There are also other responses. Wonder and worship. Gratitude and joy. Comfort and encouragement. Faith and hope.

And since Scripture has relevance for all of life, the personal as well as the social, the spiritual as well as the political, all sorts of responses are possible as we seek to live life moved and guided by God's word.

Reflection

God's word comforts and challenges us. It is the light that enlightens and enlivens us.

2 Corinthians 9:6–8

April 21

A Community of Faith for All

The church of Christ can never be parochial, tribalistic, or exclusive. Since Christ died for all, the church is for all whether one is rich or poor, white or black, male or female.

Biblically and theologically, it is clear all who come to faith in Christ are included in the church. The church therefore is an inclusive community. It welcomes all. And all, whether rich or poor, are one at the one Eucharistic table.

St. Ambrose, former governor of Aemilia-Liguria, turned bishop of Milan, makes this vision clear. He writes, the church "pours the same grace not only upon the rich and mighty, but also upon men of low estate, she weighs them all in an equal balance, gathers them all into the same bosom, cherishes them in the same lap."[111]

That this vision has not always been properly outworked in the actual life of the church calls the church to ongoing repentance. For the church is only truly itself when its arms are as wide open as the love of God and when it not only confesses this oneness, but lives this out in mutual concern and mutual sharing.

While this oneness is most obvious in the common life of monks, it can also become the common life of members of parishes as Christians are involved in practical care and sharing for the sake of Christ. Worship, prayer, mutuality, and service are common to all whether one is a monk or a Christian mother, teacher, or motor mechanic.

Reflection

In what ways can you reflect the unity of God's love and wideness of God's mercy in your life and service to others?

1 Corinthians 10:31

April 22

Not What You Do or Where You Are

A lot of Christians who wish to serve the Lord spend much anxious time thinking about where they should be and the nature of their service. Far better that more time was spent regarding who they should be and what gifts they should bring to their service.

Meister Eckhart goes to the heart of this matter. He writes, "God does not look at what you do, but only at your love and at the devotion and will behind your deeds. It matters little to him what we do, but he does care a lot about the attitudes our deeds express."[112]

While this is clearly no blanket approval for doing anything and everything, including what is immoral or unjust, it does open up a very wide space for Christian activity and endeavor in the world.

Christians can find their place in many spheres of human activity. But it is what they are in these activities that is important and not simply what they do. Do they seek to serve others? Do they want to bring glory to God? Do they want to make the world a better place? These are important questions.

We can be in the right place, but have a bad attitude. We can have a wonderful ministry opportunity, but bring little love to the task at hand.

The heart of the matter is that we should humbly serve no matter where we are or what our position in life. This will bring joy and blessing.

Thought

May God's love be expressed through who we are and what we do. And may people see God in all we do, and not only our enthusiasm or piety.

Romans 12:12

April 23

Perseverance in Prayer

The first and main temptation of the Christian is to neglect prayer. It is a temptation we readily succumb to, for we so easily think God does not hear us, or that prayer accomplishes little.

Julian of Norwich believed prayer is integral to the Christian life. She wrote, "Pray inwardly, even if you do not enjoy it. It does good, though you feel nothing, see nothing. . . . For when you are dry, empty, sick, or weak, at such a time is your prayer most pleasing to me . . ."[113] This is an insight she claimed to have received from the Lord.

These words of encouragement highlight that God understands the difficulties we have in our praying. God knows we are often discouraged and prayer seems to die in us even when it has hardly been brought to birth.

Furthermore, these words suggest that even our dry prayers are a sweet fragrance to God. Even our prayerful sighs are not wasted. Thus a sigh is more fruitful than a sullen silence.

So let us then pray always. In ecstasy. In fervor. In thankfulness. In praise. In silence. In sighs. In lament. In hope. In pain. In light and in darkness.

Prayer is God's handiwork in our lives. It is our being sculpted by the breath of God. It is the Spirit coming to expression in us.

Reflection

In prayer we are most truly what God calls us to be.

Revelation 7:11–12

April 24

The Vision of God

All of the great writers before the Reformation on the topic of spirituality see the vision of God as the state of blessedness. In our contemporary world this is hardly our focus. We are more concerned about our blessings and our service.

Life in the Western world is a self-preoccupied way of life. We are primarily concerned about our own well-being and future.

This way of living has also penetrated the portals of the church. Christians also focus on themselves, and their relationship with God is largely to do with receiving God's blessings.

But there is another vision of life that has God at the center. The Franciscan theologian Bonaventure speaks of "the soul's deep affection . . . centered in God and transformed, as it were, into him." And he goes on to say that for this to take place, "then ask grace, not learning; desire, not understanding; the groanings of prayer, not industry in study . . ."[114]

In this vision neither my piety, my service, nor my wisdom are the center of attention. What is in the forefront is a desire to know, love, and worship God for who God is, and not for what God does for us.

This is the vision splendid. This is a thirst for intimacy with God the Creator, the Son as Redeemer, and the Holy Spirit as Life-giver. This is all about God and not us. This is living the Christian life in fullness and joy.

Reflection

In the vision of God all other things come into true perspective. Without this vision all other things become idolatrous. In the former is true joy. In the latter there is a tragic bondage.

Psalm 46:1–3

April 25

In the Midst of Difficulties

No matter what steps we take to protect and safeguard our lives, we live in the midst of difficulties, troubles, and sometimes in the midst of great disasters.

We live in a world where difficulties come our way. Not even our inner world is safe. There is no ultimate safe place. Not even in a monastery.

As a result, the challenge for us is how to live with the hard things that come our way, whether that be relationship breakdown, ill health, economic difficulties, or natural disasters.

It needs to be acknowledged at the outset we cannot make sense of all the things and difficulties that come our way. Some things we will never understand. Some things we just have to accept. But some things we can process into some sort of clarity.

Thomas à Kempis believes difficulties can lead to some spiritual good. He writes, "Sometimes it is to our advantage to endure misfortunes and adversities, for they make us enter into our inner selves and acknowledge that we are in a place of exile and that we ought not to rely on anything in this world."[115]

There are also other possibilities. In the light of difficulties, we may see the invitation to rethink our priorities. We may become less driven or less controlling. We may even become more compassionate and understanding of others.

But difficulties may also harden us and make us sullen and resentful. Hence, difficulties must be impregnated by grace if good is to emerge.

Thought

Only grace can truly change us. Difficulties are only the opportunities for grace.

Psalm 51:1–2

April 26

Overwhelmed

There are times where we feel overwhelmed with our personal wrongdoing, weaknesses, and sins. It almost feels as if we are trapped and deliverance seems far away. It seems change is so far away.

Unlike our attitude in the modern world—where we are more concerned about what we are not getting from God, rather than focusing on our own failures—Christians in bygone eras had a very different attitude.

This attitude is well illustrated by St. Anselm. He had a profound sense of God's holiness and human sinfulness. He writes, "Sometimes my sins drag me here and there, mocking at this wretched and tattered little man, and at other times they come in a mob and trample me underfoot in triumph."[116]

This surely is something we need to recover and grow into. I am not speaking about morbid introspection. Nor about an overly sensitive conscience. Nor about an unhealthy self-denigration. I am talking about something quite different.

I believe as we recover a sense of being enamored with God, become concerned about God's in-breaking kingdom, become concerned about the state of the church and the needs of our world, we will begin to live towards God in wholly different ways. More prayerful. More repentant. More obedient. More given to the art of relinquishment and surrender. And more aware of our sins and the ways in which we displease God.

Reflection

A fuller vision of God can make us more repentant. A greater sense of God's presence can make us more aware of our failures. But forgiveness and healing can turn us around and bring us into the places of freedom and joy.

Colossians 3:3

April 27

The Hidden Life

Ours is the information age and people are besotted with a constant outpouring of their daily thoughts and happenings. But where is the inner life? Where are the practices of reflection and meditation? Where is the life of prayer? Where are the places for stillness.

St. Jerome, the great church father and Bible translator, speaks of Paula, who from a noble family was even nobler in holiness. He writes of her, "She was hidden and yet she was not hidden. By shunning glory she earned glory; for glory follows virtue as its shadow; and deserting those who seek it, it seeks those who despise it."[117]

In this testimony about a remarkable Christian woman, St. Jerome has a particular challenge for us in the twenty-first century. We seek fame and notoriety. We want to be known for who we are and what we do. But there is a whole other way of living the Christian life.

This other way is the hidden life. The life of prayer. The life of stepping out of the limelight. The life of forsaking position and prestige. Monks live this kind of life. But we too can be cloistered with God in the midst of life through the practices of solitude and prayer.

This is a life that chooses downward mobility. It knows the way of the "desert." It knows the art of relinquishment. It is a life that knows how to wait, not simply how to act.

This life too has its power and influence, but only in totally unexpected ways. In this way of life God uses our nothingness for his glory.

Thought

Flee to the "desert." There you may find God and yourself. And you may yet be a harbinger of a better world.

Jeremiah 18:5–6

April 28

Sculpted by God's Hand

That God is a magnificent sculptor is clearly evident in the beauty and diversity of nature. But God's creative activity is also evident in the diversity of cultures and in the human lives shaped by grace. It is also evident in God's healing and renewing activity.

Bonaventure uses a powerful image to speak about God's beautifying activity in our lives. He writes, "Love is always preceded by negation, a sculptor never adds anything; rather he removes matter leaving the noble and beautiful form in the stone."[118]

The thrust of this imagery is that God wants to uncover what is good and beautiful in us. This uncovering is to reveal to ourselves, as well as to others, the gifts and abilities God has already placed within us.

What is so sadly true of most of us is we have become encrusted, like an old sunken ship, with barnacles that hide who we really are. And we have clothed ourselves with our social self, sculpted by the values of our culture rather than allowing our truer identity to shine forth.

As a consequence, things have to be stripped away and God's shaping hand needs to bring the true, the good, and the beautiful out into the open. This sculpting process may be difficult for us.

All of this means, of course, that we have to learn to submit ourselves to God's creative activity rather than always trying to fashion and refashion ourselves in the endless round of self-creation.

Reflection

To yield to God's creative work is the safest place to be.

Luke 7:47

April 29

Surprises in God's Kingdom

It is so easy for religious people to become self-righteous. They think they are better and more favored than others. But the God of abundant grace may well lift a terrible sinner out of the ash heap of a decadent life while a religious person languishes in his or her shallow religiosity.

While some Christians are more openhearted and generous in their attitude towards other people, others are more rigid and intolerant. The latter attitude is often held by fundamentalists who know exactly how others should be and act. This can lead to a judgmentalism that factors out the triumph of God's grace.

The biblical story clearly points us in a very different direction. An insignificant people are raised up to bear God's witness to the surrounding nations. People who practice justice are in God's orbit more than those who make abundant burnt offerings. The poor rather than the religious establishment hear the words of Jesus with gladness of heart. And pagans are ushered into the faith rather than those to whom it was first offered.

This very long story demonstrates how God works in unusual and surprising ways. God's way is the way of the upside-down kingdom.

The unknown author of *The Cloud of Unknowing* knows this vision. "And yet it often happens that some who have been hardened, habitual sinners arrive at the perfection of this work sooner than those who have never sinned grievously. God is truly wonderful in lavishing his grace on anyone he chooses."[119] The author highlights God's surprising ways.

Thought

See others through the eyes of God's great generosity. And see yourself not as a person of entitlement, but as a hungry person seeking bread and wine.

Galatians 4:19

April 30

Christ Formed in Us

The great grace in the Christian life is not simply what we believe and confess nor how we serve and what we do, but what we become. And it is becoming partakers of the new humanity, with Christ as the New Adam, which most clearly marks who we are.

To believe is one thing. And belief is important. To serve others is also important. This flows from our faith. It is the practical outworking of what we believe. But other things are equally important.

A reshaping at the very core of our being is central to our belief and to our service. This is being formed in Christ. This is the mystery of the being of Christ ever more taking shape in us.

The great Irish missionary, St. Columbanus, in one of his sermons talks about this. "Let Christ paint his own image in us"[120] is this saint's way of putting it. This is a wonderful, artistic image of Christ's way with us.

Paint, sculpt, form, shape—these are only some of the ways in which we try to describe this inner work of the Holy Spirit. And this is all about renewal and the new creation.

This work of the Spirit we are invited to welcome. We are encouraged to yield to the Spirit. And we are to pray that the Spirit may do this magnificent artistic work in us.

As Christ is formed in us we will love the words of Christ, emulate the way of Christ, and continue his mission in the world.

Thought

People formed into the life and way of Christ are living signposts of the New World.

JULIAN OF NORWICH

2 Chronicles 2:6

May 1

The Mystery of God

The word "God" does not sit well with many people. The word conjures up ideas of authority and power gone wrong. But the God of the Scriptures is a seeking and healing God rather than a distant or oppressive God.

We are often faced with two problems. The one is where we project our unhappy experiences with human authority figures onto God. The other is that our descriptions of God are one-sided and may well fail us, particularly when we go through a major life crisis.

The medieval Christian mystic Richard Rolle helpfully points us to the mystery of God, rather than to static formulations. He writes, "God truly is of infinite greatness, better than we think; of unreckoned sweetness; inconceivable of all natures wrought; and can never be comprehended by us as he is in himself in eternity."[121]

All of our language regarding God can only go so far. Whether we use the more philosophical language of infinity or eternity or the language of personalism and call God lover and healer, we are merely on the outskirts of the mystery of God. And at the outskirts we will remain.

And when we think we have more clearly understood who God is in the face of Jesus Christ, we suddenly find Christ's way eludes us and we struggle with understanding the mysterious workings of the Holy Spirit.

Thus, our language of description can finally only become the language of worship and adoration.

Thought

Love does help us to see more clearly.

Matthew 22:21

May 2

Where to Draw the Line

The early Christians drew a line somewhere regarding their faith and as a result received a martyr's death. Modern Christians no longer know where to draw the line since tolerance and relativism have become dominant values.

Much of what the early Christians did may surprise and even upset us. But what is abundantly clear is that many had the courage of their convictions.

St. Ambrose is one such outstanding Christian leader. He told the emperor of the day, "Do not burden yourself, Sir, with the idea that you have any right as emperor over the things of God." This was in the context of the emperor wanting to reclaim for secular use a Christian basilica. Ambrose continued, "You have been entrusted with jurisdiction over public buildings, but not over sacred ones."[122]

This poses a challenge for us, not only in where to draw the line in the relationship between church and state, but also where to draw the line in the personal outworking of our faith in the public arena.

At what point in an academic setting do I say, "I can no longer teach this"? Or in a work setting, "I can no longer do this"? Or in a political environment, "I can no longer support this policy"?

And so the questions of morality and ethics press in upon us as we seek to be faithful to the way of Christ.

Prayer

Lord, help me in my lack of discernment. And give me greater courage when you have shown me the way. Amen.

Psalm 69:29

May 3

A Protective Shield

In the modern world our protectors are often doctors and scientists. We have little sense that we daily need the protection of God. And yet in earlier times Christians primarily looked to God as the source of all help.

In Celtic spirituality there was a profound sense that everything was to be birthed in and surrounded by prayer—the body, relationships, the home, the farm, the land.

In "The Breastplate of Laidcenn" the general prayer, "O God, defend me everywhere with all your impregnable power and protection. Deliver all my mortal limbs guarding each with your protective shield," led in more specific directions so that every part of the body was prayed for. The prayer goes on, "Protect, O God . . . my shoulders . . . arms . . . elbows, cups of the hand . . . fists, palms, fingers with their nails."[123] Even the more intimate parts of the human body were prayed over for God's loving protection and care.

A number of things are important for us here. The first is that this reflects a life of prayer. *Everything* was prayed about and prayed over. Secondly, in this approach to life everything had to do with God. God was central. And thirdly, God was seen as the great life-giver, carer, and protector.

In the modern world it appears we have many "saviors." While we should be thankful for all the good that comes our way, we need to recover the vision of God as the source of all good and as our careful protector.

Thought

To pray in relation to all the activities of life would make God more central to our existence.

1 Timothy 6:18

May 4

A Spirit of Generosity

We live in a world where we are very calculating. We are willing to give, but this must somehow benefit us as well. The gospel calls us to a whole new way of radical generosity.

Ours is a profoundly materialistic age. And we live ever wanting more. Even in our generosity we want something for ourselves. The spirit of acquisition, which Meister Eckhart calls "the commercial spirit," has possessed us. We are therefore more "demonized" than we care to admit.

This German Christian mystic has an answer for this kind of possession. He writes, "do all you can in the way of good works, solely for the praise of God." And he continues, "You shall not ask anything in return for it and then your efforts will be both spiritual and divine."[124]

All of this suggests that we are invited to move from self-preoccupation to live for God and for God's glory. And living this way calls us into a life of relinquishment and living with open hands. It calls us to great generosity.

This way of living invites us to move from a focus on self-regard to living to bless others. Other-person-regarding is a way of self-giving that calls for sacrifice. It may well call us into suffering.

This calls for a deep conversion as the fruit of grace. It is the outworking of the life of Christ being formed in us.

Reflection

Do I wait to be dispossessed? Or do I voluntarily live a great renunciation?

Titus 2:11–13

May 5

Formation in Goodness

No matter how much we seek to attribute the growth of the fruit of the Spirit in our lives to the mysterious working of this third person of the Trinity, we do need to forge practices and disciplines in our lives that facilitate the growth of goodness.

It is wholly appropriate for us to acknowledge God's work in our lives that fills us with grace, faith, hope, and love. Surely we can confess, all that I am is due to your goodness and healing presence, O God!

It is one thing to acknowledge God as the source of all goodness. But this does not mean we just wait for things to come our way. We are not to be passive but active seekers of the grace and goodness of God.

Everywhere in the biblical story people are encouraged to seek and pray, and with this comes the call to develop practices in our lives that channel all that God gives us.

The unknown author of *The Cloud of Unknowing* makes a good point, "Genuine goodness is a matter of habitually acting and responding appropriately in each situation, as it arises, moved always by the desire to please God."[125]

What this means is that we also give shape to our own life. We have values shaped by the gospel. But we set priorities. We develop certain disciplines and habits. We live life in a certain way.

These habits give a rhythm to our lives. And as a result, we don't have to ask ourselves each time will I do this or not. We just go ahead and do it, particularly when this has to do with the practices of prayer.

Reflection

What habits in my daily life have I formed in loyalty to Christ?

John 15:16

May 6

We are the Fruit of God's Choosing

Yes, of course we choose to believe the gospel and to follow Christ. And we need to continue to choose daily to follow in the way of Christ. But our choosing is shaped by God choosing us.

Thomas à Kempis had the right perspective. He writes, "To serve You does not appear so special to me; rather, what is outstanding and marvellous is that You have chosen one so pitiable and unworthy for your service and have numbered him among your beloved servants."[126]

In our narcissistic age, we think God should be grateful because we have decided to play on his team. We have been good enough to choose God and therefore God should be pleased with us. Here we are at the center of things.

But it is really the other way round. We should be marked by deep gratitude and joy that God has reached out towards us. We should be thankful God has called us and has poured his grace and goodness into our lives.

And the fact that we have been called adds no credit to us. This does not give us special status. It only means that out of the love that has been shown to us we are to extend love to others.

Our special calling is at best a calling to servanthood where we follow the movement of Christ from privilege to embracing the cross.

Thought

Election is unto servanthood, not privilege.

Revelation 22:1–2

May 7

The Grand Vision

Christian belief has a grand end in view. New heavens and new earth, the healing of the nations and a lived reality where God is glorified and there is no more sorrow and death. This grand vision we are to live now in anticipation and hope.

Christians are invited to live their lives today in the light of this future hope. Thus Christians live towards a grand future in prayer and anticipation. And they express this prayer in faithful service.

This future vision, however, does not make them insensitive to the realities and needs of today's world. This is so because this future world is straining to come to fuller birth in the present world.

The power of renewal not only awaits the future but also makes the future present. St. Anselm has a vision of this present in-breaking of the reign of God. He writes, "By you the world is renewed and made beautiful with truth, governed by the light of righteousness. By you sinful humanity is justified, the condemned are saved, the servants of sin and hell are set free."[127]

There are other things we can also say. By your Spirit people are renewed in faith and love, the church is empowered, movements of justice emerge, and the face of the earth is renewed.

But however we may understand and express this grand vision it will always be a vision lived in prayer and hope and costly service.

Reflection

God's future is breaking in amongst us.

Luke 18:13

May 8

The Heart Cry of Prayer

God is not necessarily swayed by the abundance of our words. It is the heart's cry that wings its way to the compassion of God.

The seventh-century ascetic St. John Climacus talked about the simplicity of prayer. He reminds us, "A single word of the publican touched the mercy of God. A single word, full of faith, saved the good thief."[128]

This cry of the heart is not a prayer we easily or readily come to. We are usually so preoccupied with so many things that we can't identify what is going on inside of us, let alone that we have been able to work out what it is that we most desire to bring to God.

Thus the prayer of the heart is a prayer we need to sink deeply into and is to be soaked by the practice of solitude and careful listening. This listening is a practice directed at our inner being and the movement of the Holy Spirit.

It is when we are able, beyond all the blockages and all the distractions, to see our own deepest need in the light of God's mercy and grace, that we may come to the cry of the heart. This cry is not the prayer of circumstances, but the very breath of our inner being and longing.

This may simply be: Lord, forgive me; Lord, please heal me; Lord, give me courage; or Lord, help me follow your guidance; or Lord, give me healing hands. This is no grandiose prayer. It is the prayer we pray in our very living.

Prayer

Lord, bring my prayer life to a deeper honesty and intercession. Amen.

Job 13:24

May 9

Be Found

Our looking for God, our wanting God, and our prayer to God can often be self-interested. We want something from God or want God on our terms. There is a whole other way to be in relationship with God.

Meister Eckhart notes that God "is a hidden God" and goes on to make the strange comment, "the more one seeks Thee, the less one can find Thee."[129]

There are at least two important dimensions to what this mystical writer is saying. The first is God must be encountered not only in revelation, but also in mystery. And as such, this is a way of recognizing God's radical freedom beyond our conceptions of who God is and what God should do. To surrender to God's mystery is the way of humility and faith. Thus we embrace the darkness of God's mysterious way with us.

The other dimension is that our relationship with God is as much about being found as it is about finding. God reveals himself when he chooses. And God's revelation is as much about mystery as it is about knowness. Thus, while God is "bound" in his essential being, God's relationship with us is one of radical freedom.

Our seeking, therefore, has to give way to being found. In this way God is truly the God of surprises. And embracing God in his radical otherness is being led on paths of faith and surrender.

Thought

Let God be God. Not one of our own making, since such a God is finally idolatrous.

Hebrews 12:1–2

May 10

Surrounded by the Faith of Others

In our contemporary world we think our faith response to Christ and the gospel is simply what we do with the aid of the Holy Spirit. But there is usually much more to the story. Family and the faith community often carry us into the life of Christ.

St. Jerome makes reference to what a believing family can do in carrying someone into faith. He writes, "The one unbeliever is sanctified by his holy and believing family. For, when a man is surrounded by a believing crowd of children and grandchildren, he is a candidate for the faith."[130]

None of this means a person does not have to make a personal faith response to the guiding presence of the Spirit and to the invitation of the gospel, but it does mean there is a great blessing in being surrounded by people of faith. There is, therefore, much more to our story of faith than simply our own commitment.

To be part of a family of faith or the Christian community means we can be carried by others. Others can lift us up. Others can nurture us. Others can pray for us. We are part of others in the faith journey, including those who have gone before us throughout the ages.

Thus, not only the Spirit but also family and friends can carry us to the heart of Jesus. And so prayer is the midwife that can help bring others to spiritual birth. And the mysterious communion of the saints sustains us in ways we cannot comprehend.

Reflection

Others can and do carry us to the heart of God.

Psalm 46:10

May 11

The Practice of Silence

Ours has become an age of incessant talking. Usually this is no longer face-to-face. The challenge for us in all of this is two-fold: the praxis of a greater solitude and the need for face-to-face relationships.

In the rule for monks written by Columbanus there is the mandate for the practice of silence. It reads, "it is right that he [the monk] should keep silence except concerning those things that are beneficial or necessary."[131]

In our world of endless chatter there is a challenge for us in this admonition. While the readers of this book are probably not monks, we do all need to create an inner solitude. Such a place can be a source of vitality, renewal, and wisdom.

We do need to find places of stillness in our lives. In fact, it is a wonderful discipline and this could become a rhythm in our daily lives.

Stillness, however, is only ever the first move. What we hope for is the gift of solitude. This is coming to an inner stillness in the presence of God. To be in such a place is to be loved and nurtured and it is in this place of shelter that we can know both the comfort and the direction of God.

Solitude is thus a birthplace. Here our inner life can be renewed. Here healing can be received. Here wisdom may come to us. And here we may more deeply fall in love with the God of all grace and goodness.

Thought

Stillness can be the productive place for the presence of God. It is a way of preparing the way for the Lord.

Romans 12:3

May 12

Accepting Limitation

The Christian faith is eschatological and therefore we lean forward into all we may yet become in Christ. But this does not mean we can become everything and anything in this life.

One of the exciting themes in the Christian story is that through the grace of God in Christ and the renewing work of the Holy Spirit we can grow in wholeness, maturity, and spirituality. We also grow into becoming women and men of purpose, vocation, and service.

But this does not mean we become some universal persons who transcend time and culture. We remain rooted in our particularity with our genetic inheritance, personal biography, giftedness, and socialization.

While Christ heals our alienation and wounding, he does not seek to change our personality. In our createdness we remain precious to God.

St. Thomas Aquinas in his letter of counsel to a student is, therefore, to the point when he advises him, "Do not concern yourself with things beyond your competence."[132]

This is certainly not advice that says just remain ignorant. Nor is it an argument against growth and development. It is simply a call to humility and accepting personal limitation.

Even with the generous outpouring of gifts through the Spirit on the people of God, this does not mean one person has all the gifts. The opposite is true, we all have gifts we share, but we need others to share their gifts with us.

Thought

Accepting limitation is grace not a lack of faith.

Proverbs 8:14

May 13

Knowledge and Passion

*It is important to think, but also to act. It is important to feel,
but also to reflect. It is important to have light and insight, but
also to have passion and purpose.*

The movement of God in our lives is not simply to bring us knowledge and understanding. It is also to heal us and give us purpose and direction. The Christian life can be lived with passion.

Thus God's salvific work is multi-faceted and comprehensive. It engages all of who we are, transforms every part of our lives, and energizes us to love and service.

St. Bernard knows something of God's dynamic activity. He writes, "The revelation which is made by the Holy Spirit gives light so that we may understand, and fire so that we may love."[133]

This reflects the wide-ranging action of God. We need to be enlightened so we may know who God is and what God has done for us in Christ. In this light we also need to know ourselves and recognize our need for forgiveness and healing. And we need to understand how we may now live to the glory of God and for the well-being of others.

But we also need to be empowered to action: to love and to serve and to give ourselves for the blessings of others. This empowerment may be needed in the call to go the extra mile.

Thus our knowing needs to be full of love and therefore practical and beneficial. And our loving needs to be full of knowledge and therefore must be wise and discerning.

Prayer

Lord, may I become knowledgeable and loving at the same time. Amen.

Isaiah 45:22

May 14

Always Turning

The secret of living the Christian life is not to be stuck in systems and patterns of understanding, morality, faith, and service. It is to remain dynamically linked to the God who continues to call us into relationship, fidelity, and commitment.

The heartbeat of Christian existence is not the security of a religious system, no matter how carefully that has been orchestrated or sculpted. Rather, the heart of Christian experience lies in the dynamic relationship between the creature and the Creator, the sinner and the Savior, the human being and the God who makes himself known.

St. Augustine understood well the relational nature of religious experience. He writes, "the true good of every created thing is always to cleave fast to thee, lest, in turning away from thee, it lose the light it had received."[134]

The Christian life, while shaped by theology, ethics, liturgy, the spiritual disciplines, and Christian community, at heart has to do with the experience of the presence of God. It is first and foremost about relationship and all our religious systems are meant to safeguard and enhance this relationship between creature and Creator.

St. Augustine speaks of an active cleaving to the God who draws near to us and in whom we live and have our being. Thus we need to make commitments that foster relationship. This certainly calls us to a life of repentance, a life of prayer, and the journey of faith. Thus the secret of the Christian life is always turning to the Great Giver of life.

Thought

Always turning, never neglecting.

Numbers 6:24–26

May 15

In the World and Not Afraid

Both the world of nature and the social world are gifts from God to sustain life. We inhabit these worlds but they should not finally define who we are. We are more than all social definitions of who we are.

St. Ambrose used the analogy of a stormy sea and a fish to make the point that the world's troubles need not overwhelm us. He writes, "There may be a storm at sea, but a fish swims. . . . [There may be] all kinds of waves and currents and fierce tempests . . . [but] you too must be a fish so that the world's waves do not swallow you up."[135]

The way to live the Christian life is not to try to be something else or to escape from the world. That is impossible. It is to live fully in the world, but to be different.

This being different has to do with the fact that our reliance is on the God who sustains and keeps us in the midst of life. It is faith in the God who is present with us, even in the midst of difficult circumstances, trials, and challenges.

The impulse to escape, while seemingly a strategy of survival, is the way of death. The way of life is to be kept, sheltered, nurtured, and cared for in all the vicissitudes of life.

This calls us to such levels of faith and trust so that when the winds blow and the seas foam and roar we do not drown and are not overwhelmed. To be held in God's safe hand in the midst of difficulty is the place of greatest safety.

Reflection

I do commit myself into your care, O God. Be my support and shelter.

Hebrews 13:2

May 16

Radical Hospitality

In our age, where we almost exclusively go out of the home in order to entertain friends or guests, we are being invited to recover the wonderful tradition of hospitality. In exercising this gift of creating welcome for the guest, we often experience the grace and presence of the hidden Christ.

The heart of the biblical story is about the restoration of relationships between God and ourselves and others. And at the heart of this restoration lies the blessing of welcome through the practice of hospitality.

This biblical tradition has always been practiced in some shape or form in the long history of the Christian church. But it has come to its most concrete expression when Christian communities have practiced radical hospitality, which has included taking in the poor, the needy, and the marginalized.

This vision also lies at the heart of Benedictine spirituality. St. Benedict in his *Rule* writes, "All guests who present themselves are to be welcomed as Christ for he himself will say: *I was a stranger and you welcomed me.*"[136]

That there is grace in what seems to be the risky or burdensome practice of hospitality is one of the surprises of living the Christian life. Just because something may be difficult does not mean it is not graced.

But when the guest is served in the way one would serve Christ himself, then hospitality becomes an embodied reality and a spiritual discipline full of the surprises of grace and goodness.

Thought

Open your life. Open your home. Care for the guest and widen your heart.

Ephesians 5:18–20

May 17

A Never-ending Quest

Coming to faith in Christ is a home-coming. But we are also called to continue the journey of faith. Thus, we are people on the road.

Some Christians have wrongly gained the idea that coming to faith in Christ ends one's search. The opposite, however, is true. The search begins, but with a new center, a new orientation, and a new purpose.

This ongoing search is not so much to find faith in Christ, but to find the Christ of faith. It is more specifically to find Christ in Scripture. It is to find Christ more fully in our hearts. And it is to find Christ more clearly in the world and in the stranger.

This desire to know Christ and the way of Christ is the great never-ending story and the never-ending quest. This desiring is the winsome work of the Spirit within us. It can be the heart's true desire.

St. Anselm well understood this present, continuous movement of the Christian life. He writes, "Always filled, always you drink."[137] One could continue—always found, yet always seeking. Always blessed, yet always yearning. Always home, yet always journeying.

There is nothing static about the Christian life. It is a journey of faith and obedience. It is a life that ever needs to be renewed by the Spirit.

This means that there is something hourly and daily about the Christian life. This day I seek Thee, O Lord. This day give us our daily bread.

Thought

Your mercies, O God, are new every morning.

Psalm 37:39

May 18

In the Hard Times

Faith forged in fair weather is still faith. Faith formed in difficult times is faith purified in the fire. We usually experience both in the journey of life.

Thomas à Kempis puts these words into the mouth of Jesus as he speaks to us, his followers, "Your patience and humility in time of adversity are more pleasing to me than your great consolations and devotion during times of prosperity."[138]

This does not mean we should seek the hard times so we may be more spiritual. Such times will come without us seeking them. And for many Christians living in the impoverished majority world, or Third World, such times always seem to be present in the struggle for basic survival.

But for all of us, life is never just fair-weather sailing. There are head winds and there are storms. And there is loss and the most painful of disappointments.

Thus, disappointments, breakdown in relationships, betrayal, ill health, loss of opportunity, all come our way. And when they do, it is easy for us to blame God for not preventing these difficulties.

Rather than blaming the God who has given us the painful gift of living in freedom, we need to heed the call to humility and commit our lives into God's care in the midst of hardship.

In the hard times there is sustaining grace that we do not receive in times when things are going well and there is plenty.

Reflection

I do want to commit myself to the God who has not rescued me.

Isaiah 6:1–5

May 19

Desire for God

In our modern world we are cajoled into desiring much, but God is not on the shopping list. However, blatant consumerism has left us dry and empty and so it could well be that the secret desire for God may yet win our hearts.

In the practice of faith different Christian groups have set different priorities. For some, the liturgical life is their heartbeat. For others, it is charismatic renewal. Others see the practice of the spiritual disciplines as key. Others again see service to the poor or the work for justice as the center of the practice of faith.

But there is something much more fundamental that should undergird all of these responses and activities. The author of *The Cloud of Unknowing* identifies what that is. The author writes, "one loving blind desire for God alone is more valuable in itself, more pleasing to God and to the saints, more beneficial to your own growth . . . than anything else you could do."[139]

This does not mean our worship, prayer, and service are not important. What it does mean is seeking that leads to contemplation and longing that leads to revelation are much more the fuel that moves us spiritually than anything else.

This means that we need to heed the wisdom of the Christian mystics, and not be moved simply by our rationality or our spiritual routines. Rather, we need to be moved by the inspiration and creativity God gives.

Reflection

One blinding revelation and one clear call from God can mark and orient the whole of one's life. These blessings may more truly define who we are and who we need to become.

Isaiah 42:6–7

May 20

Illumination

Modern Western Christianity has been marked more by rationality than by revelation. Thus, our faith is more of our own doing than it is the product of God's enlightening and renewing activity.

The Western person has been inculcated by the false idea that we can know everything and do anything. This means we can also control God or dismiss him. Or, as is so often the case, we can use God for our own ends.

In the West we live with little respect for God, our worship is self-interested, and our service is self-seeking. And the issue for us is more what *we* can do with God, as problem or possibility, rather than what *God* may do with us.

We need to recover humility before God and rediscover our creatureliness before the Almighty. In other words, we need to gain a truer picture of ourselves.

Meister Eckhart, in one of his sermons, emphasizes that we can't just discover God, nor control him. All of our dealings with God call us to receive from him and to live in ongoing surrender and openness. He writes, "When God divinely enlightens you, no natural light is required to bring that about."[140]

In a tired Western church lacking depth and discouraged by the meagerness of its activism, a whole new sense of God's transcendence needs to fall like summer rains on parched earth.

The challenge, therefore, is not so much to find God, but to be found by God.

Reflection

Come visit us again, O God of love and power.

Exodus 15:26

May 21

Healing

Healing can come to us in many ways. Medical doctors and counselors can be agents or channels of healing. So can anointing with oil, the laying on of hands, prayer, and participating in the Eucharist.

Some people see everything around them as some sort of threat. Both the world of nature, society at large, and other people are seen through fearful eyes.

Others see other people and the things around them as neutral. Their orientation in life is what they themselves do and what they make of their own lives.

Others again, with eyes of faith, see the world and other people as upheld by God's hand and bathed in love. This, however, does not mean all of life is rosy and all is well. Rather, they believe all can be made well.

Julian of Norwich has this vision. She writes, "He shows us our sin so quietly, and then we are sorry; . . . we turn to see his mercy, and cling to his love and goodness, for we realize that he is our medicine."[141]

This is a vision of our frailty and of God's great generosity. It sees God as the great Restorer and as the One who makes all things well. God is our medicine.

This means healing comes in forgiveness, grace, and mercy. God's presence is itself a healing presence where embrace brings wholeness.

Prayer

Lord, restore me through your healing presence. Amen.

Jeremiah 1:4–5

May 22

Discerning One's Calling

In the contemporary world the emphasis is on forging one's career. In the world of Christian spirituality the challenge is to discern God's will for one's life and to be marked by that call. This gives one's life purpose and direction.

John Hus makes the point that anyone wishing to enter a monastery should "take counsel with the Holy Spirit," should be "conscious of the motive of his desire," should have in view that he "be of benefit to the Holy Church, and be open to the possibility that God may be calling him to another vocation."[142] Thus, God's call should shape our life. This gives our life purpose and direction.

The heart of the matter is not where one ends up in the service of God, in the church, or the wider society. What is at stake is to know God's will for one's life. This involves the recognition that in Christ we are now no longer the masters of our own destiny.

In faith we have embraced Christ as both Savior and Lord. Christ's renewing and healing activity in our lives has turned us around. And so we have moved and continue to move from self-will to seeking and doing what Christ asks of us.

In this we demonstrate our deep connection to Christ. And in this, we carry on Christ's presence and ministry in our world.

Christ's salvation brings us to new life. Christ's call upon our lives shapes our purpose, vocation, and ministry. This is a blessing in which we may live rather than a burden we have to carry.

Thought

In the salvation and call of Christ lies the purpose of one's life.

Luke 16:18

May 23

The Tyranny of Money

Ours is an age obsessed with security and much-having. One of the signs that our liberation in Christ has been effective is when the power of money has been broken in our lives and we are marked by generosity.

It is a serious perversion of the gospel when the message of the church is that having Christ is only and always about gain, both spiritually and materially. Belonging to Christ has to do with something different: with conversion, transformation, and an ongoing reorientation.

We are converted *from* our own selfish and sinful ways and converted *to* the purposes of God's kingdom in Christ. In this movement the focus of our lives moves from what we think we need and should do, to one of seeking God's purposes. In this way we learn to grow into the gifts of hospitality, generosity, care, and the practice of charity.

The early church father, Polycarp, clearly understood this and warns us about the power of money. He writes, "Anyone who does not avoid love of money will be polluted by idolatry."[143]

Polycarp does not say such a person is simply selfish. He says such a person is in bondage. Money has become a god. Money thus becomes a controlling power.

And there is only one way to freedom. This is the grace of Christ converting our hearts and pockets. It is growth in compassion and in love of neighbor. It is responding to the cry of the poor.

Reflection

What do I have? And what do I need? What do I not need? What should I give away?

John 17:22

May 24

The Church's Unity

The modern church is pockmarked by divisions. The splinterization of the church continues with unabated pace. We desperately need healing in a house of welcome that has become deeply divided.

The first major split divided the Western and the Eastern churches. Then came the Reformation. And now the division within Christianity has reached the point where a single church is now its own denomination. We will soon have a Christian being his or her own pope.

While we can't turn back the clock to Christianity's primitive beginnings where things seemed to be much better, even though there were the problems of unity and diversity, we can begin to change our heart attitudes and begin to practice a local ecumenism where churches in fellowship with each other work in cooperation to serve Christ in their neighborhood.

In this journey of the healing of the house of faith, St. Cyprian can encourage us. He writes, "the Church, bathed in the light of the Lord, spreads her rays throughout the world, yet the light everywhere diffused is one light." He believed the church is "a single whole" even as it "spreads far and wide into a multitude of churches."[144]

In seeing that we are one in Christ through the Spirit, we are challenged to overcome our bigotry and differences and indifference. And we want to take up the challenge to outwork this spiritual unity in as many practical ways as possible. Unity in the Spirit must come to practical expression. This unity must become an embodied reality.

Prayer

Help us Lord. Our divisions harm your name. Amen.

Luke 6:32–36

May 25

Beyond the Household of Faith

One of the dangers of any religious group is for it to become inwardly focused and to care only for its own. The call in the Christian faith is always a call to also care for the neighbor.

It is ever so easy to divide the world between those who belong to us and all the others. An insider-outsider mentality seems to be intrinsic to most of us. And exclusion so easily becomes an attitude and a practice.

One implication of this attitude is that we give preferential treatment to our own. And we may even end up neglecting others.

The Christian faith, however, is moved by a different set of values. All people are made in the image of God and therefore all should be given respect, justice, and care. We are called to love, even the stranger and the enemy.

Maximus the Confessor had this to say, "The one who imitates God by giving alms knows no difference between . . . [the] just and unjust." He goes on to say the Christian "distributes to all without distinction according to their need."[145]

This inclusive generosity comes from a love without boundaries. It is a love that, for the sake of Christ, responds to all, even to outsiders and enemies.

That the Christian church has not always practiced such love is written large on the pages of history. But through forgiveness, healing, and grace we can show such love, so that a new world may be born.

Thought

Love has all equally in view.

1 Corinthians 15:45–48

May 26

The New Adam

For some, Christ is only a ticket to heaven. For others, Christ is emulated and followed in some way. But in the biblical story Christ is the embodiment of what a new humanity may look like.

We have created in our own imaginings many ideas and images of what Christ came to do. Much of this reflects more of what we think rather than showing something significant about Christ.

In older times Christ was seen more as a kingly figure. In our time Christ is seen more as some sort of psychologist who helps us get well.

In the biblical story, however, Christ is much more than any of this. He is the savior and the healer, but he is also the demonstration of what it means to be fully human and what a new humanity should look like.

St. Cyril of Alexandria echoes this profoundly Pauline vision. He writes, "Christ is for us a pattern and beginning and image of the divine way of life, and he displayed clearly how and in what manner it is fitting for us to live."[146]

In this way Christ points us to how we should live with the Father and how we should serve in the power of the Spirit; how we should be committed to God's purposes and how we should pray; how we should build community and be instruments of healing; how we should resist the religious establishment; and how we should be peacemakers and serve the poor.

Thought

Reread the Gospels. It is clear what Jesus was about. We are called to live in the same way.

2 Thessalonians 2:13

May 27

The Trinity

The recovery of emphasis on the Trinity has brought a deepening of the life of faith and service in the Christian community. While the salvific work of Christ continues to receive its rightful emphasis, the creative and sustaining activity of the Father and the renewing work of the Spirit are also rightly in view.

The early church father St. Irenaeus gives emphasis to the way the members of the Holy Trinity are dynamically interrelated and how, in our approach to God, the Trinity is to be in view. He writes, "Therefore one cannot see the Word of God without the Spirit, nor can anyone approach the Father without the Son."[147]

While this doctrine will always remain a confession of faith that is shrouded in mystery, we are encouraged by the vision that the God of the Bible is no static and isolated heavenly entity. Rather, God is a community of "persons" existing in mutual love, harmony, and cooperation. Each is involved in the other's activity. Each is there in and for the other.

This gives us a powerful picture of the way we, the people of God, are to be in relationship and to be for the other. In this sense, the community of faith is to be an icon of the Trinity.

In the beautiful work of the Trinity we can hold together the work of salvation, the importance of the created order, and the work of the beautifying Spirit. Thus, the healing of persons and communities, the concern for our fragile earth, and the visionary power of the Spirit should all be part of our vision of what we are called into and what we need to be concerned about.

Thought

Worship God as the Triune God—Father, Son, and Holy Spirit.

Romans 8:22–23

May 28

Sojourners

Although coming to faith in Christ is a homecoming, we are still on a journey. That journey is towards greater conformity to Christ, service in the world, and the anticipation of a new heavens and a new earth.

The Christian lives in between the times—the time of Christ's first coming and the hope of Christ's return. The Christian also lives in the blessedness of the in-breaking of the reign of God and the longing for a fuller manifestation of God's kingdom.

Moreover, while the Christian is to be deeply immersed in the normal realities of life—including family, work, government, recreation, and art—the Christian is also out of step with aspects of the world's ways. Being more loyal to Christ than to holding worldly values, the Christian will always be a sojourner.

Thus, the Christian is a pilgrim. He or she is in the world but is not of it, for the longing is for the world to come. The Christian, therefore, while deeply involved in the issues of our time, is a gazer into the world waiting to be born.

St. Anselm knew this only too well. He writes, "I weep over the hardship of exile, hoping in the sole consolation of your coming, ardently longing for the glorious contemplation of your face."[148]

This is a reflection of this in-between state where Christ is with us, but the fuller revelation of his presence awaits a future time.

Thus we wait. We long. We hope. We pray. We serve.

Reflection

To be a sojourner is to be a marginal person.

1 Thessalonians 5:6–8

May 29

Distracted

Contemporary Western Christianity is marked by an austere minimalism. Christians don't read their Bibles. They come to church once every three or four weeks. And they only expect the church to serve them.

Western Christianity is not in good shape. It lacks depth and is far from robust. Some have called it a consumer Christianity that is largely culturally captive.

The key theme of this kind of Christianity is that nothing much should be demanded of the church's adherents. This also means that nothing much is expected.

To some extent this is not new. Christians have often settled for some sort of mediocrity or minimalism. Anastasius II, the Patriarch of Antioch, writes, "If the reading from the divine Gospel is somewhat long, we are irritated and we fidget about. When the priest is offering prayers, if he prolongs them even a little, we grow dismal and distracted."[149]

But the movement of the Christian life is not towards some sort of reductionism. It is towards *growth*. It is not the desire for less now that we know Christ, but the desire to grow in intimacy and commitment.

In this growth we need to take on board the blessings and burdens on being part of the Christian community. We need to contribute to its life and suffer its foibles. We need to receive, but also give. We need to serve, but also be willing to suffer.

No one can grow in Christian maturity isolated from and critical of others. The movement of life is to grow in Christ and in the service of others, and this requires patience as well as faith.

Prayer

Lord, help me to go deeper in my life of faith, prayer, and service. Amen.

Hebrews 10:32–36

May 30

Patience

What we truly are does not necessarily surface when all is going well, when life's setting is safe and there are no clouds of danger on the horizon. It is when difficulties and troubles come that we have the opportunity to tap into our deeper resources.

The medieval Christian mystic Richard Rolle, the hermit of Hampole, understood well that life's storms can bring out what is most true in us. He writes, "in peace no man is called patient, but when he is pulled with wrong; then he should see if he has patience."[150]

Therefore, to always pray for calm waters and to complain to God and others when things are not going well, is to miss the point. Difficulties are moments of opportunity. This does not mean we should wish for difficulties. They will come anyway.

The point in all of this has to do with growth. It has to do with being shaped by the good responses we make in hard times. These are responses of grace. And it is these responses of goodness that help make us into the persons we are becoming in Christ.

Goodness leading to maturity and wholeness is not only the product of fair weather. It is more often the fruit that comes from times of difficulty.

This means we need to embrace difficulty and bring it to God in prayer. It means we have to go through difficulties rather than around them in order to gain what such circumstances may surprisingly offer us.

Reflection

Suffering and surrender can lead to patience.

Isaiah 57:15

May 31

Testing

There is security in the Christian life. God will not leave us or forsake us. There is also vulnerability in living the Christian life. We are often fickle in our relationship with God.

Thomas à Kempis sounds a clear note of realism, "I have never encountered anyone, no matter how devout and religious, who did not sometimes experience a withdrawal of grace or a decrease in devotion."[151]

The Christian life is not only lived while sailing on an even keel. And the road of faith is not only a straight line. And Christian growth is not only a regular movement upward. And the life of faith is not without its doubts and difficulties.

It is all far more complex since our relationship with God swings with our moods, our health issues, life circumstances, the state of the church, and the pressures in our world. Yet surprisingly, despite all of this, our underlying faith may remain steady and vibrant.

Experience seems to suggest, however, that our spiritual fervor is much more likely to wane and wander when all is going well with us rather than when we are facing crises. Thus, in the good times there lies the temptation to forget and to neglect.

Our response in all of this, first and foremost, should not be to try harder when things are not going well or the dark night of the soul is upon us, but to commit ourselves more fully into the hands of God. In the decrease of our devotion we all the more quickly should run to the heart of God.

Thought

Even in our down times God can hold us.

ST MECHTHILD OF MAGDEBURG

John 21:15–19

June 1

Dealing with Issues

That we want to escape from our problems and difficulties is a natural impulse. That we have to face difficulties involves both courage and the hope that good things lie on the other side.

That we are escapist in our basic orientation is already evident in the Genesis saga of human rebellion against God. Our first parents ran and hid. We tend to do the same in making excuses, blaming others, rationalizing our actions, or moving on as if nothing has happened.

The wisdom of the Christian story, and the long history of the church's re-enactment of that story, is that wrongdoing needs to be faced and forgiven. The further dimension of this wisdom is that no matter how far you run you will always take yourself and your unresolved past with you.

One of the desert fathers had this to say: "If a trial comes upon you in the place where you live do not leave that place; . . . wherever you go you will find that what you are running from is ahead of you."[152]

The challenge for us in all this is to work things through in the setting in which we presently find ourselves. If things are difficult at work, don't just assume another job is simply the answer. If you are in a relational crisis, don't just assume finding new friends is the only answer. Instead, you may need to face things about yourself, as well as things in relation to others.

Thought

Problems can be the painful mirror for self-discovery.

Matthew 9:14–15

June 2

A Balanced Life?

Life is to be lived beyond both legalism and promiscuity, beyond a careless freedom and an oppressive asceticism. Life is to be lived in joy and responsibility.

If the Christian life is to be a small repetition of the life of Christ, then such a life can hardly be based on a narrow legalism. Jesus lived his life in the joy of doing the will of his Father, in contrast to the narrow religiosity of his day.

Moreover, if the Christian life is to be lived in the grace of Christ and in the power of the Spirit, then such a life is lived in the movement and energy of God and not according to rigid rules. A life animated by spiritual forces will always be more meaningful than a life framed by legalism.

John Cassian, one of the key framers of early monasticism, was concerned that monks should live the Christian life in personal devotion and community, in freedom and responsibility, and in self-denial and joy. He writes, "Too much self-denial brings weakness and induces the same condition as carelessness."[153]

To live the Christian life in the balance of grace and obedience, joy and relinquishment, service and Sabbath, self-care and oriented towards others, speaking and the practice of silence, and worship and the work of justice, will always be a challenge. To live this way of life requires passion and discernment and wisdom and gentleness.

To live a more balanced life means we have to face and deal with the compulsions and insecurities within us.

Reflection

One should not try to do more than what God asks and what God provides.

Ephesians 1:17–20

June 3

Being Enlightened

If the modernity project was primarily about rationality and technology, it could be that the twenty-first century may usher in a more integrated way of being, thinking, and doing. Maybe imagination could play a greater role in determining life.

The major contours of the biblical story can never be reduced simply to a knowledge of God. It also has to do with the revelation of God and the vision of God. And more than this, it also has to do with the worship of God, the community of God, and the service of God.

The great Franciscan theologian Bonaventure reflects this integrated vision of our entering into the ways and mysteries of God. He writes, "The reader might think that reading is sufficient without heavenly anointing, or thinking without devotion, or investigation without admiration, or mere observation without rejoicing, or effort without piety, or knowledge without charity, intelligence without humility, endeavor without divine grace."[154] Clearly, if the reader thinks this, the reader is wrong. Heart, mind, and hand belong together.

Living the Christian life is about restoration and wholeness. We are restored to God, to ourselves, to others, and to nature through the healing action of God. And we grow into wholeness where mind and body, spirituality and sexuality, worship and work, and self and neighbor form a mosaic of celebration and joy.

Mind, passion, emotions, and doing are to be woven together in a tapestry of the grace of God.

Reflection

Much doing without much prayer and joy will become a beast of burden.

Colossians 4:12

June 4

Resident Aliens

Living the creative tension of being oriented towards God and spiritual matters, while at the same time being fully immersed in the issues and challenges of our time, requires much prayerful discernment and courage. Sadly, we tend to go one way more than the other.

Clement of Alexandria, the early church father, clearly highlights the dialectic we are called to live: "Let us turn away from life as transient residents in this world and do the will of the one who called us."[155] Had Clement only said the first part, then we could readily charge him with promoting a world-denying spirituality. But he goes on to call us to seek and do the will of God. He calls us to do the will of God *in our world*.

The basic rhythm here is to turn *from* in order to turn *to*. It is to say no in order to say yes. It is being freed from worldliness in order to do God's will in serving in our world.

What is clear in the biblical story is that doing the will of God is not only related to the life to come. It is also very much related to the life of faith and service we are called to live in the here and now.

And this calling is not only to build the community of faith and to share the good news of what God has done in Christ. It is also to build the human community, to bless secular institutions, and to contribute to the common good for the sake of Christ.

Prayer

Lord, help me to be truly linked to you while being involved in the challenges of our time. Amen.

Psalm 91:1–4

June 5

The Three-fold Action of God

What God does is never marked by singularity. God does not do only one thing. Manifold are his works. Diverse is his love and care towards us.

It is very easy for us to hold a reductionistic view of God. And usually that has to do with only seeing what blesses and benefits us.

Thus in the enthusiasm of Charismatic renewal we celebrate the power of God through the Spirit, but we fail to be thankful for God's providential care for our world. Or we are grateful for God's healing activity in our lives, but we fail to see God's passion for justice in relation to the poor.

Julian of Norwich, however, gives us a much bigger and more comprehensive picture of the action of God. Talking about a hazelnut she says, "God made it . . . God loves it . . . God preserves it." In this example she sees God as "the Creator . . . protector and the lover."[156]

There are many other ways of expressing this theme. We may speak about God as creating a world, routing an enemy, and building a people. We may speak of God as healer, sustainer, empowerer, guide, refuge, and nurturer. We may speak of God as redeemer, but we also need to acknowledge God's lordship over our lives.

In all these things we need to be careful that we maintain *both* the language of distance *and* that of intimacy. God is Sovereign. But God is also friend.

Reflection

In all of the manifold ways that God acts, we are to be thankful and rejoice.

Isaiah 6:1–5

June 6

Naked before God

Much of our identity is a social construction. We are shaped by family, social institutions, and the culture of which we are a part. But we also inhabit an inner world. It is this world, lived before God, that is to determine the way in which we live and act in the outer world.

We are all familiar with the language of the inner self and the social self and with the idea of the true self and the false self. We may also hold that we have an active and a shadow side to who we are.

We are also all too aware of how much we are outer-oriented and how a life of constant externalization has left us inwardly impoverished. Modern communication technology has left us on call 24 hours per day.

Thus the great challenge for us in the twenty-first century is the recovery of our *inner* world—a world of reflection, solitude, prayer, and contemplation.

St. Francis reminds us of the centrality of this inner world. He writes, "What a person is before God, that he [she] is and no more."[157] This leaves most of us at a pretty shallow level.

This then is a challenging vision for us who have made our social persona the mainstay of our identity.

To live the Franciscan vision means God needs to become central to our existence. It means friendship with God needs to be cultivated. And this means a life of devotion, worship, and service in the will and love of God will need to develop. This is truly a revolutionary way of living in our time.

Reflection

I can only live well before God in the grace of forgiveness and in the power of the Spirit.

Psalm 143:8–10

June 7

The Ascent to God

In the long history of Christianity the ascent to God has been a major preoccupation. Embedded in this vision is the desire to be both close to God and to be like God. It should not surprise us that many pathways to this ascent have been mapped out.

The ascent to God, or the quest for union with God, is at the heart of spiritual desire. The impetus for this is both the human longing for transcendence and the work of God's Spirit within us, leading to conformity to the being and ways of God. The Spirit emanating from God in turn draws us to God as the source of our life.

The work of the Spirit within us, however, does not call us to be passive. We are to cooperate with the Spirit's promptings. One key response on our part is yieldedness. Others are longing and seeking.

In this quest surrender surely is an important theme. But so is relinquishment. This is the factor Thomas à Kempis highlights. He writes, "As long as there is anything that holds me down, I cannot freely fly to You."[158]

What holds us down may well be our sin and wrongdoing. But it may also be good things that hold us back. In relinquishment we surrender the good for the greater good of pleasing God and drawing nearer to him. This calls us to careful discernment lest relinquishment becomes an unhealthy masochism.

Prayer

Lord, help me to desire you above all else. Amen.

James 5:16

June 8

Confession

While Martin Luther sought to retain the sacrament of confession, this discipline has largely been lost in the Protestant tradition. It has become all the more lost in our present culture where sin is a mistake rather than an affront to God.

In direct proportion that the holiness of God has become problematical for many in our time, so the notion of sin has become a weakened reality. Sin is seen as mistakes or small aberrations in our behavior that impact others in unhelpful ways, rather than as thoughts and actions that grieve the heart of God and go against his will and purpose.

Clearly, on this point a huge shift will need to occur if God is to become more central to our thinking and action. And a recovery of the practice of confession both directly to God and to God in the presence of another will need to take place.

But confession is not a magic fix-all. St. Cyprian long ago pointed out that, "Confession does not guarantee immunity from the snares of the devil, nor provide lasting security against . . . temptations."[159]

The Christian life is lived in the ever-present tension of growth in Christ and the failure to walk in the ways of God. Thus, confession is called for again and again. Thus, we may say we are called to live a confessional spirituality. This spirituality calls us not only to grieve our sin, but to rejoice in God's forgiveness and to embrace the strengthening work of the Spirit within us. But even when we are stronger, confession is still called for, even if this is only for what we have failed to do.

Reflection

Confession can repair the wrong and empower us for the good.

Romans 8:14

June 9

The Blessed Spirit

While we may see the Spirit as God's gift to us, the Spirit is not our possession. Rather, the Spirit "possesses" us. And more significantly, the Spirit belongs to all who are in Christ Jesus.

Contemporary Christianity can learn much from the wisdom of the church in earlier times. One of the main reasons is that we are too locked into contemporary views and values and therefore need the corrective voice of the other.

One of our contemporary problems is that our rampant individualism has affected our relationships and our sense of community. Our Christian faith and life has become highly privatized and church for many has become irrelevant.

St. Basil points us in another direction. He writes that the Spirit is given "to everyone who receives it" and is "given to him alone." But he immediately goes on to say that the Spirit "sends forth grace sufficient and full for all mankind."[160] In other words, the Spirit is both personal and communal.

This communal dimension of the Spirit's work is a particular challenge for us today. If Christians have the presence of the Spirit in common, then there is the possibility of a common faith, common relationships, a common calling, and a shared life of worship and service. Clearly, we stand in need of a new Pentecost in our day so that a common life in the Spirit will become a source for our spiritual sustenance and a witness to the world.

Prayer

Come Holy Spirit, and make us one. Amen.

Ezekiel 34:11–12

June 10

The Hound of Heaven

We have become so human-centered that even our focus on the blessing of salvation is on what we do in finding and turning to God. Clearly, the prior emphasis lies with God finding us.

Our human-centric world has deeply invaded the consciousness of members of the Christian church. So much so that the church itself has largely become a self-energized and self-perpetuating institution. In case you doubt this, just look at the ratio between prayer and the church's many other activities.

This emphasis has also affected our relationship with God. We seem to be operating on the premise that so much depends on us, for God seems to be largely absent. And so we think we need to find God with little sense about the Spirit's prior work in us.

St. Augustine sees things differently. He explains, "even if they have abandoned thee, their Creator, thou hast not abandoned thy creatures."[161]

So if the Creator has not abandoned us, then surely God the Redeemer is ever present and the Spirit is ever brooding over our souls, the human community, and the creation.

The problem is not that God is not present, even if that is a hidden presence, but we have lost our spiritual sensitivities and can no longer see and hear. We need to be silent enough to hear and open enough to receive.

Prayer

Come to us, O God, even when we don't seek you. Amen.

Hebrews 12:1–2

June 11

The Joy of Obedience

We have this idea that adherence to the way of God is hard and burdensome because it cuts across the way we want to live. We therefore need to discover that the way of obedience is a life of joy.

In the modern world we cling to the notion that happiness lies in much-having and in the experience of unfettered freedom. If only we can do whatever we like, the happier we will be, we think.

But the wisdom of the saints of the past points us in another direction. For them, happiness lay in who and what they lived for. And central in all of this was to live life in the love and purposes of God.

Hildegard of Bingen, the twelfth-century German mystic, believed that the one "who strongly does the good he [she] ardently desires" in the light of the divine command "shall dance in the true exultation of the joy of salvation."[162]

The idea that there is joy in obedience is a wisdom one can only discover in walking this unusual road. And we usually only enter upon this road when we have become tired of the folly of our own ways and are willing, with the Spirit's help, to walk in the ways of the Lord.

While this journey at first may seem to be very arduous and self-sacrificial, it is a road of increasing lightness of step and the blessing of joy.

Thought

Our own way is burdensome. The way of Christ is a lighter burden marked by joy.

Psalm 51:10-13

June 12

A Gentle Transformation

God's way with us is not one of negation but one of cleansing and renewal. While we may need to be stripped bare, God's love clothes us in new garments.

Our contemporary view of God is hardly marked by great generosity on our part. We often see God as demanding and less than available. Clearly, in this view of God we may merely be repeating the way in which others have treated us and we treat others.

We also tend to see God as thinking much too badly about us. God, we claim, thinks of us in wholly negative terms. We are always a problem to God. We are only ever sinners.

St. Anselm had a much warmer and more generous view of God. In prayer he exclaims, "Most kind Lord, acknowledge what is yours in me, and take away anything that is not yours."[163]

In this view of God's dealing with us we see a warm embrace and a gentle transformation. There is both God's affirmation and his healing and renewal.

What is of note in St. Anselm's prayer is that he does not simply see the good in us as being of our own doing and making. All is of *God*. In both the story of our general formation in family and society, as well as in the story of our regeneration and healing through Christ, God is wonderfully and mysteriously at work in us. God both preserves and renews us in his work of grace.

Prayer

Strengthen what is good, renew what is dormant, heal what is broken, and carry me forward into your love, O Lord. Amen.

James 1:13–16

June 13

Temptation

To say one is tempted is to acknowledge a lot; namely, one has a sense of right or wrong, one can be led astray by outside or internal forces, and one has a sense that this invitation should be resisted.

Most of us have a regular conversation going on inside of our heads that revolves around what we may or should do, and what is not a good idea or unacceptable. Thus, on a daily basis we make choices between right and wrong. And guiding these choices is usually the basic value framework by which we have chosen to live.

But we don't consistently live our values. Out of our routines, in different circumstances, in a different place, and in times of stress and difficulty, particular temptations may come our way.

Evagrius Ponticus, an early church father influenced by Platonic thinking, recognized that the unexpected could come our way and things could arise from the subconscious. He notes, "Many passions are hidden in our soul, but escape our attention. It is sudden temptation which reveals them."[164]

That being the case, temptation is an invitation not simply to resist the temptation, but a journey to a much greater self-awareness. Temptation says as much about what is in us as it does about a malignant force or being that is trying to lead us astray.

Prayer

O Lord, lead us not into temptation. But when it comes, help us find sustenance and clarity with you. And draw us more deeply into your grace, your ways, and your embrace. Amen.

Romans 8:18

June 14

Martyrdom

In the Western world we are living with the idea that all physical suffering can somehow be overcome by medical technology. But suffering is an integral part of life. It is also a key dimension of living the Christian life, where grace calls us not away from suffering but to deeper suffering.

Christians in the first three centuries of the Christian era, but also subsequently, were willing, by following Christ, to embrace the possibility of a martyr's death. They believed in a baptism in water, a baptism in the Spirit, and a baptism in blood. The latter was a baptism into martyrdom.

The early church father St. Ignatius not only saw martyrdom as a possibility, but he welcomed it as a way of discipleship. He writes, "So that I may not merely be called a Christian, but actually prove to be one,"[165] he wanted to embrace a martyr's death.

Martyrdom for the faith is once again occurring in the non-Western Christian world. But it poses a challenge for us in the West with our easy-going Christianity. Western consumer Christianity is certainly not marked by martyr's blood.

But there is a place where we can start. We can begin to live a more prayerful life. We can live more sacrificially. And we can begin to make the concerns of our brothers and sisters in Africa, Latin America, and Asia our own concerns. This means a radical identification with them even at a cost to ourselves.

Reflection

In what ways do I need to give up some aspects of my life for the sake of the reign of God?

Mark 12: 29–31

June 15

Loving God

The biggest challenge facing contemporary Christianity is not first and foremost church renewal or missional renewal, but a revitalization of our love for God.

St. Bernard of Clairvaux, who brought about a revival of monasticism in twelfth-century France, is well known for his reflections on the nature of Christian love.

The first degree of love, he says, is when you love yourself for your own sake. The second is when you love God for your own well-being. The third is when you love God for God's sake and not simply for the blessings you receive from God. But the fourth, and clearly the highest form of love according to St. Bernard, is when you love yourself for the sake of God.

This form of relationship has to do with a merging of love of the one into the other. One's very breath and being has to do with God. To explain this merging St. Bernard speaks of "a drop of water . . . disappear[ing] completely in a quantity of wine." And further, "it is necessary for human affection to dissolve in some ineffable way and be poured into the will of God."[166]

He goes on to say that we cannot make this happen and the soul can only hope to attain this as a gift of God's grace.

But the invitation for us is clear. Far too self-preoccupied and utilitarian, we are called to a deeper love.

Prayer

Win my heart, Lord, in order that I may surrender it to you.

Luke 7:47

June 16

Having Been Forgiven

While we may want to live towards others from the position of competence and strength—and possibly even live towards God in this way—there is quite a different way of living. At its heart this other way is to live in gratitude and humility. And this includes receiving the blessing of forgiveness.

Our world is marked by a certain cruelty. It is a one-up-manship and a relentless competitiveness that we have chosen to live in our world. Always with our guard up, we have constantly to better ourselves in relation to others.

There are, of course, other ways to live. Most basic, this is to live more communally and cooperatively. And one can live with thankfulness and generosity. And to live well in relationship, one cannot do without giving and receiving forgiveness.

The fourteenth-century Dominican mystic Henry Suso looks at the power of forgiveness in relation to God. He notes, "The more mercifully I am dealt with, the more tearfully I afflict my soul, because I have been ungrateful to so devoted a Beloved and so faithful a Father."[167] The point is clear. Mercy issues into gratitude. God's generosity enlarges our soul to extend goodness to others.

Applied at the horizontal level, forgiving others leads to inner freedom and being forgiven issues into the joy of relational freedom.

Reflection

Without the practice of forgiveness a sustainable world becomes impossible. With forgiveness there is always the hope of new beginnings.

Psalm 27:8

June 17

God Alone

Life in the modern world is such that we think we can have everything. We can have happiness, health, careers, enjoyment, and spirituality. We can have all of our wishes and all of God's purposes at the same time. We may need to discover that things don't quite work that way.

To try to have everything is to embark on a unsustainable lifestyle. One of life's early discoveries should be that we have to live with limitation.

The problem with trying to get as much as we can, and to hope for everything, is an equally impossible road, for what we get will never satisfy us and our hopes will always outrun us, for enough is never enough.

Instead, we should live according to a certain purpose. And for the Christian that purpose is to seek God's will and direction for one's life. And in that quest of listening and discernment the focus should be on the worship of God rather than on our self-determination about the path we are to take.

To put this more clearly, if we seek God we will find our way in life. If we only put ourselves in the picture we will lose our way.

Meister Eckhart has put this clearly, "to seek nothing and to set out only for God himself, is to discover God who gives the seeker all that is in his divine heart."[168]

And the all in God's heart includes not only our salvation and healing, but also the unfolding discovery of our life's purpose and joy in relationships and in our vocation.

Reflection

In seeking you, O God, I find myself.

2 Samuel 11:13

June 18

Addictions

To avoid the pain of living or to escape from particular problems, we have always tried to find ways of escape that dull our pain. The use of certain drugs is one such strategy. Sadly, this leads to addiction.

While addiction may be a pressing problem in the modern world, it has always been part of the human condition. The impulse to escape *from* our problems is generic to our humanity. And since this impulse is so strong never mind that it may lead to other problems.

St. Augustine understands some of the psychology at play in addiction and when we seek to move out of our addictions. He notes, "And the worse way, to which I was habituated, was stronger in me than the better, which I had not tried."[169]

Here lies the problem. The world of my addiction, whatever form that may take, is at least the world I know, and while it is destructive it gives me some comfort. The world of freedom, through conversion and healing, is still such a strange world, that even though it beckons me I dare not enter it.

This is a picture of the person in conflict, bound to a problem, but longing for deliverance. This is also the problem at the core of conversion. We are bound to what is familiar but brings us no happiness, while we are afraid of God's call to change and be healed. Somewhere in all of this we need to find the courage to try the new. This calls for a deep surrender.

Reflection

How can I hear more deeply the call to be free and whole?

Mark 8:34

June 19

Cross-bearing

While there is a lot of morbid language and sentimentality around the topic of the cross and our need to carry a cross, the heart of this imagery is the freedom we will discover in cross-bearing.

It is true that in life we all have to live with limitations and difficulties regarding some of which there are no answers. Bad things happen to all of us.

While in common conversation we call this having to carry our cross, cross-bearing in the Christian tradition means something quite different. It means voluntary relinquishment in order to more truly follow Jesus.

Thus, at the heart of the Christian tradition cross-bearing is the way of discipleship. It is the way of the *imitatio Christi*. It is accepting and embracing that the way Jesus lived his life, even unto death on a cross, is the way in which we also need to live our lives as we seek to be like Jesus. Thus, both service and suffering will be key to the way in which we live our lives.

Thomas à Kempis in his discussion of this topic makes the helpful comment, "If you should throw off one cross you will surely find another and perhaps one that is even heavier."[170] His point is clear. Bearing the cross of Christ, while it may seem heavy, is in fact lighter than bearing the cross of a life without the grace of God and the power of the Spirit. Or to put that differently, living life in our own self-determined way may leave us with heavy burdens.

Thought

Redemptive suffering brings healing to our world. We too, in our small ways, are called to this.

Matthew 5:4

June 20

Mourning

While thankfulness and rejoicing are important dimensions of the Christian life, so is mourning. We mourn the loss of all we could and should be.

In his reflections on conversion, St. Bernard of Clairvaux talks about the role of mourning in conversion. We mourn our sin, obstinacy, and lack of surrender and obedience. But mourning can't only be about regret, it also needs to be full of hope. Thus he writes, "Let him mourn, but not without holy love and in hope of consolation."[171]

Mourning, however, can play a much larger role in our lives. We mourn not only for ourselves, but also for others and for the church and the world.

We can mourn for or with others not only in their loss, but also in the failure to be what they could be. And this dimension of mourning can be applied to many of the situations in which we find ourselves: a Christian ministry losing its effectiveness; an institution not realizing its potential; a government not fulfilling its mandate; a world gripped in the madness of war; nature groaning under the weight of exploitation.

To mourn is more productive than to grumble. In mourning we grieve the pain of loss, we look for consolation and we prepare ourselves to live in the hope of something new coming into being. Mourning, therefore, is not dismal. It is hopeful.

Reflection

In mourning we lay the ground for a new morning.

Romans 6:8

June 21

The Great Reversal

The Christian faith is no rational enterprise. It is a matter of faith. And it is embracing the mystery that God does things in such surprising ways.

If much of twentieth-century Western Christianity was too enamored with rationality as a way of being in the faith, that is hardly the case now. And certainly this was not the way in which Christians in earlier times understood the faith.

St. Anselm in the eleventh century understood the faith in deeply personal but also paradoxical terms. He writes humans "might kill life," but Christ came to "destroy death." He continues, we humans "condemn the Savior," but "Christ came to save the condemned."[172]

His point is clear. God does the opposite of what we would do or might expect. Why create when one is already marked by fullness? Why redeem and make whole a humanity marked by resistance or indifference? Why care at the cost of suffering? Why not simply turn away? Why should God the giver of life embrace a sacrificial death?

Thankfully, God is not like us. And therefore there is the full scope of hope for inner renewal and for transformation in our world. Long after we have given up, God continues to love and to make whole.

Reflection

In contrast to what we would never do, we see God's different way of infinite mercy and grace.

Psalm 42:1–2

June 22

The Longing Heart

It is not what we have that truly defines us. It is what we long for that shows the true colors of our values.

In the contemporary world human longing seems to focus on material well-being, success, and the ability to influence others. The quest for happiness also continues to be key concern.

For the Christian, the longing heart has other priorities. Most basic, these have to do with the search for a deeper relationship with God, prayer for the fuller in-breaking of God's kingdom, the longing to serve others better, and the hope in the life to come.

The desert father Macarius of Egypt purportedly wrote about the quest of Christians, "the more insatiable they are of the heavenly longing ... the more they seek on with diligence."[173]

This longing for God and the things of God's kingdom is no mere human effort. It is a gift of grace. It is also no quick matter. It is a lifetime preoccupation. It is not simply a burden. It is also a joy.

The longing heart is not only the restless heart, it is also the focused heart. It seeks for God and the ways of God.

It is also an open heart. Open to the quest for friendship and understanding. But also open to the surprises of God.

Prayer

Lord, help me live beyond the predictable in my relationship with you. Lead me to new places with you. Amen.

Matthew 5:4

June 23

Identification

Despite the individualism characterizing our contemporary thinking, we are more bound together in the human community than we care to admit. One outcome of this connectedness is that we are willing to identify with the needs and issues of others.

A world marked by indifference is a world that would become unsustainable. A world marked by mutual concern and cooperation is a world that nourishes and empowers us.

In Christian thinking there is a very strong emphasis on relationships and care for the other. The common faith that we have in Christ and which is nurtured by the Spirit draws us together into a common life, common friendship and care, and service.

But this sense of commonality is also to be extended to those outside the Christian community. St. Clement of Rome, one of the very early church fathers, expresses this well. He writes, "You mourned for the transgressions of your neighbors: you considered their shortcomings to be your own."[174]

This expresses the depth of identification to which one might go. Not only can we identify with others in care and service, but also in intercessory prayer and burden bearing. We can mourn for our own sins but also for the sins of others. In this we vicariously stand in the place of the other person.

Thought

How much am I willing to carry another's burden?

Psalm 37:7

June 24

The Virtue of Disinterestedness

At face value we would never call disinterestedness a virtue. Instead, we might call it a vice, for to be in relationship demands love, care, and interest. But in Christian spirituality disinterestedness is seen as a blessing, not a problem.

Meister Eckhart, the German Christian mystic, has written much about this topic. He notes, "Disinterest is best of all, for by it the soul is unified, knowledge is made pure, the heart is kindled, the spirit wakened, the desires quickened, the virtues enhanced."[175] He regards disinterestedness as a great spiritual quality.

At core what Eckhart means by this is an inner disposition that is *the heart in repose*. It is a spirituality of surrender and waiting rather one of striving and asking. It is a spirituality of receiving rather than first and foremost one of giving.

This poses a challenge for us. Much of our relationship with God, our involvement in church and in our prayer life is oriented around our needs, concerns, and what we can get. Thus, we love God for the blessings and benefits we receive.

But there is also another dimension that we can grow into in relation to God and spiritual matters and that is not to demand but to love and wait.

To attempt to live this way in relation to God is not to deny that we have needs but that our needs are not always the primary focus. To love God for who God is and not to demand is an attitude of surrender and humility.

Prayer

Lord, teach me to wait on you, to wait for you, and to wait with you in order to do your will. Amen.

Psalm 19:1

June 25

Loving God and All Things

In the history of Christian spirituality there has persisted the faulty idea that in order to love God well one must not love other things. But clearly to love God well is to love all that God has made.

Dualistic thinking has long plagued the history of Christianity. In this we elevate one thing over another—the soul over the body and the spiritual over the material.

This kind of thinking has led to one-sided ascetic practices and to unhelpful ethics where certain dimensions of life are celebrated and others are denigrated. Thus fasting is seen as spiritual. The enjoyment of food is seen as having nothing to do with spirituality.

St. Augustine, however, gives us a much more integrated perspective. He writes, there is a place "where time does not snatch away the lovely sound, where no breeze disperses the sweet fragrance, where no eating diminishes the food there provided. . . . This is what I love when I love my God."[176] Here we have a beautiful vision of love of God and love of beauty.

While we are to love God above all others and all other things, we are to love others and the gifts of creation as well. Prayer and food are gifts from God. A home and temple are both places where God can be worshipped. Contemplation and love of nature are both part of the goodness of life.

In loving God we are to love all that comes from God's good hand. Beauty, art, music, celebration, fun, play, are all part of life lived to the glory of God.

Reflection

I need new eyes to see all of life as God's great gift.

Matthew 7:3–5

June 26

Self Insight

That we see the faults in others but not in ourselves is a well-known human trait. We, therefore, need to find mirrors in which we learn to see ourselves more truly.

The quest in the spiritual journey is to know and see God more fully and clearly. But in this quest one can't know God more fully and remain blind to oneself. The knowledge of God does come from the knowledge of self and it comes by revelation. But since knowledge of God involves repentance, faith, and humility, this knowledge involves self-knowledge.

St. Isaac the Syrian makes the point rather strongly. He writes, "He who sees himself as he is, is greater than the one who raises the dead."[177]

Leaving comparisons to one side, his challenge is clear. One may do great deeds in the name of God, but to be blind to one's own strengths and failings is a great loss.

What this means by way of further implication is that in the face of God, in the light of Scripture, through the work of the Spirit, and in relationship with others, we are led to greater light and truth about ourselves. Thus self-insight is part of the spiritual quest. This quest is to know oneself in the love of God.

The great mirror in all of this is Christ who both embraces us, shows us our faults, and forgives and heals us. And in being healed we know ourselves more truly.

Reflection

In being loved we can see ourselves more truly.

Isaiah 11:1–5

June 27

A Righteous Judge

We face two contemporary problems. One is we have so emphasized the love of God that we have lost the notion of judgment. And we are so used to the perversion of justice we can hardly conceive of a God who judges fairly.

The biblical narrative is quite clear about two interrelated themes. One is God redeems and heals his people and calls them to fidelity. This theme is the magnificence of God's grace and generosity. The other theme is God's people are judged in history and there is final judgment at the end of time. Clearly, the Christian life is lived in the tension of these two themes.

St. Gregory of Nyssa in commenting on the justice of God at the resurrection makes reference to what a good judge would do. He writes, "To evaluate the way a person has lived, the judge would need to examine all these factors: how he endured suffering, dishonor, disease, old age, maturity, youth, wealth and poverty; how through each of these situations he ran the course of his life."[178]

The belief that the God of all the earth will be even more gracious than such an earthly judge is comfort for us all.

As a consequence, we can live the Christian life not in the fear of a final judgment but in the call to love and obey God in our daily lives. And our future is in God's gracious heart.

Thought

Justice marked by grace is the way the whole world should function.

Proverbs 8:27–31

June 28

The Playful and Purposeful Trinity

There are those who have a very mechanical view of God. They
see God as the powerful and unchanging heavenly machine.
But God is personal, dynamic, loving, and eternally interactive.

The German Beguine mystic St. Mechthild of Magdeburg has a delightful understanding of the nature of God and the relationship between the Father, the Son, and the Holy Spirit.

Several themes stand out in her visionary writings. The one is the delight and joy in the relationship of the community of the Trinity. The other is their joyful interpersonal communication. The third is their amazing cooperation in willing to play various roles and take on certain tasks in order that the heavenly purposes they are determining will be realized.

She sees the Son speaking to the Father as follows, "With your blessing Father, I will freely take on human nature despite its pollution, and I will wash its wounds through my innocent blood."[179] This kind of communication she sees taking place amongst all members of the Trinity.

The challenge in this for us is not only to think about the Trinity in a different way, but also to take inspiration from this way of interacting. If only we could relate to others in a spirit of love, cooperation, and service, what a difference this would make to our churches and institutions. Thus, the love and cooperation in the Trinity should shape our relationships.

Reflection

Joyful service coming from mutual cooperation will impact our world.

Psalm 103:2-5

June 29

God the Giver of Good Things

We can see ourselves as self-made women and men. In that way we only see what we have done and achieved. We can also see ourselves as persons to whom much has been given.

There are many ways in which we can understand the shape of our humanity. Clearly, there are biological and many other formative factors. There are also the choices we make, the training we undertake, the work we do, and the relationships we nurture.

Even in noting this we can already see we receive so much from others. Even our biology is a gift. So is our family. So are friends.

Recognizing the way in which so much has come to us from others calls us to a profound thankfulness. And this is the royal road to live the good life.

St. Benedict takes this one step further. He writes, "If you notice something good in yourself, give credit to God."[180] This expresses a vision of life where God's pervasive presence and influence is seen, not only in the ministry of the church, but in all the dimensions of life. God in nature. God in family. God in the human community. God in our schools, institutions, and neighborhood.

With this vision, thankfulness to God becomes the pervasive reality of our lives rather than a self-congratulatory self-sufficiency.

Thought

Thankfulness is the oil of all good human effort.

Psalm 141:2

June 30

Prayer

Prayer is not mere self-talk. It is not wishful thinking. It is not simply a form of self-catharsis. It is, instead, a communion with God. And it constitutes one of the key disciplines of the Christian life.

The German mystic and Dominican preacher Johannes Tauler has often been called the first Protestant before the Reformation. His writings had a profound impact on Martin Luther.

In one of his sermons on the reality of prayer, Tauler simply states, "The essence of prayer is an ascent of the mind to God."[181] As such it is foremost friendship with God.

Leaving aside the fact that all spatial language in relation to God is inherently problematical, we may say this upward move is also related to an inward move. And either move can come first.

If we go inward in the contemplation of self-reflection, we will find many reasons to open ourselves to God, for there is much inner healing that still must take place. If we seek the face of God in contemplation of transcendence, this God will also encourage us to reflect on our life and to turn our attention to the neighbor in love and service.

The turning to God in worship and listening is to keep life centered and focused. It can also be the inspirational center of our lives. It is *the* relationship that empowers the whole of our life. Thus, prayer is the food and drink of our life.

Prayer

May I gain an attentive heart, O God, that seeks your friendship. Amen.

JULY

ST FRANCIS

Galatians 4:19

July 1

Suffering Love

Love is relational. It links us to others. And it binds us to those who are in difficulty and are suffering. Love then suffers with and suffers on behalf of others. This is a true love.

One cannot be a serious reader of the Pauline Epistles without being struck by the fact that the apostle not only taught his hearers the faith but that, like a woman giving birth, he agonized them into the spiritual life and growth.

In this St. Paul showed not simply his pastoral care, but his deep love for the members of the early house communities. His was a suffering love because the early churches were full of problems and difficulties.

Lady Julian of Norwich writes, "The higher, and greater, and sweeter our love, so much the deeper will be our sorrow when we see the body of our beloved suffer."[182] Julian is referring here to the disciples' love for their suffering and dying Lord.

But this love for Christ needs to be extended to the suffering church, the body of Christ. And the church is suffering and bleeding. While in some places this is the suffering of persecution, in many other parts of the world it is suffering because it has lost its own way. It is suffering akin to that of a parent for a wayward son or daughter. And how hard is such a scene for loving parents. In a similar way we need to love the church today.

Prayer

Lord, give me a love that hangs in on the bad and difficult times and continues to love and serve. Amen.

1 John 3:18

July 2

Our Work Reveals Us

While we may think that how we explain and justify ourselves in relation to others is what we truly are, this is hardly the case. It is what we persistently do that best reveals who we are.

William of St. Thierry talks about how in doing the commandments of God one understands oneself. In doing "one begins to understand his own works and to understand his own affections."[183]

This is a profound spiritual and psychological insight. Our work most clearly reveals us. We are known by our actions.

We see this most clearly in the life of Jesus. It is not only in what Jesus said that we can see what he came to do. His purpose and passion shines most clearly in what he *did*. And in the followers of Jesus we can most vividly see their discipleship in what they *do*, not simply in what they say.

In this context we are not so much talking about the fact that your paid job reveals who you are, though it may. The emphasis is more about the passion and vision you bring to your paid and voluntary work and when you are not working. It has to do with what you prioritize and value.

The challenge in this for most of us in the Western world is that despite what we say, we are really addicted to middle-class mediocrity, security, and self-interest.

Reflection

The work I do and how I do it is a great mirror.

Matthew 3:1

July 3

The Solitary

The biblical narrative is strong in its emphasis on people-hood and community. But it also acknowledges the place for individuals to know and do the purposes of God.

The Christian story is basically a communal story. It is about people formed by their relationship with the Father, the Son, and the Holy Spirit and further formed by their common life of worship, teaching, sacraments, fellowship, and service.

In monastic communities, religious orders, and many other forms of intentional Christian community, this formative dimension of the Christian life is brought to an even deeper expression.

But all of this is not meant to make a person a "groupie" and foster dependency. This is not a new tribalism.

Monastic communities recognized the place for the solitary hermit. St. Benedict writes, "Thanks to the help and guidance of many, they [the hermits] are now trained to fight against the devil. They have built up their strength and go from the battle in the ranks of their brothers to self-combat in the desert."[184]

Thus, formed in community they have the resilience to live the solitary life of faith and service. This is an important vision for us today. From isolation we move to community in order that some may move to a holy isolation of prayer or prophetic service.

Thought

The road to maturity does lie through formation.

Titus 2:11

July 4

The Wideness of God's Mercy

Religious groups spend much time seeking to define who is in or out of their group. But being deeply embedded in one's tradition should prepare a person for great generosity of heart, not a narrowness of spirit.

In the contemporary world there has been the healthy move to overcome narrow religious sectarianism and bigotry. But the way to do this is not through unhealthy reductionism and finding the lowest common denominator.

Another move—possibly a most surprising move—needs to be made. And that is to become so deeply immersed in one's religious tradition that one can transcend it to possess a great generosity of heart. To be grounded gives one the ability to fly.

No one will ever doubt the profound religious depth and commitment of the desert fathers and mothers and their commitment to a life of prayer on behalf of the world. But this did not lead to a pious narrowness.

One old desert brother was asked about God's generosity and forgiveness. He responded, "Tell me, beloved, if thy cloak were torn, wouldst [thou] throw it away?" He said, "Nay, but I would patch it . . ." The old man said to him, "If thou wouldst spare thy garment, shall not God have mercy on His own image?"[185]

Reflection

Depth of faith, generosity of heart, and grace to all are the marks of maturity.

Psalm 55:17

July 5

A Habitual Spirituality

The Monastic tradition has taught us the importance of rhythms in our day and regular religious practices. Contemporary Christians live without such routines and lack centeredness and integration.

The experience of many contemporary Christians living busy lives in urban centers is one of fragmentation. We are forever pulled in many directions—family, friends, work, schooling, church, recreation, etc.

In this busy round of activities, we find it difficult to find a place for solitude and regular prayer and meditational practices continue to be our biggest challenge. We seem to be just too busy for these things.

The unknown, late-fourteenth-century author of *The Cloud of Unknowing* and *The Book of Privy Counseling* makes a simple-but-helpful point: "with experience, this interior work becomes a spiritual habit."[186] In other words, prayer and other meditational practices should not be left to one's whim or circumstances. They need to be cemented into the daily rhythm of one's life.

A daily practice can become a way of life. And this can sustain us in busy, easy, or difficult times.

Spiritual practices need to become the bread and butter of our lives rather than the leftovers of our spare time. These practices ground us, and surprisingly they empower us for the other activities of the day.

Reflection

Daily solitude can become the productive place for listening, hearing, and renewal.

Matthew 22:37–40

July 6

The Heart of All Things

There is much that is good and much that is needful. But the heart of all things for the Christian is to love God with all that one is and has.

Throughout the history of the Christian church there have been periods of great apostolic endeavor, times of theological controversy, times of reformation, and times of great devotion. The twelfth and thirteenth centuries were particularly a time of renewal in the love of God.

The prayer of St. Francis expresses this well: "With our whole heart, our whole soul, our whole mind, with our whole strength and fortitude, with our whole understanding, with all our powers, with every effort, every affection, every feeling, every desire and wish, let us love the Lord God."[187]

This song of love of God with our whole being poses a particular challenge for us. We are more at home in the service of God rather than in the love of God. This extravagant love of God is something that does not seem to characterize our faith communities.

So it is a time for us to ponder. Are we possibly missing the heart of all things? Have our concerns for our fragile world, issues of justice, and our preoccupation with economic security, robbed us of all things? Has God ended up in a pious corner of our lives rather than being our major focus and from whom our energy comes to respond to the issues of our time?

Prayer

Lord, capture my heart. Amen.

John 3:8

July 7

The Blessed Spirit

Ever the mysterious One in the Trinity, the Holy Spirit—often neglected in the history of the church and in the awareness of Christian experience—is the faithful servant behind the scenes.

The person of the Holy Spirit may be regarded in our stumbling language about the third member of the Trinity as *the action of God*. The Spirit makes things happen. The Spirit animates, enthuses, empowers.

St. Basil was practically enamored with all that the Spirit could do. He writes, "Hence comes foreknowledge of the future, understanding of mysteries, apprehension of what is hidden, distribution of good gifts . . ." His list goes on and concludes that the Spirit not only makes us like God, but we are "being made God."[188]

While this kind of language makes us nervous and we would draw the line at being made *like* God, what is clear in Basil's writings is that the Christian life has everything to do with the Spirit. The Spirit not only gives certain gifts—an emphasis of contemporary Pentecostal movements—but also sanctifies us and makes us more Christlike.

Since the Spirit works quietly behind the scenes, a greater awareness of and sensitivity to the Spirit is certainly one of the challenges facing us today.

Reflection

Do we need a new outpouring of the Spirit in our time?

Psalm 25:8–10

July 8

Thinking about God

In so many ways the idea of God has become problematical for us in the modern world. For many scientists, God is a hang-over from a pre-scientific age. For others, God is oppressive. But in Christ we can see the heart of God.

Julian of Norwich has put it well. For the person of faith, who lives a life marked by hope rather than despair, his or her view of God is key. She puts this as follows, "For of all of the things our minds can think about God, it is thinking upon his goodness that pleases him most and brings the most profit to our soul."[189]

And so it is. To believe in the goodness of God in both good and hard times is one thing. But to actually *taste* the goodness of God is quite another, especially in the dark places of life.

Faith is never only belief. It is also trust. And trust is experiential. Thus, we may know the goodness of God not only because of the words of Scripture, but because we have experienced the goodness of God.

This does not mean life will always be smooth sailing. It does not mean no hardship will come our way. The goodness of God is sometimes most powerfully experienced in the valleys and difficult times of our lives. At such times, God's sustaining presence and comfort is an expression of God's goodness. And sometimes that sustaining presence is there in a way we don't recognize till much later.

Thought

May I ever think of God in faith and love, not in doubt and anger.

Romans 6:3–4

July 9

Sacramental Grace

In our scientific, rationalistic, and pragmatic world, we are all desperately seeking to recover the power of the symbolic and artistic dimensions of life. The church fathers and mothers had such a view of life. The power of the sacraments marked their spirituality.

At the heart of Christianity lies the word about God's revelation in history. This is a word that invites us into the salvation God offers. It is also a word that guides us how to live in this salvation and express it in our lives and world.

But living this life of faith is a profoundly mystical experience. It is life in the Spirit. And this life is sustained by the word of God, life in community, and through the sacraments.

The sacraments, especially baptism and the Lord's Supper, open up for us the power of the symbolic. St. Cyril of Jerusalem makes this abundantly clear. He writes, "Christ's crucifixion was real, His burial was real, and His resurrection was real: and all these He has freely made ours, that by sharing His sufferings in symbolic enactment we may really and truly gain salvation."[190]

The point is clear enough. By faith and in the Spirit in a mystical way through the sacraments we participate, enter into, the key dimensions of Jesus' life and death and resurrection. Thus, we become joined to him. We are identified with him. His life becomes our life.

Reflection

We don't simply believe in Jesus. We are joined to Him. He becomes normative for our life.

Romans 12:1–2

July 10

Transformation of the Mind

Earthbound and self-preoccupied, a deep work needs to occur within us if we are to be oriented to the things of God. In this we need the power of God's love and spiritual practices that continue to reorient us.

That we are most basically self-oriented is a fact of life. Self-regarding rather than other-regarding is stamped within us. And this life orientation can have a most unfortunate and destructive outworking. Neglect and abuse of others are two of the more obvious indicators.

That we need a change of heart and mind is the offer of God's redemption in Christ. That the work of grace needs a long appropriation is what sanctification is all about. In grasping what God offers we need to develop holy habits. What God wants to give we need to receive, hold, and nurture.

St. Maximus the Confessor discusses this. He notes, "Where the mind devotes its time it also expands."[191]

His challenge is clear. The mind won't suddenly move from self to God. This will only happen over time as we through the love of God seek the spiritual way to be and live. In this reorientation the spiritual practices are necessary. Prayer. Reflection. Ascetic practices. Humility. Relinquishment. Attentiveness.

Reflection

The embrace of grace can be in a moment. The outworking of grace is a lifetime.

Ephesians 3:18–19

July 11

Christian Growth

Coming to faith in Christ is sheer gift. Growing up into Christ is sheer grace. But we are called to respond and cooperate with God's action within us.

In the flowering of Christian spirituality in the Middle Ages there was a great preoccupation with the various phases or stages of growth in the Christian life. St. Bernard of Clairvaux was one such an exponent. He spoke of three stages of the progress of the soul. He writes, "First there is the forgiveness of sins; then the grace to do good; then the presence of him who forgives, the benefactor, is experienced as strongly as it can in a fragile body."[192]

While it is appropriate to embrace the theme of growth into Christian maturity and while we understand where Bernard is going in moving us to a contemplative union with God, this kind of language is less than helpful. Intertwined processes rather than stages mark the Christian's journey.

Thus, in correcting Bernard's stages we may note a powerful sense of oneness with God may occur at the very beginning of one's faith journey. It may also reoccur at various times in one's lifetime. Furthermore, forgiveness of sins pervades every phase of the spiritual journey. And Bernard's emphasis on moving from doing to contemplation is also unhelpful. Far better to think of doing good and experiencing God's presence as belonging together.

Thus, far better than to think of stages is to think of three continuous themes or rhythms in the Christian life, or three streams constantly watering a lake.

Prayer

Lord, may these three themes be ever present in my entire Christian journey. Amen.

Deuteronomy 5:12–15

July 12

Work and Play

In Western culture we work hard and play hard. Since life is all about productivity and winning we even play in order to work harder. And there are plenty of different kinds of pills to help us stay afloat. But we need to learn a different rhythm where solitude and Sabbath become important parts of our lives.

The medieval Dominican mystic Johannes Tauler has some surprisingly practical advice for us in the twenty-first century. He suggests that in a well-integrated and "solidly transformed person" it is key that "work and enjoyment become one and that the one remain unobstructed by the other."[193]

We seem to know so little of this kind of integration. Seldom do we see work as a form of enjoyment. And those who do so are blessed indeed.

But Tauler gives us a lead to think about further kinds of integration. Can we integrate rest into our work? Can we bring work and prayer closer together? Should contemplative practices form an important part of our work-a-day world? The possibilities are endless.

What is more basic in all of this is that this is a challenge to live with a different rhythm: less driven, less preoccupied, and less busy. And with a greater emphasis on prayer and reflection in our ordinary day maybe we will become wiser, healthier, and more effective persons.

Since productivity and effectiveness are related to creativity and creativity springs from inner resources, we may need to bring God more to work.

Thought

Review the patterns or rhythms of your life; there may be things that need to be more fully integrated.

Deuteronomy 31:6

July 13

For the Whole of Life's Journey

Some Christians operate on the idea that God only shows up occasionally, usually in times of crisis or difficulty. God is thus seen as the interventionist God rather than the life-sustaining God.

The German mystic Hildegard of Bingen had a profound sense of God's direct involvement in people's lives. She also believed the entirety of a person's life was in God's hand. And furthermore she believed the end of life here could only come if a person had fully completed God's purpose for their existence. She writes, "I [God] do not take his spirit from his body before his fruits have fully ripened."[194]

This not only brings an important perspective to the euthanasia debate, but it also suggests that God has a purpose for the whole of a person's life, not simply for the best years with its youthfulness and energy.

This is particularly relevant for an increasing aging population in which people can easily feel that since their working life is over they are no longer able to make a contribution to society. Some even feel they are just a burden.

Hildegard's perspective is that God has a purpose for the whole of one's life, including the latter stages. This then is a picture of a God who is involved and brings to fruition all the phases of one's life. This is truly God Immanuel—God *with us*.

Reflection

What fruit still needs to be born in my life?

Proverbs 9:6

July 14

The Weakening of the Powers

While we may have naïve notions about the extent of our freedom, we are more constricted than we care to admit. And while there are social powers that influence us, there are also inner powers that plague us.

There are many ways in which we are moved by inner forces. Habits, forces, passions, and weaknesses all sculpt our inner world.

Clearly, though these forces are at work within us, it does not mean we are helpless and change is impossible. Conversion and healing are two powerful factors that can bring about significant change.

St. Augustine in his deep reflections about the inner condition of the human being, especially the problem of human sin, notes another factor that can bring about inner change. He writes, "My passion had ceased to excite me as of old" because passion had become "a grievous burden" and he wished no longer to live "in such servitude."[195]

One way of viewing the point that St. Augustine is making is that sin overplays its hand. Pleasures turn into nightmares and at that point their power weakens.

This opens the way for change and transformation. When the old passions no longer hold their full sway, the longing for a new way becomes the time that grace, already at work within us, can come to fuller expression.

Reflection

The weakening of the old beckons the new.

Psalm 46:10–11

July 15

Distracted

This must be the time where we have become the most distracted people ever in human history. Constant movement, constant messages, and constant communication are part of the fabric of ordinary life. We need to find solitude not only for our spirituality but also for our sanity and health.

One of the biggest challenges facing us has to do with our identity and spirituality. Our identity in the modern world is always in a state of flux. We are constantly trying to reinvent ourselves. Thus, we carry the burden of making ourselves.

At the same time, our spirituality is minimalist and pragmatic. Prayer is difficult. And the practice of solitude almost impossible. We suffer from an overdose of distraction.

What should encourage us is that to practice solitude and to be inwardly centered has always been difficult, even for monks of a much earlier time. John Cassian writes, "No sooner does the mind discover some other opportunities for spiritual thoughts then something else breaks in and what was grasped now slips and glides off."[196] So it is not just us; monks were also distracted.

But difficulty in the spiritual disciplines of solitude, reflection, and meditation should be seen as an invitation. For these practices, rather than being the extra in our daily routines, are really the bread and butter of our existence.

Thought

Our well-being is rooted in a spiritual centering in the presence of God.

1 Samuel 15:23

July 16

Idolatry

In the biblical story idolatry is an important and discordant theme. It is the flipside of love of God, because it is the love of other gods. The nature of the love God asks of us is an exclusive love.

Idolatry is not simply an issue that belongs to a hoary and primitive past. It is as much an issue today as it was in the ancient world.

The reason why it is an issue today is because some central themes in human experience and spirituality never go away. Two issues in particular stand out: deviancy and substitution.

In deviancy we want to do our own thing. We rebel. We go our own way. We don't want to obey the voice of God. We are willful and stubborn.

In finding substitutes we demonstrate that while we are rejecting God we have a need to create alternatives. We create our own gods. Thus, we continue to be god-worshipping creatures.

The early church father Tertullian has this to say: "The principal charge against the human race, the world's deepest guilt, the all-inclusive cause of judgment, is idolatry."[197] He spends much time pointing out that this sin virtually includes all the others.

What is particularly grievous about this sin is that we acknowledge our need for God but want a god of our own making. Thus, it is the elevation of the self. And it is the most blatant refusal to go God's way.

Thought

In rejecting idolatry we acknowledge God's lordship in our lives.

Galatians 5:16

July 17

The Pendulum Swing

On the wider screen of history we can see that in times of significant change there is often an over-reaction. We go to extremes that become unsustainable. This also happens in personal religious experience.

It is all too understandable that young persons undergoing a profound spiritual experience think that in following Christ they should suddenly give away all they have, or drop out of university, or become a monk or a nun. And it may well be that they should do this. But this call should be tested over time. It can't just be a temporary, enthusiastic reaction.

Evagrius has some wisdom at this point. He writes, "Do not turn into a passion the antidote of the passions."[198] Basically, what he is saying is don't turn into a compulsion your hoped-for solutions to your compulsions. That is simply exchanging one compulsion for another.

What this means is that one's natural aggression should not be turned into spiritual or missional aggression. And to solve the problem of gluttony don't become an anorexic ascetic.

One's inner problems are not simply changed by outward constraints. Something much deeper needs to occur. Healing of the causes of our compulsions will have a much greater effect.

Reflection

Life and vocational choices need to be made from a healed self rather than a reactionary self. And time, advice, and discernment are to be part of the process in making important decisions.

Romans 13:8–10

July 18

A Communal Identity

*In our contemporary world marred by an unhealthy individu-
alism and by a church that has succumbed to similar values,
the challenge of a communal identity remains a prophetic call.*

The biblical story is the story of a people. The work of Christ was to bring
into being a new humanity anticipating the fullness of the new creation.
And the work of the Spirit is to break down barriers and form people
into a community of one heart, one set of beliefs, common life-sustaining
practices, and cooperation in service to the world.

This movement towards commonality is always under threat. It is so
today. It was so in early Christianity.

The unknown author of the *Epistle of Barnabas* acknowledges this:
"Do not withdraw within yourselves and live alone, as though you were
already justified, but gather together and seek out together the common
good."[199]

In this call to commonality, the author seems to suggest that
Christians need each other in the growth of faith. No growth without
community seems to be the theme.

This poses a key challenge for us. Consumer Christianity, which
characterizes much of today's Western church, needs to become a servant
Christianity where we bless others, but where we are also open to the
goodness of others towards us.

Prayer

Lord, renew your church into a community of faith, love, and service.

1 Samuel 3:10

July 19

The God of Great Sensitivity

There are people who believe God is the God of great generality. God is too majestic and global to be concerned about a mere individual. But in the biblical story it is clear God sees you and me.

The German mystic Meister Eckhart has a very generous and deeply personal view of the way God works with us. He writes, "God does not work in all hearts alike but according to the preparation and sensitivity he finds in each."[200]

This view of God as the personal and sensitive One who engages us carefully, dynamites the view that God is remote and arbitrary in his dealings with us. And it undermines the idea that God only deals with humanity in broad strokes.

Eckhart's view means that, while God's salvation is general in that Christ died for all, the application of that salvation to our lives is deeply personal. And this opens up for us the great mystery of the profoundly personal workings of the Holy Spirit in each of our lives. It also opens up the vision that we need to respect the sacredness of who we are, in the outworking of common spiritual practices.

As a result of the Spirit's activity conversions are different, the practice of faith is different, our life's callings are different, we pray in different ways, and the Spirit gives different gifts.

Reflection

And so God's differing dance with us generates creativity, diversity, and beauty.

1 Corinthians 13:1–3

July 20

What Lies Within Us

It is good to be productive and active. But one must also be reflective, for one's action comes from an inner disposition, the source of which must be understood.

One can't simply divide up the world into troublemakers and peacemakers. That is far too simplistic. But it is true that people function with various orientations or basic dispositions. Some people are hopeful. Others are skeptical. Some people are open to new ideas. Others are solidly closed. The list goes on.

Thomas à Kempis speaks of two different life orientations. He writes, "The man who is discontented and disgruntled has a heart filled with suspicion; he himself has no rest nor does he allow others to possess it." On the other hand, "The man who dwells in perfect peace suspects evil of no one."[201]

The key point being made here is not simply that there are two different life orientations, but what we are within impacts all of what we seek to do. The basic consequence of this is that we need to become attentive not only to our actions, but also to our motivations. And what becomes important is not only *what* we do, but the *way* in which we do it and *why* we do it.

This is the reason why great activity or great sacrifice of itself is never commended in the biblical story. If great things are not done in love good fruit will not appear. Better to do small things with great love than great things without it.

Prayer

Lord, purify my heart and give me eyes to see the inner chambers of my being in the light of your grace. Amen.

Deuteronomy 29:29

July 21

A Limited Vision

While there are many things we can know about God because these are talked about in Holy Scripture, there is so much that remains unknown to us. We, therefore, need to be aware that what we so confidently assert about God may be more a reflection of ourselves and our values.

St. Anselm in faith and reflection sought to understand not only the ways of God—that is, God's action among us—but also the very *being* of God. He wrestled, for example, with the question how can God both punish us for our wrongdoing and be merciful towards us in our sinning. He finally came to this insight, "I only saw you in a certain degree and not as you are."[202]

There is a tension between what God reveals and what remains hidden in the wisdom of God. Furthermore, we struggle with grasping what is revealed. And all claims about the knowability of God's hiddenness should be met with deep concern. We may be treading where angels only tremble and worship.

Does all of this mean our God is the stranger God? To some extent the answer to this is, yes. This should not surprise us. Who fully understands himself or herself, or a friend, or a spouse? But one can still be comfortable and assured that all is well, even when all is not known or understood. So much the more can this be the case with God.

Thought

Relationships are always sustained by faith and trust, not only by knowability.

John 15:11

July 22

Joy in the Kingdom of God

God is not first and foremost a God of demand, but a God of grace. Grace energizes and frees us. This leads us into joyful service.

Richard Rolle, the hermit of Hampole, in his reflections on what draws us into desiring and seeking to do God's will, moves away from pragmatic reasons into the realm of joy. He speaks "of the mirth of the Heavenly Kingdom"[203] as an invitational power.

This is a challenge for us. Duty rather than joy seems to be our spiritual diet. This clearly needs to be turned around.

The notion of mirth in the reign of God can have several dimensions. One is the joy in the community of the Trinity. The Father, the Son, and the Spirit are eternally glad in and with each other. Secondly, there is joy in heaven when a sinner repents and God's will is done on earth as it is done in heaven. And finally, joy is ours when we go God's way, do God's will, and fulfill God's kingdom purposes.

It is not difficult to see that joy is a much more powerful motivator than duty. And it is obvious that living in joy is far more precious than to live in duty or unhappiness.

The joy of the kingdom of God is all about grace and God's sustaining presence. It is a gift, not the product of our good activity or service. And joy is a reality beyond all our circumstances.

Reflection

Joy can be like a well with fresh water ever bubbling to the surface.

Isaiah 44:28

July 23

God's Love for the World

We see the world and its ever-present problems and feel that God has abandoned it. But based on God's love and with the eyes of faith we do see the signs of God's goodness.

The late medieval mystic St. Catherine of Siena was preoccupied with the vision of God's ongoing involvement with our world. God spoke to her, there are "many . . . roads and ways I use, through love alone, to lead them [humanity] back to grace."[204]

Rather than abandonment, she saw presence. Rather than rejection, she saw salvation. Rather than condemnation, she saw welcome.

This way of seeing the world has life-giving implications. First of all, it draws us into the very nature of who God is. God is love and God's love is a pursuing love that brings healing and salvation. Secondly, it draws us into a particular way of seeing the world. We see the world not simply in terms of its problems, but in the light of what it is and can become in the love of God.

This is a vital and integral spirituality which probes the heart of God and probes the pain of the world. And it recognizes that God's way of reaching out to the world is varied and multi-faceted.

We will, therefore, need new eyes to see the footprints of God's concern for humanity. Not only in the work of the church, but also in the affairs of society, God's healing presence is seen with the eyes of faith.

Reflection

A new way of seeing comes from a renewed faith.

John 20:26–29

July 24

A Tested Faith

We cannot live the whole of faith's journey on the springtime of our faith. Faith too has its seasons. Faith needs to be tested in the winter storms.

There are many things that eventually will begin to probe the delicate nature of our springtime faith. Such a faith will be tested in the long haul of the Christian journey. Such a faith will also experience the blast of doubt. And temptations will come our way to deny God's way and promises.

Julian of Norwich is therefore right when she writes, "if our faith met no opposition it would deserve no reward."[205] And we may add that an untested faith would be a faith that would never come to maturity.

The delicate nature of faith is due to the fickle nature of the human condition. We are restless. We get bored. We want more or want something else. And in the final analysis we always want to do our own thing rather than go God's way.

As a consequence of faith being so fragile, we need to live more and more in the grace and goodness of the faithfulness of God towards us. We are held by much more than we hold onto in the goodness that God gives.

And this is what makes faith stronger. It is not our faith that sustains us, but God's grace that holds us fast.

Reflection

Even our faith needs to be given and sustained by the goodness of God.

1 Corinthians 11:23–26

July 25

The Eucharist

God comes to us in the word. God comes to us in the sacraments. God comes to us in the community of faith. God comes to us in the mysterious workings of the Holy Spirit.

The very nature of God is not static but dynamic. God is the joy of the community of the Trinity. God is the creator and sustainer of all things. And God is ever engaging the community of faith with God's presence and gifts.

In this self-giving of God, spawned by love and not by need, we are invited into a dynamic relationship with this generous God. This is the God who nurtures us.

This invitation and calling is such that we may increasingly become like the God who redeems us. Nurtured into God's likeness rather than commanded into God conformity is the way of God with us.

William of St. Thierry sees the Eucharist playing an important part in all of this. He writes, "For to eat the Body of Christ [in the Eucharist] is nothing other than to be made the body of Christ and the temple of the Holy Spirit."[206]

In this feast of the self-giving of Christ we celebrate both what Christ has done on our behalf and what we are to become—a self-giving community of faith serving the purposes of God in our time. Thus, the Lord's Supper is the place where our life of faith is nurtured and we receive food and drink for our service to the world.

Thought

The God who gives calls us to self-giving.

Luke 7:33–35

July 26

Friendship

In our time when friendships are fragile and uncertain partly due to the high mobility of our lifestyle, a deepening friendship with God may help us to recover the value of our horizontal friendships.

In the ancient world friendships were all important. That world, largely without contracts and other forms of legal obligations, depended on the word of a trusted friend.

In the face-to-face, older world marked by relationships, families, guilds, and religious communities, good friendship was seen as a virtue. And God, though seen as powerful and other worldly, was also seen as a friend—as the great trusted one. St. Thomas Aquinas wrote, "Charity signifies not only the love of God, but also a certain friendship with him."[207]

This friendship exists first and foremost within the Trinity. The Father, the Son, and the Holy Spirit reflect an amazing friendship of reciprocity, mutuality, cooperation, love, and care. And this is extended to us. The great Friend becomes our Befriender. Christ is the gift of the friendship of God. And the most permanent expression of that friendship is the quiet friendship of the Holy Spirit—the Go-Between God.

In the grace of this friendship with God, our friendships can become relationships of beauty, service, and care.

Thought

To be there for the other is one of the great gifts of friendship.

Luke 6:20–26

July 27

Living Upside Down Values

The way of Christ is a strange way. It is living life with totally different values. One needs to be marked by the grace of Christ and sustained by the Spirit to live this way.

The idea that the desert fathers and mothers went into the desert to escape reality is a profound misunderstanding of their way of life and their mission. Rather, they went into the desert to pray in order to find a new reality. What they looked for was a deeper relationship with Christ in order to lay the basis for a renewed church and a better world.

This vision of a new way of life and a new world in the shambles of the old drew them to become visionaries of what was yet to come—a further in-breaking of the reign of God. And in order for that to come into being they began to live as if this new world had already come.

One of the desert fathers, Abbot Macarius, taught his monks the following: "If to a monk scorn hath become as praise, and poverty as riches, and hunger as feasting, he shall never die."[208]

Here were a few contours of the new way, of an upside down way. Others could readily be added: Forgiveness instead of revenge, community instead of isolation, humility rather than power, service instead of self-seeking, peacemaking instead of anger. This list goes on. It is this new and strange way that anticipates the fullness of God's final future.

Thought

Don't wait till the end. Live the future now.

Mark 8:34

July 28

Bearing the Marks of Christ

*In ancient Christian spirituality there was the belief that one
could become so identified with Christ that one could even end
up bearing the scars of Christ's crucifixion.*

On the human level we know something about the deep bonding that can
occur between marriage partners and close friends. That bond can be so
deep they can anticipate each other's thoughts and wishes. And when one
dies the other often also quickly passes away.

Spiritual identification can occur at an even deeper level. Not only
does the salvation of Christ impact us and Christ's words guide us, but
the presence of the Spirit and the life of prayer can draw a person into a
profound connection with Christ.

Bonaventure, writing about St. Francis, notes, "a heart burning
fervently with the love of Christ crucified can receive the imprint of the
Crucified Lord himself on his cross."[209]

While St. Francis purportedly experienced the stigmata, we all must
bear the marks of Christ in some way. Some may more fully than others
carry his healing ministry. Others may be characterized by the prophetic
passion of Christ. Some may be community builders like Jesus. Others
may be persons of prayer. As we are all marked by Christ's love, we will
also carry his sufferings.

Reflection

To be so identified with Christ as to bear physically the scars of his
suffering is an identification with Christ that enters more fully into all that
Christ is and sought to bring into being.

Exodus 3:7–10

July 29

God Attentiveness

It is what we most attend to that reflects our values and commitments. In the West our self-preoccupation is a chronic malady. We need the deepest of conversions.

The unknown author of *The Cloud of Unknowing* points us moderns to a solution for our deep unhappiness. We are both materialistic and self-preoccupied, but also deeply unhappy to the point where the therapeutic industry needs to rescue us.

The author's wisdom is, "Attend more to the wholly Otherness of God rather than your own misery."[210] To which we could add, do this rather than attend to your own wants, pleasures, and preoccupations. In other words, make *God* the central focus of your life and its purpose and direction.

But note that we are challenged to attend not to the convenient God—the God of blessings and fair-weather, the God who is our butler—but to the radically different God. This is an invitation to attend to the God who will take us elsewhere, who is not willing to leave us in the familiar places of our own making.

This is the Exodus God. This is the God who calls us to conversion. This is the God who heals us. This is the God who turns our world upside down.

This kind of attentiveness is scary and unsettling and therefore needs to be deeply marked by grace and faith and love.

Thought

God is also the great disturber.

Luke 19:8–10

July 30

Making Amends

Saying sorry has become such an emasculated concept in the modern world. And this will remain a trite concept unless it is savored with the fruit of repentance.

The English medieval mystic Richard Rolle understood the power of the love and grace of God in Christ. He spoke of Christ "stabling" in us. But he also understood our wrongdoing cannot be cheaply and easily dismissed.

He therefore speaks of our need to make amends for our wrong deeds and suggests the following steps, "*Fasting* because he has sinned against himself; *prayer* because he has sinned against God; *alms* because he has sinned against his neighbor."[211]

What Richard Rolle highlights here for us is a way of repentance rather than a cheap apology. And he does this because he takes the holiness of God and the reality of sin much more seriously than we do in the modern world. And since we have trivialized the moves this mystic makes, his suggestions are not a part of our spiritual practices. But they should be!

While we may not want to take on board the precise formula of Richard Rolle, we do need to take on board the concept of making amends, the practice of restitution, and the movement towards reconciliation. Well-being in relationships can only be fostered in the wake of such practices.

Reflection

Doing wrong does invite us to making right.

John 1:35–42

July 31

The Following of Christ

*To be a disciple of Christ never requires blind following. Rather,
it is to be a committed-but-thoughtful following, and as such,
it is a self-giving marked by freedom.*

Some people cast religiosity into the sphere of blind faith, fanaticism, and spiritual coercion. But it need not and should not be like this. Spirituality should be marked by grace, joy, and a thoughtful response to the God who calls us into fellowship, well-being, and service.

Meister Eckhart echoes this. He talks about an intelligent rather than a literal discipleship. He writes, "We should take care to follow him [Christ] intelligently."[212]

Such a following of Christ does not mean that we carefully calculate everything we do and that we are without passion and commitment. It also does not mean we decide how to outwork the Lordship of Christ rather than to live in obedience. But it does mean that we know what we are doing, that we count the cost and follow Christ from a place of willing surrender.

Blind faith marked by fickleness and irrationality is not what we see in the life of Jesus. Jesus communed with the Father in heaven and willingly sought to do God's will. We are called to do likewise as we follow in his footsteps.

Obedience born out of prayer and reflection is the kind of obedience that marks the Christian. Obedience stemming from blindness, self-willed passion, or fear is not what God calls us to.

Thought

Faith does not throw the mind away, but renews it.

WILLIAM OF ST THIERRY

Ephesians 3:14–17

August 1

Inner Transformation

The blessing of grace moves us into right relationship with God and with ourselves. We move from the false self to the true self.

The tragic outworking of sin is alienation. The blessing of grace is restoration. And one out-working of restoration is to be restored to ourselves in the light of Christ.

What this means is that in coming home to God in Christ through the Spirit we can now also begin to come home to ourselves. This on-going inner transformation is a work of grace that restores us to the person God has meant us to be.

This person of God's intentionality is not a person of human autonomy. Not a self-made person, but a person marked by God's healing and renewing presence. Such a person is moving into the true self for he or she is becoming more Christlike, while retaining the integrity and particularity of his or her being.

St. Anselm prayed a telling prayer: "give me what you have made me want."[213] This shows the interplay between human longing and divine orchestration. It shows the deep inner work of God's grace. And it reflects the harmony between God's will and my desire.

This is the move into the true self made in the image of God and restored in Christ. It is the move into becoming Christlike, God-like.

Reflection

What God does is what I want. God's desire is my pleasure.

Acts 20:17–21

August 2

Tried by Trials

It does not matter what one's circumstances of life may be, there will always be challenges, difficulties, and trials. Life needs to be forged in the midst of trials. In the dark places light needs to found.

In the modern world there is a deep-seated unhappiness regarding the workplace. It is not so much that work is hard. It is much more that the instrumentalism that characterizes modern capitalism makes people feel used and exploited. It seems productivity and care can no longer remain connected.

Under such circumstances one may dream of a better place to be. But possibly no such place exists, not even in the monastery. Thomas à Kempis writes, "In the monastery, men are tried *as gold is tried in the furnace.*"[214]

No matter where we work and live and no matter what our relationships may be, there is no utopia. No place is without its challenges, not even the monastery. There is no magic place somewhere else. All of life has its goodness and its difficulties.

To be tried in the furnace of life, however, is not a curse. It is a hidden blessing. In such situations we can grow the virtues that make us more whole, caring, and adaptable. And most surprisingly of all, difficulties and trials create spaces where goodness, grace, forgiveness, and reconciliation can flourish.

Since the human condition is not the lull of peacefulness but more the vortex of challenge and response, grace rather than fear is needed to face such difficulties.

Thought

I am shaped in the midst of life primarily through my response to what happens.

Mark 1:35–39

August 3

Looking Both Ways

One can't just look at God. One also needs to see the world.
One can't just see oneself. One also needs to see the neighbor.
One can't just see one's extended family. One also needs to
have the nation in view.

The unknown writer of the fourteenth-century writing *Theologia Germanica* suggests that the soul of Christ "has two eyes, a right eye and a left eye."[215]

The right eye is the heavenly glance to the faithfulness and dependability of God and God's ways. The left eye sees the reality and pain of the world.

The author goes on to say that the right eye with its Godward glance should determine what the left eye sees. Thus we see the world from a heavenly perspective.

This is a significant insight. A much simpler way of saying this is that we should see the world through the eyes of faith. Or we need to see the struggles of our time in the light of the kingdom of God. Or again, it is through the contemplative vision that we should see the need for the work of justice.

The gaze of the right eye on its own can make us pious but irrelevant. The sight of the left eye on its own can make us despairing because of all the problems we see. And we may end up lacking in faith, hope, and love.

This means that the contemplative experience is multi-directional. It is both transcendent and immanent. It sees the heavenly vision and the curse of our global inhumanity.

Reflection

The movement from prayer to action in the world keeps us centered in God, for God cares as much about the world as he does about our piety.

Genesis 12:1

August 4

A Change of Circumstances

We are a world on the move, particularly in our urban centers. We relocate for a multitude of reasons, including for work, education, and a change of status. But our movement is often motivated by hope rather than necessity.

There are multiple millions of people on the move due to wars, floods, earthquakes, and poverty. They are driven by necessity. But most people on the move do so by choice. In the move they hope for a better job or a better neighborhood.

In the hope for something better one does need to acknowledge that we bring our old selves with us. A change of location does not mean a change of person.

St. Basil understood this. He writes, "I have abandoned my life in town . . . but I have not yet been able to get quit [rid] of myself."[216]

But a change of circumstances does offer possibilities for change. The fact that we are now away from familiar places opens up the way for us to see ourselves in a new light.

And there is more. The fact that we may be disappointed that the old self continues despite the new place is an invitation to probe and search more deeply regarding the person we need to be and become.

In all this, we need to trust more fully the work of God in our lives. The God who is not bound by any of our life's circumstances knows how to use these circumstances for our good.

Reflection

In every major life change lies an invitation that we need to learn to hear.

John 20:22

August 5

The Life-giving Spirit

It is one thing to be aware of the Holy Spirit in times of social change or church renewal or revival or in personal inner trans-formation. It is quite another thing to live in the Spirit when everything seems to be so ordinary.

While in the modern world we have ever so carefully segmented life, including the spiritual and the sexual, many Christian writers of the ancient world are not afraid to bring these two spheres together by using sexualized language to explain the spiritual.

St. Bernard of Clairvaux is one such writer. In a sermon on the Song of Songs he speaks of the Kiss of God. He writes, "to be kissed by the kiss, for that is nothing but to be given the Holy Spirit."[217]

This is emotive and highly significant language. And it is particularly relevant in relation to the Holy Spirit. The Spirit is so often seen as a vague spiritual force rather than as an intimate presence.

It is also relevant in relation to our view of God. God is often seen as powerful and remote. God seems to be more the absent rather than the present one.

But St. Bernard moves the categories. God can now be seen as intimate, close, and affectionate. And the Spirit is God's intimate love gift to us.

It is possible that this language will break through the rational and distant views we have of God, and so may encourage us to come closer to God.

Reflection

The kiss of God brings new life.

Revelation 12:9

August 6

Renouncing Satan

In an age where God seems remote and where sins are mistakes, it should not surprise us that the idea of a Satan has been relegated to the pages of mythology. In the older traditions of Christianity this was not so.

In the older traditions of the Christian church becoming a member of the community of faith was a thorough process. One or two years of instruction or catechesis led to the public confession of one's faith, water baptism, anointing with the Spirit, and prayer for healing and exorcism.

Thus, renouncing Satan was part of Christian initiation. St. Cyril of Jerusalem advocated the use of this formula, "I renounce you, Satan, you wicked and cruel tyrant; I no longer fear your power for Christ broke that power by sharing flesh and blood with me."[218] The prayer goes on to reject all of Satan's words, pomp, and service. The image used is that Satan is trampled underfoot by the gentle but powerful Christ.

While one extreme is to give Satan too much power, the other extreme is to dismiss him, as we have largely done in the contemporary church. This is serious pendulum swing in the wrong direction.

It is worth pondering whether the spiritual superficiality and ineffectiveness of the present day is linked to the dismissal of Satan. It is further worth reflecting on the fact that in times of revival and renewal, the reality of Satan undergoes a revival as well.

Thought

In what ways do we need to regain a perspective on the Evil One?

1 Timothy 6:17–19

August 7

Use Your Privileged Position

The immature Christian attitude to people of power, position, and influence is one of envy or criticism. The mature attitude is one that calls such persons to make use of their power and resources for others.

An unhealthy dualism does run through much of the Christian story. The basic idea is that people with power and resources can't be very spiritual, and only those who have relinquished these things can truly be followers of the lowly Jesus.

But there are other ways to think about these things. The people of God need to represent Christ as prophet, priest, and king in the world. Thus, we need the lowly Franciscan who serves the poor in the slums of Manila as much as we need Jesuit scholars who serve Christ in the world's most prestigious universities. We need the community worker and the business person who are both seeking to serve Christ.

The unknown writer of the *Epistle of Barnabas* remarks, "I urge those in high positions, if you will accept some well-intentioned advice from me: you have those among you, those to whom you can do good—do not fail."[219]

Whether these comments are for the well-to-do within the faith community or in the wider society, it matters little. The point is clear. There are those who have more than others. This is a fact of life. But this blessing places them under responsibility. This is the call to generosity, the antidote to self-serving. Such persons are also serving Christ.

Reflection

On a sliding scale we all have something to give. Giving lies at the heart of our humanity and spirituality.

Romans 7:21

August 8

Conflicted

We don't like to hear this about ourselves, but we are seriously conflicted in our inner being. There is no rock-solid core of goodness to who we are. Goodness has to be given and won in the face of our foolish selfishness, fear, and wrongdoing.

In the history of Christian thought there has been a lot of debate about the nature of evil in our world and the extent of sin in our own lives. Some see sin as learned behavior. Others see it as innate. Some see sin as all pervasive. Others see it as more peripheral.

St. Augustine wrestled hard and long with these matters and pointed out that even in the person marked by grace there is still conflict. Because we are not whole "It is, therefore, no strange anomaly partly to will and partly to be unwilling."[220] Thus inner conflicts continue.

Some may see this as bad news and as depressing. But it is really good news. If we were whole and perfect and non-conflicted, pride and ease and arrogance would soon characterize us. In the struggle for goodness, which is our lot in life, we can be marked by grace, longing, humility, forgiveness, and growth.

This conflict in our will means we are ever to be discerning, ever prayerful, and ever needing to make choices. Thus we live in anticipation of growth in our inner being and the hope of fullness of life in the age to come.

Thought

To be torn is to become candidates for healing.

Jeremiah 1:4–8

August 9

Prophetic Witness

Throughout the history of the Christian church there have been women and men who have spoken and lived prophetically. They have dared to speak the correcting and visionary word of God. Often this has been at great personal cost.

Don't ever desire to be a prophet. And don't make yourself a prophet. This is not a vocation one can choose for oneself. And one would almost have to be sadistic to desire such a calling.

Prophets are raised up by God's choosing. They seem to emerge out of nowhere. They are often the most unlikely people. But they are women and men who are burdened with the renewing word of God. They are endowed with the Spirit and they can see what others don't see and speak what many refuse to hear. And they are called to live the message they seek to bring.

Bishop Eusebius of Caesarea, the great writer of an early church history, writes, "We burn the prophetic incense in every place and we sacrifice to him [God] the fragrant fruit of a theology lived out."[221]

Eusebius recognizes that the role of prophets should be the rule in the church, not the exception, and that they are to be the embodiment of the challenging and renewing word of God. As such they are a witness, a signpost. And they are a seed sown to die in order that new life may emerge.

Without this prophetic ministry the church itself would soon become mediocre and irrelevant and society would suffer as a consequence, since despite criticism the church is the agent for much good in our world.

Thought

Without the prophetic vision, a mediocre Christianity will bring little transformation.

Matthew 26:38–39

August 10

The Scope of Prayer

Personal, as opposed to liturgical prayer, is an ever dynamic and changing reality. It takes into account one's stage of life, spiritual condition, life's circumstances, and one's present challenges and issues.

For personal prayer to have some integrity it must reflect what is happening in a person's life. It must incorporate the difficulties and the challenges the person is facing. As such, prayer is a mirror of the soul and in this kind of self-disclosure we can see ourselves more truly.

Our ancient forebears understood this all too well. John Cassian, the wise man of early monasticism, writes, "One prays another way when the life of the Spirit is flourishing, and another way when pushed down by the mass of temptation." He goes on that prayer will differ if "one is seeking the gift of some grace . . . or the removal of some sinful vice."[222]

This means that prayer is not following some constant path, but prayer reflects the fragility of our life and its circumstances. Thus, prayer is contemporary. It is spontaneous. It is agonizing. It is questioning. It is hopeful.

Prayer as language of the present moment of course needs to be reinforced by prayer as language of the universal church where we affirm the riches of the church's tradition. Thus, prayer is ever new and old.

Thought

Prayer as language of the heart is a revelatory experience.

Acts 17:22–28

August 11

Christianity and Secular Education

Very early in the church's history, the early church fathers recognized that Christian formation leading to a Christian mind-set did not exclude the need to study non-Christian literature.

Some people believe that the only wisdom is in the Bible. Others believe that wisdom from elsewhere must be accepted as long as it does not contradict the message of Scripture.

The early church fathers, in seeking to explain the biblical message to a non-Christian world, believed God's truths were also scattered in non-Christian literature and could be used to make a point of contact in explaining the gospel.

Tertullian, however, raises an interesting issue regarding these matters. He saw it is appropriate for a Christian to have a "literary education," but this does not mean he or she accepts everything. And what the Christian teacher may not do is commend what is idolatrous. In teaching idolatrous things "he commends them . . . he confirms them . . . he bears testimony to them."[223] This must not be done.

Thus Tertullian believes a Christian cannot teach subjects that are against the gospel.

What this highlights is that this church father rejects the divide we hold today between the personal and public spheres of one's life. And he believes teaching is more than information sharing; it involves attesting to, recommending, and affirming what one teaches.

Thought

Here lies a challenge for us for a greater integration of our beliefs and our vocation in society.

1 Corinthians 12:13

August 12

The Bonding Spirit

There is no need for a clearer sign that we are devoid of the work of the Spirit. Our lack of community in our churches and our ecclesiastical differences all point to the fact that the Spirit who unites and bonds us together is achingly absent.

St. Bernard of Clairvaux in his writings gives much attention to the doctrine of the Trinity. He believes the Trinity models in some way what should also be true of the community of faith.

St. Bernard believes the Spirit is the go-between member of the Trinity. He writes, "the Holy Spirit is the love and goodness of both [the Father and the Son]."[224]

If the work of the Spirit is this bonding work within the Trinity, then the grace the Spirit brings to us is first and foremost to bond us to the Father and the Son. Thus the Spirit brings us home to where we truly belong in the love and goodness of Father, Son, and Holy Spirit.

This vertical homecoming is to come to expression in our horizontal relationships. We are also to come home to each other in Christ. And we are to come home to humanity in the work of our Creator God.

As a consequence, all that separates us from what God would want us to have together is a reminder that we desperately need the power and grace of the Spirit.

Reflection

To separate and flee was part of human original sin. To be made one in Christ and with each other is the work of restoration.

1 Corinthians 15:53–56

August 13

Immortality

God is the Creator. We are mere creatures. God is immortal.
We carry within us the seeds of death. To live beyond the grave
is not our inherent possession. It is only God's gift.

It is the ultimate form of human hubris to see ourselves as gods. And it is cynical despair that, on the other hand, holds death is the end of who we are.

But the very old idea that we have an eternal soul or spark captive in a body that will decay, is a notion the early church fathers resisted. St. Justin Martyr, the great early apologist wrote, "the soul partakes of life, since God wills it to live."[225]

This is a very different understanding of the soul or inner person from that of Greek thought. For this apologist the soul is not immortal in and of itself. Only God has immortality (1 Tim 6:16). If the soul continues in an afterlife this is due to the action of God, not due to the soul's innate qualities.

But, of course, the Christian hope is much fuller than this. The issue is not the continuation of some part of us, but the fulfillment of the new creation Christ has brought into the world.

Christian hope is based on the resurrection of Christ, who as the New Adam is the trailblazer for the new humanity. This hope invites us to truly honor all of who we are—and not some part of us—and to wait for God's gift of transformation.

Thought

If in this life we are wholly dependent on God, how much more will this be true in the life to come?

Luke 14:23

August 14

Compelled

In the creative tension between God's sovereignty and human freedom and choice we tend to overemphasize the latter rather than God's sovereignty. In an age where we have become so homocentric we need to recover the power, wisdom, and love of God.

The twelfth-century German mystic Hildegard of Bingen had visions about the mysterious way God worked in human affairs. One such vision had to do with God's sovereignty in bringing people into his kingdom of light and grace.

She writes, "'compelled sheep' are those people who are compelled by Me [God] against their will, by many tribulations and sorrows, to leave their iniquities."[226]

While this seems to assume there are other people who willingly turn to God, it is probably more accurate to say most of us need to be *made willing* to turn to God. God needs to work grace in us. Our hearts need to be softened and our fears and resistances overcome.

If we could turn to God simply by ourselves, we could pat ourselves on the back and see what we have done as a virtue. The fact that God has to draw us, win us over, turn us around, truly illustrates the persistent love of God.

The fact that we sometimes need tough treatment to respond to God only highlights our rebellious stupidity and God's strong love.

Thought

To acknowledge God's strong and persistent love for us in no way undermines our need to respond.

2 Samuel 12:1–7

August 15

Self-Confrontation

There is much truth in the statement that we are most blind to ourselves. The challenge, therefore, is to find windows and doors to enter into our own defenses and self-justifications.

The rather obvious statement from Thomas à Kempis, "be more willing to correct yourself than your dearest friends,"[227] already contains one window for self-insight. This is, what you want to correct in your friends is probably what you need to confront and correct in yourself. The sins and failings we readily see in others often lie ever close in our own hearts.

But there are other windows through which we need to see in order that we may grow in self-awareness and self-insight.

The most basic for the Christian is the use of Scripture as a mirror. In reading about God's will and purpose for humanity we can see where we fail and where we need forgiveness and healing.

A further window is the feedback and advice from committed friends who love us and can more easily see areas in which we need to grow. And a spiritual companion or director can further add to our inner growth.

And the place of prayer and meditation provides a place for the ever-present Spirit to nudge us, open up spaces, and renew us. The Spirit makes Christ known to us, but also reveals our selves to us.

Thought

Self-insight is key to a sustainable way of life.

Ephesians 2:19

August 16

A Way of Life in the Gospel

For many in the modern world, Christian faith is like an insurance policy for the world to come and the afterlife. The Christian faith for many is also just an add-on while living secular values. Instead, the faith can lead us to a whole new way of life.

The point being made is clear enough. In contemporary Christianity and especially Christianity in the Western world, the Christian faith is understood and lived in a peripheral way. We live secular values, but have a faith that will get us into heaven.

The Christian faith was never meant to be lived in this way. The faith was to be a radical alternative to all other ideas and values. And the faith was to percolate into every dimension of one's life and one's role in the world.

This is the way the early church fathers understood the Christian faith. It was a way of life motivated by the love and grace of God in Christ and shaped by the gospel.

Origen is a good example. He taught and lived a radical following of Jesus. He writes, "among our agreements with God was the entire citizenship of the gospel."[228] What he meant by this was a whole way of life, including one's basic life choices, one's sexuality, one's work and service, and one's stand for Christ in the public arena. For Origen, this included a willingness to embrace torture in the following of Jesus that led to his death.

Reflection

The challenge for us is to overcome the way in which we have segmented and privatized our faith.

John 8:3–11

August 17

Beyond Legalism

One of the problems of religiosity is the development of narrow certainties, moral legalism, a work's righteousness, and communal exclusiveness. The way of Christ disturbs all of this and points us to a new way of life and to the wide open spaces of the Spirit.

Jan van Ruysbroeck, the medieval Christian mystic, despite his unhelpful categorization of different levels of Christians, is helpful in his challenge against legalism. He speaks of people who "keep with the law . . . of God . . . [but] they do not keep within the law of love."[229]

Clearly, this poses a challenge for us in the modern world. Since a narrow and bigoted fundamentalism continues in our day, Ruysbroeck's words of direction are helpful. But there is also a major sector in contemporary Christianity where an anemic law of love has become so prevalent that the law of God has become totally negated.

The way of Jesus opens up a new way. This upholds the law of God but champions grace in each particular situation. It holds the word—thou shalt not steal—but forgives the thief and empowers him or her to live a life converted to responsibility and generosity.

In this way, grace trumps law, but also reinforces it. This is a challenging way to live. It's like the river of love flowing within the banks of the law.

Reflection

The triumph of grace leads to the goodness of law-keeping.

2 Chronicles 6:12, 26–27

August 18

Confession

Despite the regression of organized religion in the modern world, certain religious practices continue to make their mark. One such practice is the liberating art of confession.

In our so-called secular world, particularly in the West, religious practices persist. They simply morph into some other form.

For private confession one now goes to one's personal therapist. For public confession one uses the internet.

The public nature of confession is an interesting phenomenon. It seems appropriate for public figures whose misdemeanors become public. But now we have the internet facilities for anyone to make public their failings and weaknesses. This could be some form of drawing attention to oneself. But it could also be a reflection of the fact that we recognize wrongdoing has wider communal and maybe cosmic implications.

St. Augustine went public with his confession. But he struggled in writing his book. He asks, "What profit is there, I ask thee [God], in confessing to men in thy presence, through this book, both what I am now as well as what I have been?"[230]

The answer to this is easy. Your book, my son, of sin and faith has continued over many centuries to be a source of spiritual nurture and challenge for many.

Thought

In another's confession, I may find the language for my own confession.

John 6:35

August 19

A Cruciform Life

The heart of Christian spirituality does not lie in certain spiritual practices. It lies in an ever-increasing conformity to Christ. This is not a process of rigid identification, but of creative reconfiguration in the mystery of grace.

A cruciform life is a life marked by the cross of Christ. This means it is marked by the blessing of Christ's death on our behalf and our calling in the following of Christ to embrace suffering.

But there is much more to this story. The cross of Christ is linked to the resurrection, and a cruciform life is not simply partaking in the blessing and movement of death, but in partaking in the power and mystery of the resurrection. New life comes from death.

This movement of death and life is clearly seen in our baptism. The old self is to die in Christ and the new self is to come to life in Christ.

This movement is also at the heart of the Eucharist. St. Anselm points this out most clearly, "by virtue of this sacrament I may deserve to be planted in the likeness of your death and resurrection."[231] The body and blood of Christ given in death becomes life giving for us. It becomes our spiritual food and drink.

Thus, the cruciform life is never simply about suffering. It is also about the joy of a new life given as the fruit of sacrifice.

Reflection

Am I willing to suffer on behalf of others to bring new life to them?

Romans 12:1

August 20

An Offering to God

There is little doubt that the good Christian will want to give back to God in some way. And usually this is expressed in some form of service to the neighbor. But maybe there are things we need to give directly to God.

We all know the receiving of gifts places us under some kind of obligation to the giver. Usually, we feel at some point we need to give back in kind. What we have received we give back in a similar way.

But how does this work in relationship with God? We can't give back to God the grace and forgiveness we have received. So usually we extend our small expressions of thankfulness and goodness to others.

There are offerings, however, we can make to God. Worship, gratitude, and obedience are central responses to God's grace and forgiveness. The unknown author of *The Cloud of Unknowing* adds another. The author notes, "concentrate on the effort to abide continually in the deep center of your spirit, offering to God that naked blind awareness of your being which I call your first fruits."[232]

Whatever unknown depths the author may be plumbing here, it is clear we are being invited to give to God the very core of our being in contemplation and prayer. Thus, this is not giving *something* to God, but giving *our very selves*.

Reflection

What do we hold back in giving ourselves to God?

Psalm 63:1

August 21

Re-finding God

The fragility in our relationship with God lies with us, not with God. God's covenant faithfulness is secure. We are fickle in our relationship with God in the changing circumstances of our life.

No matter how much we posture and pretend, our life is marked by fragility. And much of life is completely out of our control, thus things happen that we don't want or did not expect.

It should not surprise us, therefore, that in all the ups and downs of life our relationship with God will also suffer. And our very aging further complicates this as we will most likely relate to God differently in the changing seasons of life.

Meister Eckhart has some advice for us regarding these matters. He writes, "find God where you have lost him" and goes on to add that "a *good* will never misses or loses God."[233]

His point is clear. We need to come back to a good disposition and good attitude towards God if we feel we have lost God. This good will towards God is the opposite of being indifferent towards God or blaming God.

A good will towards God is marked by grace and is expressed by gratitude and surrender. When we remain open and thankful towards God, no matter what our life's circumstances, then we will be found by God.

Reflection

In finding God we meet the God who ever seeks us.

John 10:27

August 22

Christ Bearers

The great challenge of Christian spirituality is not to become a saint, but to become ever more fully conformed to the image of Christ.

There are many roads to Christian maturity and to becoming more Christlike. For some the emphasis is on growth in the knowledge of faith and for others it is growth in the spiritual practices such as prayer and meditation. Others again emphasize a different road.

St. Clare, one of the famous torchbearers of the Franciscan vision, emphasizes conformity to the life and mission of Christ as a way of deeper conformity to Christ. She writes, "By following in his footprints of poverty and humility, you can always carry him spiritually in your body. . . . And you will hold him by whom you and all things are held together."[234]

Clearly, these different ways belong together. Knowledge, prayer, and a missional following of Jesus are intertwined. But St. Clare's emphasis is important. Becoming Christlike is not simply a matter of head and heart. It is also a matter of lifestyle and thus becoming Christ bearers.

This is never a work that makes us virtuous. Rather, it is the *Christ* who holds us, who is formed in us, who grows in us, that is the basis for our response in following him.

Reflection

Living in the way of Christ will always be our most powerful witness.

Mark 9:41

August 23

The Future Life

We tend to live for this life. The life to come seems so far removed from our daily concerns. For some, it seems completely irrelevant. But we need to live the now with an eye to the future life.

One of the desert fathers who was close to death was asked by his companions whether he was afraid of dying and facing judgment. He responded, "Here I have toiled with what strength I had to keep the commandments of God: but I am a man, and I know not whether my works have been pleasing in His sight."[235] Thus we die in faith not in certainty.

While we may respond differently to the question of our mortality, most of us would not face death with confidence. Death is the great intruder and most of us feel we have not done enough in this life. There is more that could have been done. And what we have done could have been done differently.

What can give us some peace is not in relation to what we have done or not done, but in relation to the grace and goodness of God. While the Christian life is to be lived with responsibility and service, its heartbeat is the embrace of God. Death is God welcoming us home.

The challenge in all of this is to live the now in the light of the future. This is the call to live the now well and to live it to the glory of God and the blessing of the neighbor.

Reflection

While we should not serve with an eye to future rewards, we will need to account for what we have done.

Matthew 17:1-8

August 24

The Contemplative Vision

There are many ways in faith to draw near to God and to experience God's presence. But for our ancient forefathers and foremothers the most profound way was through contemplation.

The Carthusian monk Guigo II wrote the popular book *The Ladder of Monks* in which he outlined various steps in drawing near to God. These included reading, meditation, prayer, and contemplation. The highest rung was the contemplative experience.

Guigo II describes this experience. He writes of a state in which "the mind is in some sort lifted up to God and held above itself, so that it tastes the joys of everlasting sweetness."[236]

What is striking about this description is not its clarity, but its vagueness. This should not surprise us. The contemplative experience is a visionary gift. It is an experience of the presence of God that lies mainly beyond language. Only stumblingly do we try to make sense of such an experience.

This means that contemplation is not a discipline but a gift. Reading Scripture, prayer, and the practice of stillness and receptiveness are things we can do. These may be preparatory. But the contemplative experience is the fruit of a gift that may come to us at any time, but also may be in relation to these practices.

This encounter is more about who God *is* than about what God wants us to do. It is revelatory. This cannot but challenge and transform us.

Thought

The challenge for us is to prepare the ground so that fruit may come. God comes in his own time and way.

Hebrews 3:12–15

August 25

The Will

The will is the determining and volitional center of who we are as humans. By it we make choices and decisions. But our willing and subsequent doing needs to be shaped by goodness.

We have all met people who have strong personalities and a strong determination. This is a wonderful gift. To have the will to live, the will to do, and the will to try and risk is a key dimension of what it means to be human.

But this strong determination has to be tempered, just as a wild horse has to be broken in in order to become a good stock horse. Our strong determination can lead to an unchecked willfulness that can be harmful to ourselves and others.

A tempered will has nothing to do with being weak-willed and afraid, it has to do with a will being moved by goodness and not by mere self-assertion. William of St. Thierry understood this. He writes, "When the will is in union with grace helping it, it develops and receives the name of virtue and is made love."[237]

In the language of Christian spirituality, the will needs to be "captured," not in order to negate it, but to transform it. And the heart of this is a will marked by the love of God. This is a will that wants to do the will of God.

To live like this calls for the deepest of transformations.

Prayer

May my will confirm to yours, O God. Amen.

Revelation 21:3–4

August 26

What We Will Yet Become

In the religious vision of life we live in the hope of what we will yet become. The life to come is a fuller realization of what we already are.

At the heart of our humanity is the longing for fulfillment and transcendence. Even though we may be deeply thankful for who we are and what we have received, we do long for more and for completion. And every act of love is a partial expression of this longing.

One of the implications of this longing is we live with limitation and incompleteness. Julian of Norwich discusses one form of limitation. She writes, "But we shall never wholly know our self until the very last moment, when this passing life with its pain and woe shall come to an end."[238]

The point she is making is that the longing for a fuller self will not come to completion in one's lifetime, no matter how great or wise one may be.

It is, therefore, humbling to realize we are not self-made and can't complete ourselves. It is not only in the face of God that we will know ourselves more fully. But more specifically, it is through the healing and renewing power of God that we are made whole.

This fullness of life awaits us in the life to come where all will be well and we will be whole in the healing God gives.

Reflection

The human longing for completion is also a matter of faith.

Ephesians 3:18–19

August 27

Fullness of Life

Our early Christian forebears never saw the Christian life as being something peripheral or minimalistic. They saw it as the experience of the plenitude of God.

St. Gregory of Nyssa saw the Christian life as resulting from an outpouring of the divine life into the soul. He writes, "For the participation in the divine good is such that it makes anyone into whom it enters greater and more receptive." He goes on to say that this can be a continual renewing power. He writes, "the person who is nourished always grows and never ceases from growth."[239]

The picture this early church father paints for us is not simply that God sparks something in us. Rather, it is a picture of the continuous outpouring of the love and presence of God. It is a picture of an ever flowing stream.

This speaks of God's abundance towards us. It also speaks of our need for God's ongoing nourishment and care.

Thus, we need God not some of the time, as in a time of crisis or difficulty. We need God all the time. We need the constant outpouring of God's life and goodness.

This means we are to live a God-sustained life, a God-empowered life. God is thus the very source of our life.

Thought

We often only want a trickle from God when it suits us. God wants to flood our life.

Ephesians 2:20

August 28

Firmly Grounded

The contemporary church has seriously failed and short-changed its members. It has given them the impression that God would give much even when there is little commitment.

One can't be critical enough of much of present-day Christianity, especially in the Western world. The church in the West, marked by consumerism, is a Christianity of convenience with little depth. The laity in our churches are biblically illiterate and theologically naïve.

By way of contrast, St. Ignatius, one of the very early church fathers, talks of Christians being "firmly grounded in the precepts of the Lord and the apostles." He suggests this grounding is so they "may prosper physically and spiritually in faith and love."[240]

The Christian life is not simply based on an easy decision to accept Christ as Savior. Rather, it has to do with a way of life of ever greater conformity to the life and ways of Christ.

Nor is the Christian life based on occasionalism. It is a daily affair. It is living all of life in the presence of God and for the glory of God.

Nor is the Christian life simply a private matter. It is also a commitment to the community of faith. It is a communal experience. It is a life together in Christ through the Holy Spirit.

Moreover, it is a life saturated in the gospel which ever sustains, renews, and challenges us.

Thought

An unthoughtful Christianity is hardly sustainable.

Revelation 19:6

August 29

God's Rulership

We are most ambivalent about the notion of God's rulership. We are happy for God to aid us, but we are not so happy for God to tell us what to do and how to live.

It is clear that the leaders of the early church had a commitment to the notion that God was both Savior and Lord. That they were willing to live the Lordship of God is evident by their willingness to embrace suffering in their following of God's way.

But St. Basil takes this even a step further. He not only suggests that the embracing of the Lordship of God is part of one's journey of faith, but this is a much better way to live. He writes, "For He always rules our lives better than we could choose for ourselves."[241]

This simple-but-profound statement has huge implications. It maintains God's rule is a *good* rule. We should not be afraid of it, but welcome it. It also suggests we can *know* this rule. God makes his way known to us. And it also means we need to *surrender* our own way.

It is the last statement that is possibly the most challenging for us. The idea that another knows us better than we know ourselves is a challenging notion. And the idea we can most safely put ourselves in God's hands will always challenge our self-sufficiency and our sense of independence.

Thought

That God reigns is not difficult to accept. That God wants to direct my life is altogether different, for this calls me to surrender and obedience.

1 Corinthians 13:3

August 30

Reward

That we do things for many mixed reasons is stating the obvious. And since we are never pure in our motivations, we need to be in a spirit of repentance and humility even in doing the good.

There is much in the language of Christian spirituality that speaks about a pure heart. And in the area of pastoral theology we speak about good intentions.

While it is true we are capable of doing great good, our motivations for action and generosity are often less than stellar. We can do good things for the wrong reasons.

The unknown author of the *Theologia Germanica* identifies Christians who are so enlightened by the Spirit and so filled with love that "They do not practice the ordered life in expectation of reward." The author goes on, "they do what they do . . . out of love."[242]

This poses a particular challenge for us in the modern world. In our obsessively self-centered culture we need to learn to get our eyes off ourselves and we need to move beyond thinking only about what is in it for us. Instead, our service needs to be for the other and other-regarding.

This calls for a deep conversion. By the fire of God's love we need to be made whole so that the love we extend to others is for them alone.

Reflection

To become disinterested in ourselves and interested in the other for the sake of the other is true virtue.

1 Timothy 1:12–14

August 31

Struggles of Life and Faith

In the great spiritual longing and quest to become more Christlike and holy it is important we don't lose the language of failure and vulnerability.

One of the great hindrances in the spiritual quest is the emphasis on piety and the failure to recognize sin and failure. As a consequence, people wear the cloak that all is well with them.

A far better way to live the spiritual life is in acknowledging our struggles. This is often far more encouraging to others than an unhealthy triumphalism.

St. Jerome in a letter seeking to encourage and challenge a monk has this to say about himself: "I am no experienced mariner who has never lost either ship or cargo." And in further self-revelation he writes, "Lately shipwrecked, as I have been myself, my warnings to other voyagers spring from my own fears."[243]

This honesty is both refreshing and disarming. In this language one can find comfort. And indeed such is the Christian life. No one has a smooth journey. No one is beyond failure and the need for forgiveness.

It is with this kind of openness that we can be an encouragement to our sisters and brothers in the faith. This brings hope. This is life giving. And our challenge to others is far more likely to come home with this kind of humility.

Reflection

Little comes from self-protected piety. Much comes from loving vulnerability.

RICHARD ROLLE

Psalm 90:9–12

September 1

Facing Our Mortality

In the Western world in particular we live in a death-denying culture. But we also live in a death-perpetrating culture. We are thus strangely ambivalent about the subject of death.

That the Western world has overcome its earlier barbarity and has become the benign Father Christmas to the rest of the world is a myth. Violence is still a part of our DNA and we practice it against our own unborn and our enemies. And in much more subtle ways we do the same against strangers, refugees, the disabled, and the elderly.

Our violence, in whatever form it takes towards others, is an indicator of the priority of our quest for self-preservation. And in self-preservation we go to extraordinary lengths to block out threats and go to great lengths to preserve our looks and health. It seems we can't face our own mortality.

St. Bernard of Clairvaux, however, wants us to think and live very differently. He writes, "Do not think death is a long way off, for it may catch you when you are not ready."[244]

This does not mean we should focus on death or fear death. Rather, it means we should live our days with responsibility and vulnerability. We should see each day as God's gift to us and as an opportunity to live well in the practice of goodness.

It also means we need to seize the day for what we can do now as we may not be able to do that later in life. But above all, Bernard's challenge is to live our lives in dependence on God and in faith and hope in the God who will carry us beyond the abyss.

Thought

To live well in the light of death is to live a purposeful life.

Psalm 63:1

September 2

Pre-understanding

The philosophical idea that in understanding something one must already have some idea of it beforehand has deep theological roots.

Nicholas of Cusa once made the observation that "What is totally unknown can neither be loved nor found; even if found, it is not apprehended as found."[245]

This insight has relevance for every dimension of life, but is particularly relevant in relational knowing. You can't, for example, love someone you don't know. And the more you know someone the more you will realize how different they are to what you first thought. Thus, knowing is also always developmental.

This idea of pre-understanding is also important in relation to God. Through faith and revelation we more fully know the God we already know in some way. This incipient knowing is theologically spelled out in the belief that we are made in God's image. In some way, the mark of God is already upon us. In some way, the human heart longs for transcendence. In some way, we search for the God we both fear and long to know.

What all of this highlights is that we need to work with our apprehension and intuition. And we need to become more deeply reflective in order to touch what already lies within us in some incipient way.

That we rush over this challenge to go deeper is one of the tragedies of our modern way of life.

Reflection

What am I being inattentive to, or what have I suppressed that needs to surface in order for me to live life more fully?

Genesis 3:15

September 3

Women in the History of Christianity

Generally, women have not fared well in the long history of Christianity. They were viewed by men with eyes shaped by patriarchy and seen as temptresses and seductresses in the light of a misreading of the biblical story.

While in much of the modern world women have gained full equality, discrimination against them continues, including in other religions and in certain sections of the contemporary church.

What has sadly been forgotten in the church is the liberating attitude of Jesus towards women, the flashes of insight regarding women in the Pauline writings, the role of women in monasticism, and the Christian women in the Middle Ages who counseled emperors and popes.

One such wise woman was Hildegard of Bingen. On the issue of women she makes an important theological point. She writes, "The Devil at first conquered Man through the woman, but God at last crushed the Devil through the woman who bore the Son of God."[246]

Here lies a basis for a positive view of women in history and in the life of the church. To this could be added that both women and men equally bear the image of God and that God's redemptive work in Christ has made men and women free in the grace of Christ beyond all the distinctions that create hierarchy and inequality.

Mary, the mother of Jesus, becomes the icon of all women who in Christ seek to be obedient to God's strange call and seek to be fruitful in love and service.

Thought

Women bring forth not only new generations, but fruitfulness in family, church, and work.

Joel 2:28–29

September 4

Times of Refreshing

Much of the Christian life is lived in naked faith where there is little sense of God's active presence, even in the midst of regular religious activity. Into this uninspiring time refreshment needs to come.

In the history of Christian biography we know that prayerful and faithful brothers and sisters in the faith lived a long, dark night of soul. For some, this darkness persisted over much of their faith journey. Mother Teresa is one contemporary example.

For others, such as Hadewijch, a Beguine in the first half of the thirteenth century, the Christian life was a heavy burden. And we could refer to many others for whom the Christian journey has been one of hardship.

Thomas à Kempis' prayer, therefore, is most appropriate: "Send down Your grace from above and water my heart with heaven's dew."[247]

This prayer recognizes that the Christian life cannot only be lived with tenacity in the face of darkness or difficulty. It must also be lived through being sustained and refreshed.

While it is difficult to see God in our darkness and difficulty, God as the very ground of our being can sustain us when we have no sense of God's present grace. But nevertheless, our cry for refreshment should be our heart cry.

Thought

To thirst for the presence of God's Spirit is the most basic thirst of the Christian life.

Psalm 42:7

September 5

The Seeking Heart

The longing of our finite being is for connection with the infinite God who is both loving and personal and awesome and transcendent.

The great quest of our ancient Christian forefathers and foremothers was for union with God. Generally speaking, this union was not understood that we would be absorbed into God, but more that we would become more God-like.

This growth into greater God-conformity was based on a deep longing that knew even the cry of pain. St. Augustine articulates this. He writes, "As for myself, I will enter into my closet and there sing to thee the songs of love, groaning with groanings that are unutterable now in my pilgrim life."[248]

This expresses a language beyond rationality. This is the language of ecstasy. This is the human heart in the sway of the creative Holy Spirit hovering to bring a new reality to birth.

It could well be that in the twenty-first century, with its impatience to move beyond the rationality of the past century, we may learn again to long and to pray in this way.

This longing is more than an act of the will. It is a heart cry from the depths of our being. It is the cry beyond all forms of sensuality for a homecoming and joining that brings us into the heart of God.

Thought

One can't be self-obsessed and a Spirit-inspired ecstatic at the same time.

John 15:4–5

September 6

Generativity

The movement of goodness in the human being is always to bring something into being, to create, to "give birth." Goodness thus wants to leave traces, to leave a legacy.

St. Anselm is well known for using feminine language in relation to God. He writes, "And you Jesus, are you not also a mother?" He goes on to explain what he means by this. He notes, "For, longing to bear sons into life, you tasted death, and by dying you begot them."[249]

Here St. Anselm is talking about the generativity of Christ. Christ, the ultimate source of goodness, wants to bring more of that goodness into the world through others and is willing to pay the price of suffering to do this.

So what about our generativity? So what about the desires to do good that lie in us spawned by the creative Spirit. What about the hopes and dreams we carry to build community, to see people reconciled, and to see people experience shalom?

In seeing this come into being we need to follow the way of Christ. Christ's way will need to be replicated in us. And therefore, we too, like a woman in the agony of childbirth, will need to surrender ourselves to the birth process with all the implications of penetration, fruitfulness, gestation, waiting, and the pain of giving birth.

May our lives thus become fruitful in joyous self-giving to family, church, and world.

Thought

Generativity and pain belong together.

Genesis 18:22–33

September 7

An Interactive Relationship

*Some so stress the power and sovereignty of God to the point
that we become mere puppets. Others so stress human freedom
that God is only a vague influence. The truth lies elsewhere.*

The Genesis narrative pictures humans as made in the image of God and
given responsibility to determine their lives and shape their world. This
suggests significant delegation of power and responsibility to humans.

But the biblical narrative is not advocating mere self-determination
so that we can do whatever we like. Rather, the outworking of our responsibility must remain God-like, God-shaped, and we remain accountable to
God. Thus, our responsibility is to be outworked in the presence of God
and in a dynamic relationship with our Creator and Redeemer.

Within this awesome dialectic of freedom and responsibility, faith
and obedience, the unknown author of *The Cloud of the Unknowing*
suggests that "God, the Lord of Nature, will never anticipate man's choices
which follow one after another in time."[250] This means the God who empowers and guides us will not directly prevent us from making choices
either in doing good or evil. We are not puppets in God's cosmic scheme.

What God will do is, in time, help us to see the blessedness of
the good and the folly of our evil. Thus, God guides us in the reflective
moments of our life so that we may gain a heart of wisdom.

Thought

In a small way, when parents delegate responsibility to their growing sons
and daughters, we can see something of God's way with us.

Ephesians 1:7–9

September 8

The Blessing of Contemplation

Most Christians are familiar with reading the word of Scripture and praying words to God. The challenge for us is to grow in the art of seeing.

The great Christian virtues of faith, hope, and love have everything to do with seeing. Hope sees a future. Faith sees the presence of God. And love sees the person to be loved, whether loveable or otherwise.

Seeing is as much a matter of the heart as it is a matter of the mind, as it is a matter of faith.

True seeing, according to St. Clare, is the contemplative experience of "seeing with the eyes of the Spirit."[251] Thus, contemplation is not merely the human activity of reflection. It is much more. It is the gift of insight as the fruit of God's presence and wisdom.

This kind of seeing is seeing things with new eyes. It is seeing through the dominant values of our time to seeing what ought to be, and what could be. This seeing is therefore both radical, critical, and eschatological.

But it is not a negative way of seeing. Seeing with the eyes of the Spirit is seeing that leads to renewal, seeing that restores, and seeing that makes us whole. This is because the Spirit turns our eyes to the vast spheres and possibilities of what God has done in the grand redemptive work of Christ.

Thought

The challenge of our time is to see the world with new eyes and to act accordingly.

Psalm 37:4

September 9

The Mystery of Reciprocity

While God is the source of our life, we are to live our life by forging values, developing disciplines, making choices, and living our gifts and passions.

No matter how spiritual you may think you are, this does not mean God lives your life *for* you. God lives *in* you by his Spirit, but you have to live your life. This means you have to make choices and you have to take responsibility. But all of this is to be done to the glory of God.

An ancient desert father once gave this advice, "What therefore thou findest that thy soul desires in following God, that do, and keep the heart."[252]

This means the Christian is to look in two directions at the same time—upward and inward. Upward is looking for God's direction in the following of God. Inward is coming in touch with what we most deeply desire.

Clearly, these two movements must impact each other. They must be reciprocal. And to live the Christian life well means that what we most deeply desire is what also pleases God.

This is not the product of the movement of a bland conformity. Rather, it is the mystery of reciprocity. What we want is what God wants. This is the movement of love. Love brings God and humans into a dynamic relationship where we grow in loving what God loves. To live like this is to be truly converted and inwardly transformed.

Reflection

To become more godly will always remain a key purpose of life.

John 11:25–27

September 10

A Good Dying

The power of our longing for eternal significance clashes with the sheer reality of our mortality. But death need not be the bitter end, but the peaceful surrender.

Gregory of Nyssa is to the point when he speaks about the threatening nature of death. He writes, "When we see those who are dying, we do not easily accept the sight, and when death approaches, we flee from it."[253]

The death of another clearly draws us into the domain of personal loss. And it confronts us with our own mortality; we face what we mainly suppress.

The approach of our own death may be fraught with many issues and challenges. We are not yet ready to leave the familiar. We feel there is more we must do. We are afraid of the passage of death. And we are uncertain about what lies beyond the grave.

In the light of this we are forced to come to terms with what good dying looks like. Such dying acknowledges all and more of the above. Good dying faces loss and pain; it does not deny it. But good dying does involve thankfulness for the years and for all that has been given to us. It involves embracing our mortality. And most importantly, it invites us into the embrace of a God who promises to carry us over the abyss.

Therefore, the resurrection of Christ remains normative for us. For Christ was and is the pioneer of our salvation and the life to come.

Reflection

We want to remain upright, but we need to learn how to fall. Death is the final falling and the great standing upright.

Matthew 9:14–15

September 11

Asceticism

The art of self-denial and relinquishment is an intrinsic part of living the Christian life. Often this is a struggle. But one can come to a place of surrender.

The German Christian mystic, Meister Eckhart, is well known for not majoring on strategies for living the Christian life, but focusing on what is most fundamental. His is an ontological spirituality. This has to do with what we *are*, not simply how we act.

In the light of this Eckhart makes the point, "best of all is the person who can go without because he [or she] has no need."254

This takes the act and challenge of self-denial to a whole other level. This is no longer the daily struggle of letting something go. This has to do with a radical inner transformation leading to a place of certainty and peace that one can live in a particular way without certain things.

With the present proclamation of the spurious gospel of plenty, rather than the gospel of sacrifice, and in our world of continued exploitation, this kind of surrender becomes all the more telling.

The resolution that I don't need to live in a certain way is a much more permanent marker than what I will give up. Asceticism, usually the relinquishment of the good for the sake of the reign of God, thus becomes a way of life.

Thought

Leaving aside some of its extremism in ancient times, the central idea of asceticism needs to be recaptured for a prophetic, contemporary Christian spirituality.

Mark 15:34

September 12

Uncertainty

While we may long for certainty and the security it brings, much of the Christian life is marked by mystery and uncertainty. The very nature of faith is the anticipation of things that don't lie securely in our hands.

St. Anselm's encouragement may at first seem very strange to us. He writes, "Let us live with uncertainty as with a friend."[255] But this counter-intuitive statement opens up some important insights.

While certainties are helpful, they can also become the rigid places in our lives. And certainty over time can easily become arrogance.

Uncertainty, on the other hand, is an open and fragile space in our lives. Such a space can, therefore, become a place for longing, for sighing, for seeking, for crying, and for revelation.

While uncertainty can lead to despair, it can also move us forward. Thus, the seeking heart draws us into new territory.

Furthermore, the quest for knowledge and wisdom is never premised on certainty, but on uncertainty. I don't know, or I am not sure, is the starting point on the royal road to understanding.

St. Anselm thus suggests that uncertainty is not to be feared, but is to be welcomed. And in the whole gamut of Christian experience it is probably the dark night of the soul that ushers us most deeply into an uncertain space.

Reflection

Not to be sure and not to be secure is grace that can lead to the seeking heart.

Jeremiah 6:20

September 13

Beyond Pragmatism

The modern world, including the church, is enamored with outcomes. It is what we achieve and do that is so much in focus. But Christian spirituality challenges us to tap into a more fundamental reality, that which moves and motivates us.

The English Christian mystic Richard Rolle brings us to the heart of this matter. He writes, "the virtue of charity surpasses without comparison all fasting and abstinence."[256]

This is a relevant challenge for us since we can so readily revert to law, legalism, and routine. We can so easily think that the acts of our spirituality and service, particularly those sacrificially made, have virtue in themselves. Thus, we want God to be impressed with what we do, be that in our prayer or our work for justice.

We need to realize this kind of thinking misses the point. A more basic issue is not what we do but *why* and *how* we do it. One can be proud in one's acts of humility. One can serve others for self-aggrandizement. One can be generous to be well liked.

Thus, in our much-doing we need inner renewal and purification. And in our acts of service we need to tap into the subterranean stream of the love of God shed abroad in our hearts by the Holy Spirit. This is so that what we do and the way in which we serve will come from a good place.

Thought

Love needs to permeate all we seek to do.

2 Peter 3:13

September 14

In Between the Times

As someone once said, Christians are too late for the world and too early for heaven. Christians live in between the death and resurrection of Christ and the final fulfillment of all things. Thus, Christians continue to be God's expectant people.

The greatest Dutch poet of the Middle Ages, the Beguine Hadewijch of Antwerp, recognized the anticipatory nature of living the Christian life. She writes about "a fidelity that allows itself to rest peacefully without the full possession of Love."[257]

What this means is that while we reach out in faith for fullness of life in God, we are at the same time at peace with what God has given to us in our lifetime. Thus, strange as it may seem, longing and acceptance can go together.

This attitude needs to spill over in all areas of life. Our relationships, our work for justice, our pastoral work in the church, and the calling to work for spiritual and social transformation. These all carry the marks of the now-and-not-yet dimension of Christian faith.

The challenge in all of this is that we remain faithful in our calling, whether much or little is accomplished. Sometimes in revival or renewal we see much, at other times we see little of the in-breaking of the reign of God. Either way, our faith need not waver, although in hard or dry seasons of the spiritual life our faith will be sorely tested.

Thought

Faithfulness is not based on completion or perfection, but is anticipatory. It waits, longs, and works toward what will yet be.

Ephesians 2:8–9

September 15

Faith

Faith is basic to the way one lives life. It is also a central motif in Christianity. In faith one embraces Christ and God's word, and in faith one lives a life of worship, prayer, and service.

St. Thomas Aquinas helpfully sets out the dimensions of faith. He writes, there is "the object of faith ... the act of faith ... the habit of faith."[258]

The *object* of faith is what one believes in. Basically, this is God revealed in God's word. This means one accepts God's revelation in Scripture regarding who God is, God's way of salvation, and how we are to live in the light of God's promises.

The *act* of faith describes the nature of one's belief and trust. This is the existential dimension of faith. This is a gift and capacity awakened and growing within us where one grows through the Spirit in one's relationship of trust in God.

The *habit* of faith has to do with the patterns and structures of sustainability. While faith is dynamic, it is not an ever new discovery. Faith can become a way of life and an ingrained reality. And as such, it is maintained by participating in the faith community, by spiritual friendships, by practicing the spiritual disciplines, and by Christian service.

While some speak of naked faith, meaning nothing can be seen, it is more correct to speak of realized and expectant faith.

Reflection

We experience both the presence of God and we long for what is yet to be.

John 13:12-15

September 16

The Problem of Elitism

Any ideological group tends to make distinctions between those who are committed and those who are less faithful. This issue has also plagued Christianity.

In the early centuries the Christian church had to wrestle with the problem of members who in time of persecution denied the faith and when these troubles were over wanted once again to join the church in its worship and sacramental life. In the meantime, others had died for their faith.

This, together with the problem of dualistic thinking that elevated the soul over the body, made for all sorts of distinctions in the church, including that of priest over laity.

The medieval Christian mystic Jan van Ruysbroeck in his writings reflects these problems. He distinguishes "faithful servants" who are "called [to] the outward or active life" and the "inward friends of God" who are called to the "hidden way of ghostly [spiritual] life."[259]

Clearly, this buys into the problem of elitism and ruptures the fundamental unity of the community of faith. *All* Christians are to be both friends of God and servants of Christ. The inner and the outer life is one seamless tapestry.

Against every form of elitism the challenge from Jesus for us to be servants and to be childlike wars against all the distinctions we are prone to make. An active life not rooted in meditative spirituality is unsustainable.

Thought

At very best we are only unprofitable servants.

1 John 4:7

September 17

The Motivational Center

Our growth into maturity cannot bypass the need to reflect even more deeply on what it is that moves us. Is it security? Is it the need for significance? Is it the longing for power?

No matter how secure and important our position and role in the world may be and no matter how great our social standing might be, we are all marked by inner fears and insecurities.

This inner and outer ambivalence and its lack of resolution means we are conflicted creatures. And it is in the cracks and fissures of these inner conflicts we may gain some insight into what really makes us tick and what really motivates us. For some, this may be the naked need to be in control, for others it may be the need to be needed.

St. Catherine of Siena wrestled with these matters. She writes, "no virtue . . . can have life in itself except through charity and humility."[260] What she is saying is that the virtue of courage, for example, needs to be motivated by something deeper. Not pride. Not bravado. But by humility and love. I act courageously because love calls me to care for someone in a place of threat. Thus, courage is not about ego. It is about service.

In living the Christian life there is no deeper motivational core that can move us other than love sourced and inspired by the love of Christ. This makes Christ truly the Lord of our lives, for he is Lord not simply in terms of what I believe, but how I act and who I am.

Prayer

Lord, may the love you have for me deepen my love for others. Amen.

Psalm 46:10

September 18

The Gift of Solitude

In the practice of stillness one may be given the gift of solitude. This gift is not a naked solitude, but a meditative presence of the God who not only comes to us, but is at the core of our being. And it may be an experience of the God who not only speaks, but is also silent.

Our experience of the contemporary urban world is one of movement, distraction, busyness, communication invasion, and stress. We feel fragmented and harassed.

We thus feel a desperate need for quiet and refreshment, but we fear stillness and we seldom know the blessing of solitude. Even our churches add to our informational overload rather than lead us beside still waters where our soul can be restored.

The French cleric, James of Vitry in writing *The Life of St. Mary of Oignies*, assures us, however, that "silence and stillness please our Lord so much."[261]

Clearly we, who think that only our exuberant worship or our practical service pleases God, need to hear this invitation. This is an invitation to friendship and inner revitalization.

God is happy with our Sabbath practices, not only with our service. And so let us embark on the challenging journey of creating the spaces for stillness and reflection in our busy routines. Not only will this de-stress us, it may also make our work more effective. Not only will this aid our health, it may also deepen our fragile friendship with God.

Thought

Reflection is always a gracious self-confrontation.

1 Samuel 8:10–18

September 19

Every Gift Has Its Shadow Side

Just as much as every paradise has its snake, so every good thing has its probable problems. And there is a shadow side to our goodness.

While one may say one can never be too honest or too courageous, it is nevertheless true that being too honest can lead to gullibility and being overly courageous can lead to fool-hardiness.

And taking this same dilemma in another direction, every gift and ability we have has its downside and potential difficulties. One's very ability to serve well may lead to a lack of appropriate self-care.

Meister Eckhart understood this well. He writes, "When one is hot . . . [one] gets little comfort out of clothing."[262]

He is right. And this is true in every sphere of life, including the spiritual. The gift of friendship may lead to undoable obligations. The use of the gifts of Christ may lead to spiritual exhaustion. The blessing of community may lead to dependency. The ability to deal with details may mean one never sees the big picture. The exercise of the gift of leadership may lead to relational distancing. Every good thing has its potential negative side, its unintended consequences and difficulties.

As a result, the human condition is always marked by limitation, imbalance, and imperfection. Therefore, counter-balance becomes key in living life in a more wholesome way.

Thought

Every good gift and ability must be worn lightly, lest it destroy us.

Galatians 5:1

September 20

Psychological Control

We live in a world where propaganda and psychological control are alive and well. In the so-called free world we are less than free. It is, therefore, all the more important that in the community of faith we live both the boundedness and freedom of Christ.

Participation in the church is not a free-for-all. The community of faith is bound together by Word and Spirit. It comprises people who are seeking to live the Lordship of Christ. The church is an ethical community shaped by the gospel. This is its bounded dimension.

But the community of faith should never be the place of coercion and manipulation. Fear of God or fear of eternal punishment should never be used to influence people. Instead, the power of love, worship, and gratitude should shape our life together.

St. Benedict understood these matters well. He writes, "the only person who has rights over the inner life of another is God Himself."[263] Thus, while a person is a member of a church or part of a religious community, that person, nevertheless, is to be marked by a radical inner freedom.

Faith and spirituality can never be the fruit of manipulation. It can only be the fruit of the love and grace of Christ and the ever-brooding, life-giving, and empowering work of the Spirit. It is only such people who can form healthy communities of faith.

Reflection

We come to birth in the free grace of Christ. We can only live well in the wide spheres of that same grace.

John 15:4

September 21

The Indwelling Christ

*Our contemporary world is enamored with independence,
self-sufficiency, and self-effort and this kind of thinking has
also infiltrated the life of the church. But the life of faith has
very different contours.*

The world of self-sufficiency operates on the idea that everything depends
on us. But living the Christian life is primarily not about what *we* do but
what *God* has done in Christ and continues to do by the Spirit.

Richard Rolle expresses the vision "that Christ may stable [in] us."[264]
This is a very picturesque way of talking about the indwelling Christ.

To use the limitations of spatial language, Christ is *both* at the right
hand of the Father in heavenly glory *and* in the koinonia and sacramental
life of the church, and in the life of each believer.

This means Christ is embedded and embodied in us by the
Spirit. As a consequence, the Christian life is, therefore, not first and
foremost moved and shaped by our faithfulness and activism, but by the
unfolding of the life of Christ within us.

Thus, Christ is the ground of our being. The source of our life. The
motivational core of our existence.

This calls us to the greatest attentiveness and respect for the One
whom we have welcomed. Christian hospitality, therefore, does not begin
with friend or stranger, but with the welcome of Christ himself.

Thought

Christ as resident guest is the very heart of Christianity.

Mark 9:33–37

September 22

Ladders or Circles?

Our ancient Christian forebears were preoccupied with ladders. They saw the phases of the Christian life not so much as a journey, but as a climb ever nearer to God.

The great quest of pre-Reformation Christianity was further growth in union with God. Thus, God-likeness was the great longing of the spiritual writers of that time.

This quest was usually cast in moving up a ladder with some contemplative vision of God constituting the highest rung.

St. Irenaeus gave this way of thinking a Trinitarian theological foundation. He writes, "Through the Spirit one ascends to the Son, and through the Son to the Father."[265]

While this makes good sense in that the Spirit does reveal Christ and Christ reveals the glory of the Father, ladders are not the most helpful way in understanding the Christian life. Ladders bred the problem of elitism.

If one must use spatial categories, it is far better to think of interlocking circles. The reciprocal love in the Trinity places us equally in relation to the Father, Son, and Holy Spirit. And living the Christian life is better thought of as interlocking circles of love of God and love of neighbor, of prayer and service, and of contemplation and community.

Thought

Not hierarchy, but a common dance is the image for the Christian life.

Jeremiah 29:7

September 23

Grace and the City

Some Christians see the city in rather dark and dismal terms.
Far better the vision of the city as a place of common grace.

The idea that our early Christian forebears were only interested in an escapist spirituality and retreat from the big, bad world is simply not true. They did not only have a vision of retreat to the desert.

While there were some themes of a world-denying form of Christianity, many advocated a world-formative Christianity. The Lordship of Christ was understood to be for the church *and* the world.

One proponent of this vision was St. John Chrysostom. While we might feel nervous about his triumphalistic rhetoric, his vision was one of world engagement. He writes, "Christians are the saviors of the city; . . . they are its guardians, its patrons, and its teachers."[266]

Instead of the Greek gods or the Roman emperors, Chrysostom sees Christians as the protective force in the city. And not only do Christians protect the city from malevolent spiritual forces, they are to play the role of formation and blessing. Thus, Christians are to bring God's goodness and shalom into the city.

By their presence, their lives, their prayers, and their service, they are seen as the glue of a community. Such a vision we may well need to recover, as we seek to overcome a self-focused Christianity and embrace a vision for blessing our cities.

Thought

Not sin or sex in the city, but grace in the city.

Jeremiah 4:19–22

September 24

A Costly Love

Love is more than an emotional high. Love is about commitment in good and bad times. Therefore, love knows the pain of endurance.

To love well is not to love some ideal person or situation, but to love *real* people in the changing circumstances of life. The move from ideal to real constitutes the true nature of love.

To love a church or community or group of friends well is to love them *as they are*, not the way one would like them to be. This is also true of one's spouse and children.

One of the burdens and costs of love is that one continues to love even when the other is no longer responsive or heads in a different direction.

The female mystic, Hadewijch, knows something of this. She writes, "more multitudinous than the stars of heaven are the griefs of love."[267] This passionate Dutch Christian poet had particularly two griefs in mind. One was the pain of love for God. The other was the pain in seeing a broken world.

Love's burden is to love God but not see God's face or come to completion and fullness as we live between the times and in the not yet.

And in and through the love of God to see the pain in our world can break one's heart. This brings with it the cry: even now, O Lord, pour out your healing on our wounded world.

Reflection

Love knows both to cry the pain of unfulfillment and that of blessing on our broken world.

Luke 18:9–14

September 25

Beyond Self-Focus

To be self-motivated and a self-starter is a good thing. To take initiative and responsibility is to be a good human being. But to be wholly self-focused is an unsustainable way of living life.

The history of Christian spirituality that charts some of the key themes in living the Christian life, is not only replete with wisdom regarding the practice of the spiritual disciplines. It is also full of wisdom regarding maturity and relational well-being.

Our Christian forebears were not only concerned with relationship with God. They were also concerned with life in community. And they were also concerned with human wellness and flourishing. Thus, they were the precursors of modern psychology.

Jan van Ruysbroeck, for example, was concerned about people "who are bent upon themselves in an inordinate way."[268]

This can be true of anyone, including religious people. Bent upon themselves, their relationship with God, their participation in church life, and their service to others, the final analysis is all about themselves.

The challenge here is to recognize the Pharisee in all of us. We are all self-serving to a greater or lesser degree. Therefore, the grace of God needs to draw us out of ourselves and beyond ourselves. Human flourishing can only occur when regard for others complements our own self-regard.

Thought

To be wholly self-preoccupied is to build a prison for oneself.

Leviticus 27:16

September 26

Recovering a Vision of the Sacred

The modern world with its science and rationality has stripped the world of its sacredness. But we can re-enchant our world.

The modern world has reduced most things to mere utilitarianism. Sadly, this also includes the way we treat humans. While we are productive we are valued, but we don't seem to have a sacred value in and of ourselves.

This crass, functional way of understanding life and the world is denigrating and demeaning. We urgently need to recover a new vision of the world and of ourselves.

Several theological starting points are key. God is the creator of the world and the universe. We are made in God's image. The world reflects something of the glory and greatness of God. And all of life is to be lived to the glory of God.

This opens up the way for us to see everything with new eyes. *Everything* bears the mark of God and *all* of life is sacred and precious.

In Benedictine spirituality the whole of life, including work and the community, was seen as God-related. In *The Rule*, St. Benedict wrote, "all the monastic utensils and goods" are to be seen "as if they were sacred vessels."[269]

If the world was thus re-enchanted, our rapacious and exploitative behavior would end, and God's shalom could flourish amongst us.

Reflection

If all was dedicated to God, all would be sacred.

1 Corinthians 9:19–22

September 27

Many Ways

While there are always people who have a myopic view of the Christian life, the way of Christ through the Spirit opens up many possibilities for life and service.

While Christ is the one Lord and the one way for salvation in the Christian story, this does not mean there is only way to live out this salvation.

Richard Rolle emphasizes this. He writes, "there is one righteousness and many paths by which we are led to the joy of the life everlasting."[270]

This is an exciting prospect, for we are invited into the wide spaces of the love of God and the diversity of the workings of the Spirit. Living the Christian life means we can give ourselves to a life of prayer, to the work of community service, or to the world of politics.

Just as there is no one way to pray, so there is no one way to love and no one way to live one's Christian calling in the world.

As the people of God we are invited to live and outwork both the prophetic, the priestly, and the kingly work of Christ. Those who build institutions of education, care, and nurture must not think kingly work is all that is needed. They need to welcome the prophet who critiques and points the way to a new future, and the priest who seeks to bring healing to all forms of dysfunction and oppression.

Reflection

The many ways to love and serve in the way of Christ creates a kaleido-scope of God's shalom.

Acts 7:54–60

September 28

The Power of Faith

Conviction grounded in faith in the knowledge of the faithfulness of God in Christ is a conviction that can withstand the greatest of tests.

St. Perpetua was one of the martyrs in the early centuries of Christianity. She came from a well-to-do family and she had a child. But she refused to renounce her faith.

Writing of her days in prison before her death she notes, "After a few days . . . Puden, who was in charge of the prison, sensed there was some great power within us and he began to show us great respect."[271]

While in prison, St. Perpetua had several visions of being with Christ in glory. As a result, she no longer feared what she knew would befall her.

This poses several challenges for us. Firstly, deep faith can't just be rational. It has to be *existential*. And often it needs to be mystical or visionary. Secondly, it raises questions about our level of commitment. In the West we don't even want to give up a consumer lifestyle, let alone be willing to die for our faith.

To gain the power that St. Perpetua received we need to look for very different sources of inspiration. One of these, is an utter abandonment to God. Another, is to live the Christian life out of a mysticism that sees "the face" of God.

Thought

The martyrs of the church will always challenge our mediocrity.

Colossians 3:5, 12

September 29

Sinner/Saint

The longing for God-likeness will always need to be grounded in the grace of God and our ongoing need for repentance, healing, and transformation.

In ancient Christianity there was a great longing for union with God. The desert fathers and mothers and the monks of the ancient world had this as their goal and focus. But this longing was not without a deep realism regarding the need for the Spirit of God to craft goodness in the human person. It also recognized the importance of being shaped in goodness by life in community. And there was a recognition that perfection awaited its final unfolding in the life to come.

The desert father Abba Sisoes, who at the end of his life had acquired great saintliness, cried out, "I have not even begun to repent."[272] This reflects an acknowledgment that despite a life of prayer, community, and service, the Christian is still only a beginner in the journey of sanctification and holiness.

It was not only the Reformer Martin Luther who recognized that the Christian in this life remains a sinner/saint, but our ancient Christian forebears believed this as well.

This understanding of the Christian life saves us from pride and living in illusion and keeps us grounded in the grace of Christ.

Reflection

Growth rather than arrival keeps us healthy in the spiritual journey.

Matthew 25:34–40

September 30

Practical Piety

No matter how fervent and deep our piety may be, it is not complete if it is marked only by prayer. It also needs to be marked by practical service.

Gerard Groote, the founder of the Brotherhood of the Common Life in the Netherlands in the fourteenth century, appointed Florentius Radewijns as his successor. And it was Radewijns who made a deep impact on Thomas à Kempis.

Thomas was struck by Radewijns spiritual presence, his preaching ability, and his wise leadership. But he was also impacted by his practical piety.

Thomas à Kempis writes, "I once knew a leper who used to abide outside the walls of the city. Florentius would often sit beside him and talk to him."[273] Thomas goes on to say that other people with severe disabilities were converted by Florentius.

The piety of the members of the Brotherhood of the Common Life was thus multi-faceted. It was directed to God in worship, prayer, and contemplation. It was directed towards the formation and maintenance of a communal life. It was oriented towards a life of work and service in the world. And it had the poor and vulnerable in society in view.

Here we see the weaving together of spirituality and community and piety and practical service.

Thought

Spirituality links prayer and service with individual piety and community.

OCTOBER

HILDEGARD of BINGEN

Isaiah 1:18–20

October 1

Not as an Object

A person should not be treated as an object or as an "it" to be analyzed or used. A person is someone with whom we are invited into communion.

The stranger something or someone is, the more we want to withdraw and the more we put him or her into a prefabricated box. And in the dynamics of familiar relationships, the more love dies the more we will treat the other as an object.

This can also be true in our relationship with God. We can treat God as an object to be feared or to be used.

In our contemporary world, using God would be more prevalent. We see God as a grand Father Christmas. We see God as the magic worker when we are in trouble.

Meister Eckhart, however, rightly points out that, "As long as a man has an object under consideration, he is not one with it."[274] In fact, what he has done is to estrange himself from the person or thing. Objectification leads to distancing.

To make a person or God into an object is the flawed art of control. The better way is to see the other as an invitation to relationship, to communion, to wonder.

Certainly, that is how we are called to respond to God. The movement of Christian spirituality is not to use God, but to grow in communion and union with God. It is all about a love relationship.

Reflection

Intimacy torpedoes control.

Luke 19:8–10

October 2

Beyond Much-Having

While there have been unhealthy emphases regarding asceticism in the Christian tradition, the more enduring emphasis is possessions should not possess us and generosity and care for the needy should characterize our lives.

Ours is a materialistic age. Material prosperity rather than spiritual wisdom is certainly the mantra of our time.

While Christians have not always lived the simplicity of the gospel, there is an overwhelming consensus that life is not primarily about much-having. It is about much-giving.

The English mystic St. Aelred of Rievaulx raises the warning: "you toil to gain [riches] . . . , slave to keep them, fear to lose them, sorrow to lack them." And he goes on, "as you pile up wealth, you pile up fear."[275]

Clearly, the Christian life has a different focus. Possessions are not our greatest possession. The gift of grace in Christ and the blessing of the Spirit are our greatest possessions. And what possesses us is to be followers and servants of Christ in our age.

For the resources we have, be they many or few, we are thankful. And with what we have we seek to care for our family and friends, but also for the stranger in need.

Thought

The more we grasp, the more we fear. The more we give, the greater our joy.

Isaiah 61:1–3

October 3

The Empowering Presence

Christian discipleship is no methodology or technique. Nor is its source human determination. Discipleship is the fruit of the Spirit's empowering presence.

St. Francis of Assisi was undoubtedly one of the great followers of Jesus in the history of Christianity. He followed the peace-making Christ into the world of violence of his day.

What is noteworthy is St. Francis was marked by joy rather than sheer determination in following of Jesus. And this was because he had identified the true source of his commitment.

In this prayer we see the basis for his inspiration: "Inwardly cleansed, interiorly enlightened and inflamed by the fire of the Holy Spirit, may we be able to follow in the footprints of Your beloved Son."[276]

What is striking about this prayer is it recognizes the need for confession and repentance. Furthermore, it acknowledges that forgiveness of sins leads to insight and wisdom. But wisdom is, in itself, not enough. Many wise people do nothing to change the world. And so, St. Francis invokes the power and presence of the Holy Spirit to motivate and move us to follow Christ and in serve the reign of God. Wisdom needs to be enthused with the wings of the Spirit.

It is the Spirit who breaks open rigid places and inspires and renews.

Prayer

Come Holy Spirit, renew the face of the earth and inspire us in the service of Christ, the Servant King. Amen.

1 Peter 2:10

October 4

A Third Race?

*In the ancient world of Jews and pagans, Christians saw them-
selves as constituting a Third Race. Sadly, today, Christians
have little such sense of a common identity. We are tagged by
our denominational priorities and churches marked by racial
and economic differences.*

The unknown author of *The Epistle to Diognetus* noted that, while Christians were dispersed throughout the then-known world, they did not live
isolated from others in cities of their own. Moreover, Christians "follow
the local customs in dress and food and other aspects of life."

But the author goes on to point out that "at the same time they
demonstrate the remarkable and admittedly unusual character of their
own citizenship."[277] Thus, they had a distinct communal life and identity
and at the same time were connected to the broader society.

The problem with contemporary Christianity is Christians are too
immersed in the broader society and lack a sense of common identity *as
Christians.* Christian community is a scarce reality.

All the research indicates we are too much like our secular neighbors
in our values and behaviors. There seems to be no distinctly Christian
lifestyle, except amongst monks.

The challenge facing us, therefore, is to recover a common life
together where we communally express a life of worship, fellowship, and
service.

Thought

If we were truly aligned with all of our brothers and sisters in Christ in
the world, then we might well have to become enemies of our own nation.

Psalm 90:13–17

October 5

Read by the Psalter

Few Christians in the contemporary church read much of Scripture, although the Gospels and the Psalms are still read. But it is not that we should read these genres of literature, but that they should read us.

The enduring power of the Gospels is they not only tell us about Jesus, but they also tell us what we can and should become through Christ.

And the power of the Psalms is that in these prayers, laments, proclamations of faith, and words of wisdom, we can find words to express the many contours and struggles of our own relationship with God.

The fourth-century bishop Athanasius of Alexandria had this to say about the Psalter: "For I believe that the whole of human existence, for both the disposition of the soul and the movements of thought, has been measured out and encompassed by the words of the psalter."[278]

While this may be somewhat of an overstatement, the point is clear, in the Psalms we can find so many of the themes, issues, and concerns of living the life of faith and prayer. The Psalter, therefore, gives us the language of praise and of lament. And it gives us the permission to rejoice in God and to question God's way with us.

The Psalter thus provides a wide space for all of our concerns in the life of faith.

Thought

Allow the Psalter to read you.

1 Kings 10:23–24; 11:1

October 6

The Tug of Love

It is easy to say the love of God should surpass all human loves. But to relinquish the deepest of human loves calls for a Calvary and a great purgation.

Héloïse and her husband, the theologian Peter Abelard, together agreed to separate in order to live the life of celibacy. She became the first Abbess of the Monastery of the Paraclete. Nevertheless, she lived a life of the deepest internal struggle.

She writes, "It is easy to accuse oneself, to confess sins, or even to impose penances upon the body from without. But it is far more difficult to tear the longing for supreme pleasures from the heart."[279]

From her writings it is easy to see that Héloïse, while having committed herself to celibacy and serving the members of her community, still deeply loved Abelard. Here then we see the continuance and persistence of both the earthly and the heavenly love, the love of former husband and the love of Christ, and the love of the sensual and the spiritual.

Multiple loves can tussle within us: love of country and love of God, love of family and love of Christ, love of one's vocation and love of prayer, love of another and love of God's kingdom.

The reality of the Christian life, therefore, is much more one of struggle than walking a peaceful road.

Reflection

Where are the inner tensions for me as I live the Christian life?

Psalm 96:7–9

October 7

Humility

While our Christian forebears sought union with God and perfection in virtue, they also confessed their utter dependency on God for life, for prayer, and for service.

While St. Patrick is aware of all the things he did in the service of Christ, including baptizing thousands into the faith, his autobiographical writings reflect a great humility. He writes, "I have nothing of value that is not his gift."[280]

This poses a challenge for us in that we seem to have lost both ends of these poles. We neither long for union with God nor are we marked by humility.

Instead of longing to be close to God we simply want God to bless us and fix our problems. And instead of being marked by a surrendered heart to the ways of God, which is the true mark of humility, we insist in wanting to pull God into our projects, our schemes, and our ministries.

As a result, our contemporary spirituality has become too human-centered. We trouble God for the success of our projects. We neglect God when we have no pressing needs.

St. Patrick's writings have a very different flavor. He is above all concerned not with what he has accomplished, but with the honor and glory of God.

Reflection

What does it look like to live to God's glory?

Genesis 22:8

October 8

Self Help?

Self-help has become one of the helpful themes of the modern world. The idea is we can do things for ourselves rather than have to depend on experts. But we do need the surgeon and the motor mechanic. And we do need God.

The modern world, with its ever-growing efficiency and ability to sustain and enhance life, is ever seeking to demonstrate it has grown beyond the need for religion that characterized the ancient world.

But religion persists and people continue to look for sources of spiritual inspiration. One can't easily quell the inner longing for self-transcendence.

One of the continual blockages in the search and longing for spirituality is the idea that we don't need someone else to save us. We can do it ourselves. And so the central message that God has provided salvation for us in Christ is a stumbling block.

St. Catherine of Siena addresses this issue. She writes, "How foolish and blind are those who choose to cross through the water when the road has been built for them."[281] Yes indeed! And to make use of this provision of the ready road or bridge means one has to be willing to see its value and accept its availability.

Similarly, God's salvation—abundantly available and so freely offered—has to be accepted in faith and trust. This offer does place us in relationship and obligation to the giver, but the offer is made for our well-being, not our detriment.

Reflection

A helpful direction surely cannot damage our ego?

Romans 12:1

October 9

Offer Yourself

The heartbeat of the spiritual journey is not the practice of religious ceremonies. Nor is it the practice of the spiritual disciplines. It is the giving of ourselves in love to the God who redeems us.

There is a notable dynamic in life. A person who is well loved usually loves well in return. And a person to whom much has been given is usually someone marked by generosity.

And so it is in the Christian life. Much has been given to us in the salvation Christ brings, and therefore we in turn can make a response in worship, obedience, and service.

Thomas à Kempis works this out in relation to the Eucharist. He writes, "Blessed is the man who, each time he celebrates Mass or receives Holy Communion, offers himself as a sacrifice to the Lord."[282]

The Eucharist is first and foremost the receiving of a gift. The gift is none other than Christ himself in the lowly form of bread and wine. In this way, Christ comes to nourish us. He comes to make us whole.

But in the very act of receiving, we give ourselves to the giver. God's good gift enlarges us, and so we can give ourselves more fully and completely.

Receiving issues forth in the sheer blessedness of giving.

Thought

Do you want to give more fully? Then receive more deeply.

Ecclesiastes 7:15–18

October 10

Life's Ordeals

There is a fair-weather gospel that proclaims all will be well for the person of faith. But also for the Christian, life brings its challenges and blessings, its sorrows and joys.

The Christian is not promised a safe passage through life without challenges and difficulties. The Christian, along with everyone else, suffers natural disasters and the mishaps and tragedies of life. And the Christian may well suffer extra difficulties because of his or her faith or mission in the world.

St. Augustine knew this. He writes, "Is not the life of man on earth an ordeal?" And goes on to admit, "My evil sorrows contend with my good joys" and "in adversity, I desire prosperity; in prosperity, I fear adversity."[283]

So much of life has to do with the movement of goodness and its resistance. Life has its hopes and fears. Things go well for a time and then cracks begin to appear.

Our faith life is also an up-and-down experience. There are seasons of closeness with God, but there is also the dark night of the soul.

Thus, the God we need to follow is not the God of the mountain top, but the God of the pilgrimage of life. We seek to follow the God who draws close to us in the kaleidoscope of life's textured experiences.

Reflection

Let God draw near, especially in times of confusion and difficulty.

Psalm 25:7

October 11

The Spiritual Struggle

In human relationships we often see the pattern of fight and flight and then the movement of reconsideration and return. In the spiritual life it is hardly different.

There are some who think that once someone has come to faith the spiritual struggle is over. They believe the only struggle is to come *to* faith. They don't believe there is a struggle *of* faith.

But the history of the saints and martyrs of the church points out otherwise. Much of the life of faith remains a struggle.

St. Anselm is but one voice. He writes, "In all this you [God] have gone before him who fled from you, and will you not take him back when he wants to return to perfect what you have begun?"[284]

This surely is a picture of struggle in the spiritual life. But it is also a confession of hope for it speaks of a God who does not abandon us when we flee. And it expresses faith in a God who does welcome wanderers back in order to continue the work of restoration and healing.

Implicit in this prayer is a belief in the steadfastness of the God who not only first welcomed us in Christ, but who continues to welcome us in the journey of life and faith.

Reflection

God welcomes home his wayward sons and daughters.

Colossians 2:13–15

October 12

Principalities and Powers

God is as much concerned about large structures and institutions that order and shape human life as God is concerned about an individual's inner spirituality.

St. Paul's enigmatic discussion of the principalities and powers will always remain subject to much debate. Some see him as referring to concentrations of spiritual powers no longer subject to God. Others see him as referring to the large social structures that order life and that go astray from their God-given mandate.

The Christian mystic Hildegard of Bingen, in explaining one of her visions, sees the principalities and powers as referring to "God's gifts . . . [as] rulers of people in this world." These, she says, "must assume the true strength of justice, lest they fall into the weaknesses of instability."[285]

This is a potent insight. It implies that God has provided these structures for the good ordering of life. But these configurations of existence can easily lose their way when they no longer fulfill their God-given purpose, which includes the practice of justice.

Here lies a challenge for us. The institutions we create to serve and bless others need to be safeguarded from becoming self-serving and oppressive. The history of humanity is blotted with this happening again and again. Even the church as a structure of power has, at times, lost its way.

Reflection

Christ the Servant King is the shining example of the good use of power.

Philippians 4:8–9

October 13

Self-Care

The history of Christianity has been infected by extreme views and practices. But there is also an overwhelming emphasis on moderation and self-care.

St. Benedict's emphasis on moderation, care, regard for the other, and flexibility was not the only voice along these lines in the Christian tradition. With the primary emphasis on love, love of God involved love of the Christian companion and love of stranger. It also involved love of oneself.

The unknown author of *The Cloud of Unknowing* also brings us a vision of the practical concern for self-care. He writes, "For the love of God, discipline yourself in body and spirit so that you preserve your health as long as you can."[286]

Not only is there no sense here about burning oneself out in the service of God, but love for God involves appropriate self-care. Furthermore, this perspective recognizes personal responsibility for one's well-being. And lastly, it sees the connection between inner well-being and one's physical health.

This poses a challenge for us in our contemporary culture. Committed to much-having and finding our identify primarily in our work, we are focus too much on productivity and achievement while neglecting the sanctity of our inner person.

Committing ourselves to spiritual practices, including the art of contemplation, we may well become more deeply humane and healthy persons.

Thought

Do yourself a favor—nourish your inner life.

Galatians 6:1–2

October 14

Difficulty as Teacher

What we don't learn readily, we may have to learn the hard way. Life's more difficult circumstances can make or break us.

The wise person is not simply one who has read a lot. Rather, the wise person is one who has absorbed the goodness of life and has learned from his or her mistakes.

The idea that as a Christian one lives a charmed life protected from life's difficulties is not only a misnomer, it is also a flawed idea. Such a life can hardly result in the maturity that comes from responding to difficulty and suffering.

John Cassian, in setting out wisdom for the life of monks, makes this basic observation: "The Lord has allowed you to be hurt so that in your old age you may learn to have sympathy for the weaknesses of others . . . [and] to reach out to the frailty of the young."[287]

Life's difficulties can be our teacher, however brutal that may sound. And the Lord uses all the circumstances of our life, not only the good ones, to shape and form us.

The challenge here is to make sure we, whether young or not, have such teachers and mentors to assist and guide us in our life's journey. One may think it is heroic to travel life's journey on one's own, but it is the height of folly. We all need companions on life's challenging journey.

Reflection

The hard won wisdom of others can be bread and wine for our nourishment.

Mark 10:45

October 15

Virtue and Office

There are many forms of power. One is the power of position, where by virtue of an office one plays a leadership role. There is also moral power, where by virtue of one's wisdom and ability one is able to lead and serve others.

St. Clare of Assisi was rightly concerned about what would become of her community once she was no longer there. Second generation leaders don't necessarily have the charisma of founding mothers or fathers.

While founding leaders ultimately have to surrender their movement into the hands of God's providence, St. Clare did well to point out what sort of a future leader she wanted. She writes, "I also beg that sister who will have the office [of caring for] the sisters to strive to exceed others more by virtues and holy life than by her office."[288]

The focus of St. Clare was thus on *character* not simply on position.

It is distressing to note how in the contemporary world, including the church, this emphasis is lacking. We are so concerned with outcomes and growth and success, that we tend to acquire leaders who fulfill these measurements. We tend, as a consequence, to give little attention to quality, to community, and to the ethos of the kingdom of God as we choose our leaders. Rather than mere functional leaders, we need *virtuous* leaders who embody a way of life in the gospel.

Thought

Virtue ethics are key to good leadership.

Colossians 3:9–10

October 16

The Human Being

Capable of great good and foolish evil, the human being is always conflicted. And in this conflict the triumph of God over evil is always a sign of amazing grace.

St. Augustine understood evil as being the absence of the good. Where good triumphs there can be no evil, and where evil exists the good has fled.

But St. Augustine in talking about the human being makes this assertion far more dialectical. He writes, "Therefore, every being, even if it be a defective one, insofar as it is being it is good, and insofar as it is defective it is evil."[289]

This invites us into the complexity and ambiguity of what it means to be human. A human is still a human being no matter how great one's crimes. But the horrendous nature of one's madness does make one, at the same time, less than human. One is less than what one can be.

But good and evil lie within all of us. In Mafia gangs, for example, members are capable of cold-blooded murder of enemies, on the one hand, and passionate loyalty to family and friends, on the other.

But whether we see the human being as essentially good but deviant, or as essentially deviant but capable of good, it matters little. One's true identity is found in one's healing through Christ. Christ, the true image of God, is the one true human. Our conformity to him and to his way in the world is a reflection of who we are meant to be.

Thought

Christ-conformity is what marks true goodness.

John 15:7

October 17

The Word

Our ancient Christian forebears saw the Word of God as food and wisdom for the soul. We moderns neglect the Word and seek to sustain our spiritual quest by the scraps of a personal but fragmented piety.

One cannot be but impressed by the way our Christian forebears were steeped in the Christian Scriptures. Their writings are littered with copious quotes from the biblical story. Some writings are virtually the stringing together of one biblical text after another. What is even more impressive is that much of the quoting from the Bible was done from memory.

And what about us, for whom the Bible is much more readily available? The overwhelming evidence is that we no longer read the biblical story, despite a sea of new translations and Bible helps.

The advice from St. Bernard of Clairvaux may be helpful for us. He writes, "You approach the Word in trust, join with the Word in constancy, and question and consult the Word in a familiar way about everything."[290]

We are thus being invited to inhabit the biblical narrative, and the Word is to direct and shape our lives.

The challenge for us is to recognize that we can't really have Christ if we don't have his story. And we are not really following Christ if we don't live his story. We can't simply live our idea of Christ. We are called to live Christ's way of life.

Thought

Live Christ! Then live his story! And live it in the power of the Spirit!

James 1:2–4

October 18

The Forging of Virtues

While goodness may be resident within us, so is evil. Therefore,
a virtuous life is not a given; it has to be forged and shaped.

There is a well-known story of a desert father who thought that in living a solitary life of prayer he had become very virtuous. But when forced to associate with others he discovered how intolerant he was. Thus, he needed community to grow in character.

And so, it is often that we need the seemingly opposite to forge certain qualities in us. St. Gregory of Nyssa has this to say, "fear would produce obedience in us, anger courage, cowardice caution, and the desiring impulse would mediate to us the divine and immortal pleasure."[291]

Not only does this highlight the importance and value of our emotional life, but it also notes that what is negative, such as cowardice, can be redeemed. And it can lead to something good.

Thus, the redemption of our weaknesses, the appropriation of our shadow-side, and the productive use of life's negative experiences, can bring us into greater well-being. This requires both the enlightening work of the Spirit and self-work to face what moves and shapes us.

Rejection can make us more caring, failure can make us more steadfast, loss can make us live more freely. So nothing needs to be lost. All can be appropriated in the gaining of a heart of wisdom.

Thought

Don't waste your sorrows.

Philippians 1:9–11

October 19

Misreading

We not only misread texts. We also misread situations. And we misread what the Spirit of God is doing.

To be a person of wisdom and discernment is to possess important gifts and qualities. Why these are important is that so often we misread what people are trying to say and seeking to do.

And equally importantly, we so easily misread what God is seeking to do amongst us in the community or organization of which we are a part. We see a part of the picture, but miss the whole.

One of the emphases made by our ancient Christian forebears is that God does not only make his purposes known through the more normal channels. God speaks through the least and the most unlikely of persons.

One of the desert fathers had this to say: "See that thou despise not the brother that stands by thee: for thou knowest not whether the Spirit of God be in thee or in him."[292]

We usually assume, of course, that the Spirit is with us or with the most charismatic or the cleverest or the appointed leader. But we may well be wrong.

It has always surprised me how the wisest in an organization or group—and who often spoke the least—was not listened to when he or she did have something to say.

Reflection

A Christian group cannot primarily be understood along normal organizational or institutional lines. It needs to be seen, first and foremost, as a community of discernment.

John 14:18

October 20

Come, Lord Jesus, Come

We speak about the first coming of Christ in the incarnation. And we speak about his second coming at the end of the ages. But Christ needs to come to us again and again in the here and now in grace, healing, and renewal.

To cry for Christ to come to us does not mean Christ is absent. He could well be more present than we realize.

This cry usually means something quite different. It could be a cry of longing. It could be a call for the presence of Christ. It could be seeking the comfort of Christ.

This heart cry can also be a prayer of desperation. We are anxious. We are troubled. We are in difficulty. We are in crisis. And so we cry out for Christ to help us. And even if this help does not remove all difficulties, it is the call for Christ to strengthen us in our difficulties.

Thomas à Kempis has faith that Jesus will hear such a cry. He writes, "I [Jesus] have come because you have invited me. Your fears and the yearnings of your soul, together with your humility and contrite heart, have all moved Me and brought Me to you."[293]

It is true Christ comes to the humble of heart and to those who seek him. But he can also enter the proud spaces of our lives and break through our indifferences and resistances. It is especially in these spaces we need Christ the most.

Reflection

If we invite Jesus to come, he comes as both healer and Lord. Thus, his coming will not be on our terms, but on his good will for us.

1 Corinthians 12:4–7

October 21

Cooperation

Some Christians think their particular service is especially important. They denigrate what others do. But we need each other's gifts and contributions to form a tapestry of shalom and well-being.

One of the desert fathers, Abbot Pastor, highlights the value and importance of cooperation and mutuality. He notes, "If there be three in one place, and one of them lives the life of holy quiet, and another is ill and gives thanks, and the third tends them with an honest heart—these three are alike, as if their work was one."[294]

This way of seeing things poses a challenge for us in the twenty-first century. Being the pragmatists we are, we would favor the activity of the third member of this small community. And we would not think too much of the one who lives in holy quiet. We would probably classify such a person as a cop-out.

But people who meditate and pray also contribute to the well-being of their community and the world. For this way of being and living is not based on self-preoccupation. The person who prays also prays for others, prays for the disempowerment of the forces of evil, and prays for God's kingdom of peace and healing to shine in the places of darkness in our lives, our churches, and in our world.

Thought

If only our activism was more deeply rooted in a life of prayer.

Zephaniah 3:17

October 22

On-going Transformation

While we have the sense that we are the same person over time, we do change. And for many of us change is not due only to the aging process, it is also due to the changes in our world and to the choices and commitments we make.

We are both formed and shaped by our family relationships and by the socio-cultural settings in which we find ourselves. We are also shaped by our ideals, values, and choices.

But we are also shaped and changed in adaptive processes when life no longer sails along at an even keel. When new circumstances impact us, when we are dislocated from familiar places, when relational, health, or financial troubles strike us, we find ourselves in the slip-stream of ongoing change.

St. Gregory of Nyssa once wrote, "for our nature does not move out of itself but makes its progress through alteration."[295] This church father thus sees change as intrinsic to personal development. And for him, this change is primarily spiritual transformation. Entering the death and resurrection of Christ changes us. Grace changes us. The Spirit changes us. Prayer impacts us. And the movement of this change is towards greater Christ-conformity.

Reflection

Alteration. Mending. Transformation. Healing. Renewal. All these are the fruit of the Spirit at work in us.

Psalm 34:7

October 23

Angels Unaware

Along with ghosts and goblins, we have banished angels from the modern world. But angels may well be mysterious messengers and assistants who help us when we don't notice them.

While it is true the ancient world was full of strange superstitions, it is also true people had a much more sacred view of life than we do. Our modern world has been stripped bare and needs to be re-enchanted.

The biblical narrative casts a sacred view of life. God creates a world sustained by his presence. The Spirit animates all things. God's Son enters the human arena. Miracles happen. Angels are at work.

St. Augustine writes, "holy angels, who enjoy uninterrupted happiness" come to "render assistance" to us who are "still wandering."[296]

This church father seems to suggest these creatures from God's good hand are here to help us. What that help might look like is hard to spell out. But since Augustine identifies that we are "still wandering," angelic help could be supportive, interventionist, and directional.

Maybe, what we regard as chance encounters, coincidences, surprising happenings, could well have an angelic touch. Angels of which we are unaware may well be aware of us.

Reflection

I would have thought that to live life well, we need all the help we can get. Bring on the angels!

Numbers 6:1–4

October 24

Special Consecration

In our culture with its emphasis on much-having and self-gratification the call to some forms of asceticism and relinquishment is not to embrace a burden, but to enter the joyous spaces of relief.

Everywhere in the biblical story we meet the happy theme of God's goodness and abundant provision. And we meet the equally happy theme of people who are willing to consecrate themselves to God in special ways and live a life of self sacrifice. Nazirites, priests, prophets, and apostles are only some who lived in such ways.

In the history of Christianity we meet myriads of others who lived in particular ways in order to live in fidelity to the gospel and as a sign of the kingdom of God. St. Brigit was one such person.

Her biographer, Cogitosus, writes, "her parents wished to betroth her to a man, as is the way of the world. But filled with heavenly inspiration, she wished to offer herself as a chaste virgin to God."[297]

Whether one is called to this kind of commitment or to other commitments of relinquishment, this way of living is urgently called for. This is not to earn merit, but to give grace the much needed room in our over-crowded lives.

Reflection

The places of relinquishment become the empty places God can fill with his grace and purposes.

1 Corinthians 11:23–26

October 25

A Eucharistic Life

In the history of the Christian church we have rightly placed a great emphasis on the power and significance of the Lord's Supper. But eucharistic participation calls us to live eucharistically.

St. Thomas Aquinas is right to emphasize that "the Eucharist is the summit of the spiritual life."[298]

This terse statement can be understood in many ways. It can refer to Jesus' self-giving, with the Lord's Supper as its key expression of the great source of the spiritual life. As such, it can also refer to the pastoral reality of our daily or weekly participation in Holy Communion as our food and drink for the Christian journey.

But we can also understand his expression in a complementary way, namely, the most profound way to live the Christian life is to live eucharistically. That means we not only live out of the resources of the Eucharist, but we live its central themes.

Put in other words, we ourselves need to live a Paschal spirituality in that death and resurrection is at work in us and we become food and drink in the purposes of God for others.

To live the eucharistic life is "to die" in some way so others can live. This means suffering for the sake of others.

Thought

A life poured out is a life that sustains others.

Deuteronomy 15:12–15

October 26

Extravagant Generosity

The decadent and tiring quest for much-having—an evidence of the power of Mammon—can and must be subverted. Extravagant generosity does precisely that.

There is the possibility of living differently in our modern world. We could work less and pray more. We could play more and worry less. We could want less and give more.

But however we want to envision this different way of living, we need to find ways to resist and transcend the seductive voices in our culture, which link our sense of identity and well-being with much-having.

One way to denude the power of Mammon is to live, not with a sterile or legalistic asceticism, but with a joyful generosity.

The unknown author of *The Shepherd of Hermas* has this to say: "Work at what is good, and out of your labor which God gives you, give generously to all who are in need." The author then goes on to say "gifts should be given to all,"[299] irrespective of who they are.

This calls us to a generosity beyond our family, local church, and our favorite charity. That "generosity" is tribal generosity. It is, basically, caring for our own. But radical generosity may well call us as Christians to support a local Muslim youth initiative at great personal cost.

Thought

Great generosity is nothing other than to be in God's good slip-stream.

John 20:26–29

October 27

The Passion of Christ

Theological discussion persists as to the meaning of Christ's death on the cross. But whether it was a ransom to pay for our sins or an example of self-giving love, one thing is clear. In the wounds of Christ I can find healing. In the death of Christ there is new life.

Bonaventure, in a profoundly pastoral reflection on the passion of Christ, points us away from speculation about this momentous event. It is to *encounter* that he points us. He wants us to draw near. He wants us to enter.

He writes, "His feet are nailed, that he may stay there; His side is open for you, that he may let you enter there."[300] Here Bonaventure plays with the concepts of stability and movement. Jesus stays put in his time of agony. He fully embraces his death. But it is this very commitment to stability that opens the way for us to move from the places of our own "death" and darkness into the wounded side that heals us.

Clearly, this poetic reflection of Christ's suffering provides safety and healing for us. But it also means something more. In entering the suffering Christ we too enter into suffering. And like Christ, this is suffering on behalf of others so that life might come to them.

Reflection

Don't be afraid. Enter.

Matthew 11:28–30

October 28

The Unbearable Lightness of Being

*Our being in the world is not weightless. We are heavy.
We carry burdens. Much presses upon us. We move to the
weightiness of death. We need more than just to be sustained
on such a journey.*

Most of us have had the temporary experience of transcending life's more
weighty routines, the weight of the world rolling off our shoulders. In the
spring of a romance we have experienced something like this. An exotic
experience of nature can approximate this. Or a fantastic getaway holiday
can get us on this page. So can a religious experience.

But times of lightness of being are usually few and far between. We are
more the beasts of burden and of worry than dancers of the light fantastic.

Yet, St. Aelred of Rievaulx seems to suggest that in the ongoing
experience of the love of God and the desire to do God's will there is a
more sustained lightness of being. He writes, "This burden has wings, not
weight."[301]

He is right. Life in the presence of God, blown by the wind of the
Spirit, graced with the healing goodness of Christ, and therefore lived in
joy and faithfulness, is a life that is not burdensome but purposeful. And
there is happiness and lightness of being in the love of God and neighbor.

Reflection

Let us follow the joyful and obedient Son of the Father and so experience
his easy yoke.

Luke 6:30

October 29

The Wretched Face of Christ in the Poor

Spirituality can conjure up images of elitism, particularly if we think of monks tucked away from life in cloistered beauty. But spirituality must spill onto the dusty roads of life.

Mother Teresa of Calcutta was not the first person to speak of seeing the hidden face of Christ in the poorest of the poor. St. Francis preceded her and so did Richard Rolle, the English mystic. Rolle writes, "Two cloaks or one will seem enough to you; if you have five or six give some to Christ who wanders naked in His wretched rags."[302]

This identification of Christ with the poor has very deep theological roots. Yahweh is pictured as being particularly concerned for the poor (Ps 146). Jesus enters history as the poor man whom the poor heard gladly (Matt 11:2–5). And for much of the life of the church, it has sought to be a servant to the poor.

We can, of course, do no better than this. And possibly more importantly, we cannot live the Christian life well without this kind of commitment. For Christ is more likely to be found with the poor than in stained glass cathedrals.

To give to the poor has value in itself. But for us to find Christ in such a setting is a blessing we cannot do without.

Thought

Dare to stoop to serve. Christ will lift you up.

Isaiah 65:17–25

October 30

Ancient Seers

The modern church is good in creating practitioners with skills for the various aspects of church's life and ministry. But the church is not so good at creating visionaries—women and men who can gaze into the future and anticipate what will yet be.

The medieval mystic Hildegard of Bingen speaks of patriarchs and prophets as being ancient seers. She writes, they were "eminent men, who traversed the hidden ways and looked with the eyes of the spirit." She goes on: "in lucent shadows [they] announced the Living Light."[303] In this way Hildegard identifies their searching and visionary powers.

While it is true that since the coming of Christ the fuller light has come, it is not true we no longer need to search and visionaries are no longer needed. We need them all the more in this time of world darkness.

With the present struggling state of the church in the West, we urgently need women and men who can gaze into the heart and purposes of God for our time, who are deeply immersed in the biblical story, who know the heart cry of prayer, and who carry the pain of our world.

While we need pastors, teachers, and counselors for the modern church, we also need seers and prophets. May they arise in our midst or come as outsiders!

Reflection

We need doers. We also need seers.

Genesis 3:24

October 31

The Human Condition

Whatever profound insights psychology may be able to provide in helping us understand the human condition, it must address a primal reality—human expulsion from the garden.

The fundamental human condition is based on a great tragedy. St. Anselm, using gender specific language, identifies this. He writes, "He lost the blessedness for which he was made and he has found wretchedness for which he has not made."[304]

This tragic change in the human condition is called the Fall. And the resultant loss of goodness has left its mark on all of humanity.

And so we live. We are banned from our primal innocence and are far short of our final redemption. In the middle of things, we are fundamentally marked by loss and longing.

And so we try to make the most of it. We live, we love, we work, we build, we propagate, we beautify. Much of this is marked by goodness, but we are seldom content and happiness eludes us. There is no real homecoming.

Thus, the human condition is a movement towards death, while the hope of life burns brightly. It is a movement marked by conflict, while the hope for resolution and healing is ever with us. It is a movement towards autonomy when homecoming to God remains the startling invitation.

Prayer

Hear my cry, O Lord, even when it has become the faintest whisper. Amen.

NOVEMBER

ST CLARE

Colossians 3:5–12

November 1

Struggle for Virtue

There is no quick road to a virtuous life. Holiness does not fall on us like summer rain. Virtue has to be won in the struggle for a better life.

If only it were true that all is well once we come to faith in Christ. In fact, the opposite occurs. The struggle really begins.

With the birth of faith within us through the grace of Christ a new dynamic enters our old way of life. The old does not easily disappear. The new needs to grow. And sometimes within this dialectic we are not too sure what we favor and what is blossoming within us. It is, therefore, not surprising St. Augustine prays the prayer: "Grant me chastity and continence, but not yet."[305]

While he prayed that prayer in the early stages of his journey in faith, he may well have prayed similar prayers later on. And we will probably do the same.

We can identify with this struggle. We are only ever sinner-saints. We too want to live the goodness of the Gospels, but the un-wellness within us, and the way of the world, persists with us. We are, therefore, both graced and torn, virtuous and sinful, whole and needing fuller healing.

Prayers for God's radical way with us are prayers we will never pray easily. More likely, we will pray such prayers with much trepidation.

Prayer

Lord, deepen my desire to want your way with me. Amen.

Matthew 26:40

November 2

Being Distracted

Our experience of life in the modern world is one of distraction and fragmentation. To become recollected and centered is one of our greatest challenges.

A younger person may well ask, what is wrong with being distracted? What is wrong with multi-tasking? What is wrong with watching TV while doing email and texting on your mobile phone? At least life is not boring!

Indeed. It is not boring. But overcoming boredom is not our greatest challenge. A far greater challenge is to become reflectively attentive to our inner life, to the voice of God, and to our greater longings and aspirations.

The unknown author of *The Cloud of Unknowing* points us in the right direction regarding focus in prayer. He writes, there are many good things that come into our minds, but "these things must eventually . . . [be left] behind beneath a *cloud of forgetting*."[306] Or a related strategy rather than forgetting would be the practice of bracketing.

In becoming focused and attentive we gently put aside all those clamoring voices and we become open to the one thing needful or the one thing we need to hear. This inner voice with its singular clarity is the voice often most repressed, but it needs to surface to help us move forward.

Thought

The task and gift of reflective solitude is far more productive than much of our frenetic activity.

Matthew 23:8–12

November 3

The Practice of Servanthood

To serve others is a wonderful Christian ideal. But in our narcissistic age, even our service and giving to others is often self-serving. In the light of this, we are called to a deeper conversion.

In any and every social setting, in a small or more significant way, we can be of service to others. This means that we help and bless others even at cost to ourselves.

But we can take this a step further. We can also create groups, organizations, and movements that reflect the vision of servanthood. Many grass-roots Christian communities and groups attempting to live a Christian anarchist vision seek to live in a radical, egalitarian way.

St. Francis also had such a vision. He writes, "None of the brothers should be administrators or managers, . . . instead, they should be lesser ones and subject to all."[307]

This way of life is a challenge to us all. It is other-regarding rather than self-focused. It translates power *over another* into power *for the other*. It moves from the grasp for position to the practices of servanthood.

To live this way is to go against everything our contemporary world stands for. It is to go the humble way of Christ. It celebrates a spirituality of the little way rather than the big way that our society so clearly demonstrates.

Prayer

Lord, make me an instrument of your peace. Amen.

1 Corinthians 2:14–16

November 4

Discernment

Life has its routines. Life also has the constancy of decision-making. And for this—particularly in the more important decisions—we need a wisdom based on discernment.

To discern is to see something, to apprehend something. It also involves some form of discrimination, some form of evaluation.

In discerning something one not only sees, one also has to *weigh things up*. Discernment does lead to making choices.

John Cassian understands this. He writes that in discerning things spiritually we have to ask the questions: "Is it filled with what is good for all? Is it heavy with the fear [reverence] of God?"[308]

These are good questions for us moderns. These are not the questions foremost in our minds. Our questions are more personal and pragmatic. And the idea of weighing whether something is charged with the reverence of God is often far from our minds.

And yet we have to live more in this way, if we are to live to the glory of God, if God's way is to be our way, and if we are to be a blessing to others.

Clearly, in Christian communities, where people seek to live a life together, to ask such questions would not only deepen one's faith and service, but also the nature of one's relationships.

Prayer

Lord, give me eyes to see, ears to hear, and a heart that longs to know and do your will. Amen.

Luke 6:32–36

November 5

·

Radical Love

We know all about a love that is primarily self-interested. We know little about a love that is wholly other-regarding. And yet, such love is called for.

St. Bernard of Clairvaux speaks of this radical love. He writes, "I am suspicious of a love in which there seems to be anything of a hope for gaining something."[309]

But the love of which he speaks is not what we usually experience. Since love is relational, it is also reciprocal. When we love we trigger or evoke something in the other person. And the normal response of that person is in turn to love us back. We do the same when someone shows love to us. And this is normal and appropriate.

What St. Bernard is pointing us to, first and foremost, is that we should not *only* love to get something back for ourselves. That should not be our primary motivation. We choose to love *even if* the other does not reciprocate.

But he also points us further. This is to love another who cannot or will not give anything in return. To love someone who spurns our love and yet to go on loving.

This is a deep and mysterious love that must be born in the very depth of the love God has for us.

Reflection

Do I dare to love someone like this?

Psalm 145:3

November 6

Looking through a Window

It is very difficult, if not impossible, to comprehend something or someone who is very different. Sometimes the only way forward is by way of analogy.

Theologians have rightly spoken about God as the Wholly Other. And the Christian writers on spirituality have spoken about the mystery of God and God's unknowability. As a consequence, some writers have emphasized that in the Christian life we don't move from darkness to light, but we move from light to darkness. In other words, we move from the light of Christ into the darkness of God's essential unknowability and mystery.

And yet we do know something, even if we stumble and stutter in bringing that to the fore. We understand something of God through Scripture, but also through the gracious and often strange ways God works in our lives, in the church, and in society.

The medieval mystic Marguerite Porete writes, "Lord, how much do I comprehend of your power, of your wisdom, and of your goodness? As much as I comprehend of my weakness, of my foolishness, and of my wickedness."[310]

Here we have a partial knowledge of God by way of negation: What I am, God is not.

But whether our partial knowledge of God comes this way or more positively, finally what we do know comes by revelation.

Prayer

Lord, at least show me your way, even if your person remains veiled in mystery. Amen.

Luke 12:15

November 7

Greed

The West and other fast developing countries live with a perverted sense of entitlement. The basic idea is that I have a right to having and getting as much as I want. But our world is a common-wealth. Sharing lies at the heart of such a world order.

The monasteries of the ancient world were not simply places of prayer. Nor were they totally shut off from the real world. They were also places of work, hospitality, and commerce.

St. Benedict, in referring to the works of art sold by monasteries of his time, wrote, "The evil of avarice must have no part in establishing prices."[311]

This meant that this monastic leader had a sense of what was a fair price for work done. Thus, getting as much as possible was not the bottom line. Fairness was in view. And the bottom line had to do with a vision of the whole of life lived to the glory of God and to the blessing and well-being of others.

Such a view of life urgently needs to be recaptured in our time. Yes, profits are important, but so is building up social capital, empowering staff, giving back to society, and caring more adequately for our fragile world.

Greed is not good. It is destructive. Fairness and generosity are much more sustainable and life-giving qualities.

Thought

We don't need everything anyway. We only need enough.

John 11:33

November 8

Anger

In some Christian circles there are weird ideas in regard to the matter of anger. Basically, one should never be angry, for that is a sin, is the claim. But if Yahweh could be angry with his people (Zech 1:2) and if Jesus was angry with the death of his friend Lazarus then we need to rethink our concept of anger.

St. Jerome makes a simple point, "Offended love does well to be angry."[312] And so it is with betrayal. As it is with the cry for justice. As it is in the grief of loss. As it is in the pain of abandonment.

Anger is an appropriate emotive response in these and similar circumstances. Not to feel anger in the face of betrayal is a diminution of our humanity.

But to feel anger is one thing. What we *do* with our anger is an altogether different matter. So do we then retaliate? Do we hurt the other? Do we punish? Do we hate?

It is at this point the Christian story asks us to make a different move. The message is not don't be angry, but use your anger to move to forgiving love. Do the opposite to the other to what was done to you (Rom 12:19–21).

In making this move we follow the way of Christ whose gift of forgiveness gives new life to us. And whose gift we want to extend to others.

Reflection

Give another the precious gift of forgiveness.

Psalm 77:11–15

November 9

Action and Contemplation

We are invited to meditate on who God is and what God has said and done. Word and works belong together. So does action and contemplation.

The medieval Christian mystics emphasized both the active life and the contemplative life. Walter Hilton writes, "Active life lies in love and charity shown outwardly in good bodily works." He goes on, "Contemplative life lies in perfect love and charity, felt inwardly through spiritual virtues and by a true knowledge of God and sight of God in spiritual things."[313]

Rather than making the latter higher than the former, we may simply say they belong together. The active life is sustained from the wellsprings of the contemplative experience. And the contemplative experience with its vision of God gives us the perspective from which to see our world, leading to the love of neighbor.

The contemplative experience is transcendental. The activist experience is incarnational. And just as the former impacts the latter so the active life with all of its needs and challenges can draw us into the contemplative experience.

Just as love of God can move us to love of neighbor, so love of neighbor can move us towards the gracious heart of God. All the more so, when we recognize that we can only best serve the neighbor in the love of God.

Thought

Prayer should lead to action. Action must be sustained in prayer.

Psalm 103:1–3

November 10

God's Healing Presence

Prayer, the practices of meditation, and living the sacramental life all open us up to the healing presence of God. In these, and in many other ways, we may hear the gracious words: I am the Lord who heals you.

Hildegard of Bingen, the medieval mystic, celebrates God's healing presence. She writes, "O bright Mother of Holy Medicine, you have poured out, through your Holy Son, on the grieving wounds of death."[314]

Whether one thinks of Jesus, the presence of the Father, the work of the Holy Spirit, the prayers of the saints who have gone before us, or the work of angels, there can come the streams of healing.

And wherever we may find ourselves—at table with family and friends, in the midst of our daily work, in the company of strangers—God's healing presence still comes to us. God is not bound to the sanctuary or to our pious practices.

This healing presence sustains and nurtures us. It is the very source of our life. Thus, we are kept by the power of God, graced by the love of Christ, and empowered by the hovering Spirit.

God's healing presence is not simply the cure for illness, it is the very gift of life.

Reflection

We live and move and have our very being in God.

Hebrews 12:1–2

November 11

The Difficult Made Easy

There is something strange about the call of God. We think it is hard and demanding. But it may well be joyful and light.

St. Francis knew all about this strange way of God. He testifies, "When I was in sin it seemed too bitter to me to see lepers. And the Lord Himself led me among them. And when I left them, what had seemed bitter to me was turned into sweetness of soul and body."[315]

We tend to think the call of God is only ever the demand of God. And when we think this call will move us outside of our comfort zone, we tend to fear the worst.

But the call of God is never without the grace of God and the uplifting sweep of the Holy Spirit. And those whom we are called to serve, surprisingly, also bless us. Providing, of course, that we have the humility to receive.

And what we often don't sufficiently realize and understand is that in the walk of obedience there is a lightness of step and there is food and drink for the journey.

All of this means that waywardness and willfulness and disobedience make life's journey harder, not easier. God's call makes the seemingly difficult journey light.

St. Francis found joy in doing the difficult thing. And so can we in the grace of God in Christ.

Prayer

Lord, give me a willing heart, a gentle spirit, and joy in following in your way. Amen.

Genesis 5:1–2

November 12

To Be Like God

We are made in the image and likeness of God. And we are so unlike God. Becoming more like God is the hope and longing of the spiritual life.

William of St. Thierry on the subject of union with God wrote, "When this soul is free to be free in God, to cleave to God, she is made like to God through the piety of devotion and a unity of will."[316]

There is much that should be unpacked in this brief statement. One key point is that the freedom of our inner being is not any sort of freedom. It is a freedom *in* God. This means a freedom shaped by the love and goodness of God. It is a freedom shaped by grace.

But William also recognizes that such a relationship is shaped by the spiritual disciplines. He envisages a life of prayer, meditation, worship, communion, and fellowship. To cleave to God is what we do in our spiritual practices and we do so because we have been made free in the freedom of God.

What this leads to is not simply a relational unity, nor simply a unity of sympathy. Instead, it leads to a unity of purpose. It is a growth towards willing the will of God.

I long to do your will, O God. I seek to walk in your way, O God, becomes the heartbeat of our hearts.

Prayer

Captivate my heart, O God, that these things may become more and more true of me. Amen.

Psalm 34:8

November 13

Room for God

We are preoccupied and we are distracted. An inner silence eludes us. Stillness is not our daily bread. We need to be saved from ourselves.

It is one thing to realize we need to be saved from sin and wrong-doing. It is quite another thing to realize we need to be saved from busyness and distractedness, for if we are not saved from these things we will never be at peace. And we will never find God.

St. Anselm understands this. He writes, "free yourself awhile for God and rest awhile in him." He goes on, "Enter the inner chamber of your soul, shut out everything, except God."[317]

Clearly, St. Anselm is talking here about the practices of solitude and contemplation. And while we can try to find the still place and practice inner stillness, solitude and contemplation are gifts that must come to us.

To find God and to rest in God come through God's revelation, presence, and nearness. To be drawn near to God and into God is the work of the Holy Spirit.

While we can make room for God, we need to wait for God's appearing. God is not the end result of our meditative practices. He is God who comes in freedom and sovereignty, and in gentleness and care. We will always be surprised by God's coming.

Thought

Make time. Make more space. Wait. God will come in his own way.

John 17:20–21

November 14

Unity of the Body Christ

*We live with the shame and pain of a deeply divided Christen-
dom. Can the house of God be repaired and unified in truth,
love, and service in this century?*

There is, of course, a sense in which all Christians are already one. St.
Cyprian holds this idea. He writes, "there are many rays of the sun, but
one light; . . . many branches of a tree, but one . . . tenacious root; . . . the
unity [of the church] is still preserved in the source."[318]

What the early church father is referring to is the invisible or the
mystical unity of the church. All God's people are finally rooted in Christ
through the Spirit irrespective of where they worship or what fellowship
they belong to or in what age they lived.

This is so. But the matter should not end there. For the way we live
out the mystery of Christ does matter. It does matter what we believe. And
it does matter how we organize our communal life as followers of Christ.
And it does matter that on the ground we are so hopelessly divided.

So where do we start? What do we do? Clearly, we can begin by
joining in with Jesus' prayer (John 17:20–21). Surely, we should fellowship with Christians from different denominations. Surely, we can work
together on common missional projects. Surely . . . we can.

We can do these things. We must do these things.

Thought

Cooperation is a joyous but challenging fruit of the Spirit.

John 11:11

November 15

The Love of Friendship

Friendship is both a surprise and a gift, and a duty and responsibility. Good friendship should be mutually beneficial, but sometimes one needs to carry one's friend or be carried.

Meister Eckhart rightly emphasizes the negative side of friendship. He notes, "If I have a friend and love him so that he may benefit me and do what I wish, then I do not love my friend at all, but rather myself."[319] He is right of course. Such a friendship is self-serving and manipulative.

But this does not mean friendship can always be fully mutually beneficial. Friendship is not based on a tit for tat. It's not you do something for me and I will do something for you.

Friendship is grounded in something completely different. It is rooted in appreciation, regard, and love of the other person. And this love for the other is a love that is not only willing to give, regardless of response, but is willing to suffer for the other.

This kind of friendship is one of life's greatest gifts. If this lies at the heart of a marriage then, such a marriage can have staying power. If it lies at the heart of church fellowship relationships and in the realm of collegiality, such relationships can be wonderfully joyful, life-giving, and productive.

Thought

To carry and be carried lies at the heart of relationships.

Matthew 7:1

November 16

Beyond Judgmentalism

As Christians, we are to be committed to truth and the wideness of God's mercy. How we hold these two factors in creative balance will always be a challenge for us.

St. Isaac the Syrian makes it clear where he stands regarding this dialectic. He writes, "a heart aflame with love for the entire creation, for people, birds, beasts, evil spirits, all creatures . . . [and] moved by an infinite pity that is awakened in the hearts of those who resemble God"[320] is what we are called to.

Clearly, this church father has such a profound sense of the extent and power of God's redemptive activity that even evil spirits will finally be rehabilitated. And he believes this wide love should find a home in our own hearts.

Where this church father pushes us is that we should think differently about the Hitlers, Stalins, and Osama bin Ladens of this world. A most troubling thought indeed!

But whatever we may think regarding these troubling matters, we are hardly characterized by the infinite pity St. Isaac speaks about. As modern Christians we seem to be as intolerant and judgmental as our secular counterparts. And this should be another troubling thought!

Just as much as we will always be challenged by holding together justice and kindness (Mic 6:8) and loving our enemies (Luke 6:35), so St. Isaac's call will trouble and challenge us all of our life.

Reflection

In which direction regarding these matters do I err?

Lamentations 3:25-26

November 17

The Seeking God

While we have so-called "come of age" in the modern world and assume more and more responsibility for life in the world, we must never forget we are the happy recipients of the goodness of the seeking God.

As moderns we live with a dreadful burden. We have foolishly dismissed God from our world and we live as if everything now depends on us. Thus, we live without homecoming, nurture, and care and without the echo in our hearts of a God who knows us better than we know ourselves. No wonder we are so miserable and forlorn.

But we can live in a very different way. We can live in the goodness of the sustaining and seeking God.

St. Bernard of Clairvaux gives us a signal of what that could look like. He writes, "every soul among you that is seeking God will know that he has gone before you and sought you before you sought him."[321]

To live in the light of this vision means we may know we are not alone. We can also know God has an interest in us—surprising as that may seem. And furthermore, we can be sure this God is the One who is ahead of us.

This means we are not forging ahead into life hoping something or someone will be there for us. Rather, we forge ahead and act into life, sensing the pleasure and hearing the invitation of the God, who is there waiting for us and gently calling us forward.

Thought

Not life in a vacuum, but life through the welcome of God is the way to live.

John 17:26

November 18

Our Deeper Motives

In case we ever become too comfortable with our religiosity and piety, we just need to put the searchlight on our motivations. We will soon discover they are mixed and often less than godly.

Catherine of Genoa turns on the searchlight. She writes, "we end up doing our own will under many covers—of charity, of necessity, or of justice."[322]

This is very exposing. It is one thing to become aware of our wrong motivations in doing what is wrong. It is quite another matter to come to realize that in the doing of good we can be wrongly motivated, in that we are simply doing our own thing.

All of this suggests that the great good in Christian spirituality is not that we do good things, but that we live in attentiveness to God and to what God asks of us. In seeking to live this way, we are moving beyond humanity's primordial sin of disobedience and move instead into the realm of joyful listening and servanthood.

We know little about this way of life. We think we already know and so don't listen. We prefer to be independent and so we don't align ourselves with God. We prefer to act and consequently know little of the practices of contemplation.

But Catherine points us elsewhere. She believes that hearing, knowing, embracing, and doing the will of God is our greatest happiness and fruitfulness.

Prayer

O Lord, give me a heart that loves to do your will. Amen.

Romans 16:19

November 19

The Common Good

In holding things for ourselves and in being self-protective we think we enrich our lives. But, in fact, we only diminish ourselves. It is in sharing that we are also enriched.

In the outworking of our love of God and love of neighbor we are to enhance and contribute to the common good. The growth in the common good is an expression of God's love and concern for a common humanity. All are to stand under God's blessing—not just a special few.

But there is something counter-intuitive in building the common good. Since it asks us to give, we think we will suffer loss. But the surprise is that we will gain in our very giving.

St. Augustine understood this well. He writes that a person's "possession of goodness is in no way diminished by the arrival . . . of a sharer in it; indeed, goodness is a possession enjoyed more widely by the united affection of partners."[323]

Thus, the healing of the one leads that person to become a healing presence for others and as others are restored and made well so the initial person will be further enriched. This builds a community of goodness.

This Augustinian vision of the common good comes from a Trinitarian vision of our participation in the wonderful fellowship of the Father, the Son, and the Holy Spirit. The common good in the Trinity, as the ultimate good, is to have a gratuitous outworking in the common good we may all participate in.

Reflection

Build the common good in the family, at church, at work, and wherever you are. And live beyond a narrow tribalism.

Hosea 6:1

November 20

Self-Sufficient

The contemporary view of the human person is that we are both self-sufficient and self-made. We claim that we have no need of a God to sustain and guide us.

Our ancient Christian forebears had a very different view of what it meant to be human. They not only saw persons as created by God, but also as marked by God's persistent love.

Gregory the Great gives this understanding a further twist. He writes, "our hearts are healthy in a sick way, when we are not wounded in God's love."[324] He is thus expressing the strange notion that wholeness and well-being are premised on being wounded.

He is right. The first shaft of God's wounding love has to unsettle us regarding our indifference and rebellion in relation to God. A further shaft has to derail us regarding our attempts to pay God back for his goodness.

But further woundings are called for. The pride in our piety, the folly of bargaining, the illusion of having a special place before God, and all attempts to misuse God's goodness for wrong ends—all these need to be undermined.

God's wounding love de-centers us and opens the way for a new self shaped in the likeness of the Son of God, who as the wounded Man is the icon of the new humanity.

Thought

A complete person, distrust. A wounded person, follow.

Deuteronomy 34:10

November 21

What We Are Known For

The heroes of the modern world are our film stars and sports persons. Much further down the line are our politicians, scientists, and business persons. The saints who pray are not even on our radar screens.

Each society and culture values certain activities and virtues. In the ancient world the valor of the warrior was the pinnacle of human endeavor. But the ancient world also valued its saints and sages.

The latter are not even a blip on our present horizons. We place far greater honor on the doers and achievers of our time, than on those who pray. Adventurers are better known to us than monks. And in our churches things are hardly different. Activists will always trump the contemplatives.

St. Catherine of Siena, however, points us in a different direction. She writes, "a good man *is* a prayer."[325] In this simple statement she overcomes the dualism of the activist person and the contemplative. She suggests that the good person who is and does good—and such is the order—is a person who is an answer to prayer.

Thus, prayer is not simply about piety. Prayer is also about action. But again the order is important, action comes out of prayer.

Reflection

If Moses was known as the person who knew God face to face, what am I known for?

Psalm 42:11

November 22

Discouraged

The Christian journey is not sunshine highway. Rather, it is the rocky road of faith, hope, and love. There are watering holes along the way, but there are also desert places.

Thomas à Kempis in a word of encouragement for the discouraged begins with "and when consolation does leave you." In this he recognizes that we can lose a sense of God's presence; that we can become spiritually down-hearted; that we can become barren and empty; and that we can experience the dark night of the soul.

However, he does not see this as a disaster. Instead, he sees it as an important transition. Thomas goes on, "do not give up hope immediately, but with patient humility wait . . ." His call to wait is counter-intuitive. For when you are in a mess the sensible thing to do is to try to scramble out. Thomas, however, calls us to wait.

He goes on, "for God is able to give you a still greater consolation in its place."[326] Thus, the movement in the time of spiritual difficulty and darkness is not restoration but transformation.

The move from the experience of God in the light to the experience of God in the darkness moves us to a different place in our relationship with God. Surely, this brings us to a deeper place in the love of God.

Thought

Difficulties and discouragement are not simply problems. They are also opportunities.

Acts 9:1–4

November 23

The Divine-Human Dynamic

The human-to-human relationship places us in the sphere of social good. The divine-human relationship places us in the sphere of ultimacy.

In the stark relativism of our postmodern world, the reality of horizontal human relationships can only yield a vague sense of goodness and justice. And usually what this looks like is determined by the powerful and the culture-shapers of our time.

When horizontal relationships are shaped by the divine-human or by vertical and therefore transcendental dynamics, everything changes. For a relationship with the God of the biblical story brings us into a field of ethics where redemptive grace, restorative justice, generous forgiveness, and gracious servanthood become the determinants for daily living and working.

The desert father, Abbot Antony, touches on this. He is quoted as saying, "If we do good to our brother, we shall do good to God: but if we scandalize our brother, we sin against Christ."[327]

Thus, if you want to worship God, serve the one in need. And when you bless others you reflect the goodness of God. The vertical-spiritual and the horizontal-social dimensions of life are so deeply inter-twined that the one fully impacts the other.

Reflection

In serving the least, you are serving Christ, who came to bring good news to the poor.

2 Corinthians 5:10

November 24

A Final Judgment?

We are so wedded to the realities and shadows of our age that a final goodness or a final judgment means little to us. Clearly, we need to recover the grand narrative of the biblical story, which involves the themes of redemption and judgment.

In our post-Christendom world what is left of the God of the grand narrative is a benign Father Christmas. And the costly love of God in Christ has been reduced to a suburban, middle-class sense of neighborly niceness.

The bearers of the ancient wisdom were not lulled into this state of amnesia. St. Gregory of Nyssa does not mince his words. He writes, "He who has definitely pursued pleasure for this life and has not cured his misguided choice by repentance, makes the land of [the] good inaccessible to him hereafter."[328]

While this is no invitation to speculate what God may do at the final judgment, the message is clear enough: how we live now has consequences both in this life and in the life to come. Here is an invitation that goodness and mercy should not only follow us in this life, but also in the life to come.

The challenge in all of this is not fear of a final judgment, but finding grace to live in worship, repentance, and service.

Thought

The challenge of our time is to come out of the shadows of modernity into the gospel light of Christ.

Romans 10:4

November 25

The Law of Love

We cannot only live by law and structures. We also need to live out of spontaneity and friendship. The heartbeat of law in the biblical story is a framework for love.

A narrow fundamentalism and a strident legalism are often bedfellows. On the other hand, generous relativism and an ethical anorexia are frequent companions. But neither are options to live the biblical story well.

Better options are to live with grace in a framework of responsibility, goodness within structures of accountability, peacemaking in a world of violence, forgiveness in the midst of relational fracturing, and the river of love within the banks of God's law.

St. Augustine gets at the heart of all of this with the simple dictum: "every commandment [of Scripture] has love for its aim."[329] So not to steal is to love and respect what the other has and to be thankful for what one has received.

By not stealing one loves the inscrutable will of God who gives to all but not in equal measure. This calls us to a humility of heart. It invites us to rejoice with those who have much and to be generous with those who have little.

Reflection

Law gives us the direction. Love is the food and drink for all on the journey.

Colossians 3:9–10

November 26

The Imago Dei

While modern biological and neurological sciences emphasize the extent to which we are determined by the wiring and firing of our brains, the biblical vision of the human being is relational. We are made in the image and likeness of God and made for community.

Saint Columbanus, the Irish missionary, put it most simply: "It is a great honor that God bestowed on men and women the image of his eternity and likeness to his own character."[330]

This means that the focus is not on what distinguishes us from animals, nor is the focus on our sinfulness or our psycho-somatic unity of body, soul, and spirit. The focus is on our sense of the transcendent and our Christlikeness.

Thus, the human being is fundamentally eschatological and shaped by the virtues of the gospel. We are thus a small repetition of the new Adam, Christ, who is the head of a new humanity.

Neither Greek nor Jew, we are a Third Race. Not marked first and foremost by genetics, culture, and place, we are a people formed in Christ through the Spirit. And what is most significant about us is the way in which Christ has shaped our inner lives and our outward service.

Reflection

Christlikeness is not simply believing in Jesus. It is Christ taking gestalt in us.

Psalm 63:5–8

November 27

Reflection

Present-day communication technology allows us to be available and in touch around the clock. And our work-a-day world and urban realities have made us as busy and fragmented as we can possibly be. We need, in the light of Christ, to find space for reflection.

The unknown author of *The Epistle of Barnabas,* an early Christian writing, speaks of the value of a reflective praxis. He speaks of those "who know that meditation is a delight," and goes on to suggest that this meditation is to "chew the cud of the Lord's word."[331] This slowed-down way of thinking about Scripture is an important aid in experiencing God's presence and receiving nurture, encouragement, and direction.

But there is more to the reflective experience. The Word needs to be enlivened by the Spirit. The Word needs to be received in prayer. And the Word needs to intersect with the whole gamut of our lives in family, church, work, and society.

As a consequence, the reflective experience is both Word-directed, inner-directed, and outer-oriented. Put differently, we are to lift our hearts to God in worship and prayer. We are to turn our gaze to his Word. We are to ask the Spirit to guide and inspire us. And we are to reflect on our own inner world and on the state of the world.

Thought

No sphere of life is outside of the meditational practices.

1 John 3:18

November 28

Through Actions

*In our contemporary world of excessive words and promises
there is a crying need for the embodied word in concrete action.
We see this embodiment most clearly in the incarnation.*

Scholars have frequently called Christians the people of the Book, referring to the importance the Bible plays in shaping their religious practices and worldview. And the God of the biblical story has often been called the Word God.

But the God of the Hebrews and the God of our Lord Jesus Christ is not simply a Word God. This God is also the God of *action*—of healing, redemption, and transformation.

Just as the liberation events of the exodus lie at the heart of the Old Testament, so the action of God in Christ shapes the vision of the New Testament. Therefore, to be like God or like Christ involves following the God who acts.

St. Ignatius picks up this theme. He writes, "those who profess to be Christ's will be recognized by their actions."[332] And such actions are not to be arbitrary. They are to reflect the action of God in bringing deliverance, freedom, hope, wholeness, and renewal.

We are called not simply to follow the Word of God, but to also follow the Living Word, Jesus Christ. What Christ did becomes the pattern and shape of our engagement with the world.

Reflection

The Word must become a living word for us also. And this means a word that shapes our action and service.

1 Corinthians 2:2-5

November 29

Generativity

Generativity lies at the heart of what it means to be human. Generativity is not simply expressed in our sexuality, but in all we seek to do in maintaining and shaping our world. It also lies at the very core of our spirituality.

While there are people and forces at work in our world that seek to destroy, the overwhelming impulse of humanity is to create, to enhance, and to transform. This generativity is a common grace gift of God's providence.

In the spiritual realm generativity is a mostly fundamental dimension. St. Francis explores this. He writes, "we are spouses" when we are united to Christ through the Spirit. He goes on, we are "mothers when we carry Him in our heart and body" and "give Him birth through holy activity."[333]

Thus, Christ is not only birthed in us, but we birth Christ into the world through our Christlike activity. We are both Christ-bearers and Christ-birthers.

Of course, this needs to be qualified. We never *fully* bring Christ. Our service will always be a meager reflection of the glory of Christ. And the Christ we bring is always the Christ who is ahead of us. But, nevertheless, the great calling of the Christian is to make room for Christ in our lives, places of work, our churches, and in the wider society.

Reflection

In what ways are my actions a reflection of the Christ amongst us?

Isaiah 66:2

November 30

Christian Humility

Humility is not a favorite contemporary concept. It sounds too much like being a doormat and being subject to the misuse of others. But in Christian spirituality it has to do with being open and attentive to God and willing to do what God asks of us.

Make God indifferent or far removed or, worse, make God abusive or a tyrant and nearly all of Christian spirituality disintegrates. Such a God must be resisted not obeyed.

But embrace the God of the biblical story who enters the fray of history to redeem and bring shalom and you have a very different story. And follow that story through to the God who draws near to us in Christ and you swim in rivers of grace, healing, and freedom.

To such we can and must respond. And here humility plays a key role, for humility has to do with the listening heart and the willing spirit. Or as St. Edmund Rich points out, "there are two kinds of humility. One comes from truth, the other from love."[334]

What this means is that humility is a response to God's Word and to God's Spirit. It is a response of the mind and will and of the heart and spirit.

As such, Christian humility is nothing more or less than a willingness to respond to the God who loves us and calls us into his purposes.

Thought

Humility is a gift, a grace, and a way of life.

ST JOHN CHRYSOSTOM

Luke 1:38

December 1

Mary: Woman of Great Obedience

Mary's surrender to the mysterious purposes of God in the incarnation is a sign of a way of life we must all walk. We too need to live in faith and surrender to God's way with us.

Hildegard of Bingen, in a song to Mary, wrote these words: "He formed the Word [Jesus] in you as a human being; And therefore you are the jewel that shines most brightly."[335]

In these and in many other ways the church throughout the ages has lauded Mary the Mother of Jesus. And rightly so, since this humble peasant girl demonstrated a fully-orbed faithful response to a surprising message that could only bring her disrepute and grief.

As such, Mary is the icon of faith; she surrendered to the mystery of God that she could not possibly have fully apprehended. And her word, "be it unto me according your word," becomes the enduring symbol for all women and men of faith who trust God even in the midst of darkness.

Thus, we too would like to be like Mary, open and available to God. And, like her, receptive to God's will, way, and word to us, even when that word seems to be unlikely and even impossible. And finally, we would like to be like her in enduring reproach and suffering in the long walk of obedience.

Prayer

Lord, may I in some small way reflect the faith of Mary as I seek to respond to your call and way. Amen.

Psalm 51:3, 6

December 2

Conflicted

Whether I like it or not, I have to live my life between the longing for paradise and the reality of my daily stupidities, between acts of courage and foolish compromises, and between soaring faith and sinking doubt.

St. Anselm knew a lot about the conflicted nature of the human being. He writes, "If I look within myself, I cannot bear myself; if I do not look within myself, I do not know myself."[336] Thus, even though I wish there was a way around both these options, there is not. I have to face myself and plumb and embrace the depths of being.

The gift of faith, therefore, does not take me away from who I am. It is not escapist. Instead, the gift of faith allows me to see myself in the love of God, not only in the mirror of my own failure and despair.

But having seen myself in the love of God, I then find a place from which to face my own failure, wrongdoing, and sin. Thus, while faith draws me to God, it also brings me back to myself.

To see myself in the love of God allows me to face my inner contradictions and doubts and face the temptations that come my way. Face them. Don't ignore them. Nor deny them.

Thus, I live my life in the knowledge of what I am and in the hope of what I will yet become in the grace of Christ.

Reflection

It is *through* conflict that our life is forged.

Acts 2:44

December 3

All Things in Common

There have always been Christians who thought that a bit more of heaven could come on earth. One expression of this hope was for a community that held all things in common.

St. Augustine, as a North African bishop, was a cleric at the heart of the church. But he was also a person with a keen eye regarding major developments in society, and a Christian who experimented with alternative forms of living the Christian life.

Thus, he spoke about his participation in a band of friends who lived in "common households" and who had "one purse and the whole was to belong to each and all."[337] St. Augustine thus lived the Christian communitarian ideal, drawing this from a Trinitarian theology rather than only from the experience of the Jerusalem church.

This vision of institutional church *and* intentional Christian community opens up a rich, complementary way of being the people of God. The one is able to support the other in a richness and diversity of life, reflecting something of God's manifold goodness.

While the institutional church has been the dominant reality in history, intentional community in its various forms has remained an ongoing dream, even today. So despite our present-day emphasis on individualism, privacy, and self-sufficiency, we could let St. Augustine challenge us.

A common life is not simply one of difficulty and problems, it is also a life of support and growth pointing to God's final future.

Reflection

Formation can only occur well in community.

Psalm 103:3

December 4

God's Healing Presence

There are many avenues for healing and there are various forms of unwellness. God's healing presence can make us whole from our spiritual estrangement.

The unknown author of *The Book of Privy Counseling* uses a basic analogy to speak of God's healing activity: "Take the good gracious God just as he is, as plain as a common poultice, and lay him to your sick self, just as you are."[338]

There are several remarkable themes in this barest of statements. The first is that one does not need to do something special to gain God's healing blessing. There is no list of preconditions.

The second is that God does not need to do something special to be a healing presence. This is the way God is. God is the gracious and generous healer.

Third, take this God as you would medicine. Or in other words, bandage yourself with this God. This has to do with embrace. Take this God fully to yourself.

And finally, God's healing presence is not simply for a particular illness only, but for one's sick self. Thus, the illness can be spiritual, physical, emotional, relational, psychological.

Clearly, in the churches of the twenty-first century, and particularly in the West where so much of God's action seems to be lost amongst us, we need to recover a vision of this healing God.

Thought

Become a prayer for this, so that recovery in your family, church, and workplace may take place.

John 6:27

December 5

The Bread of Life

In the long history of Christendom we were made to think of Christ as second in command to the Emperor God. But Christ has been worshipped, not only in his power, but also in his humiliation.

There are Christians even today who want to maintain only regal language in relation to Christ. They want to see him as symbolizing a form of power that is the opposite of our puny existence. And, of course, they are right. The Bible *does* use that kind of language.

But there is also other language in the biblical story and there are other forms of power. The power of servanthood is one such other form of power.

St. Patrick understood this. He writes, "The Lord of the universe . . . so humbles Himself that for our salvation He hides himself under the little form of bread."[339] Indeed. Such humility. But such power. The power to sustain and enliven the whole people of God in every place and age.

And this can point the way for us who in Christ's name seek to be food and drink for others. While we may want to take the royal road to serve others, the way of humility, the little way, may well accomplish more.

The hidden life with God in the service of others may well be the only road we can walk without becoming seduced by our own seeming goodness.

Thought

Let us embrace the little way so that much good may flourish.

Deuteronomy 8:3

December 6

Knowledge of the Word

As moderns we tend to place ourselves above the Word in order to extract from it our theologies and religious practices. We need to learn to read the Bible differently.

One of the most basic ways of reading Scripture differently is to do so with reverence for God and desire to hear God's voice. In this way, Scripture is not simply some ancient religious book, but God's living voice to us today.

The Word is thus a living word and with an expectant anticipation we long for encounter: the Word speaking directly into our lives. As such, Scripture is relevant and it is formative for the shape and fabric of our lives.

John Cassian has something to say regarding receptive listening to Scripture. He writes, "If you wish to achieve true knowledge of Scripture you must hurry to achieve an unshakable humility of heart."[340] He is thus suggesting that receptivity must come from humility.

He is right, because our attitude to Scripture is often problematic and ambivalent. We are distracted listeners to Scripture. We seldom listen in faith. We doubt more than we believe.

True humility is respectful and attentive. It rightly sees who God is and who we are. It recognizes that a willing spirit and an obedient heart places us in a right relationship to God and his Word.

Thought

We don't live by the Word, but by the Living Word of the Living God.

James 2:22

December 7

Faith and Deeds

The desert father Macarius once wrote, "the soul that really loves God and Christ, though it may do ten thousand righteous deeds, esteems itself as having done nothing."[341]

The God of the Bible is the God of the Word. But God is also the God of the deed, for the Word that comes from God is a Word that is generative and productive. It is a performative Word. It *does* what it *says*.

The clearest Word of God is the Living Word, Jesus Christ, and he was the Word that accomplished the will of the Father. The Living Word brought healing, forgiveness, and new life into being.

This Living Word, Jesus Christ, is the Word that shapes us, reorients us, penetrates us, and makes us whole. Thus, in a very small way we become such a Word.

In becoming such a Word, we are not mere words. We are also deeds. Through the Spirit the love and deeds of Jesus are replicated in us. Thus, like Jesus, we too seek to be a healing and forgiving presence in our world.

This calls us to remain close to Jesus. We are to follow him. We are to be like him. And it is for his sake and in his name that we do similar deeds of love.

There is no other way to live the Christian life. It is not just about words or just about deeds. It is always about both. Thus, we are to be a small, trembling repetition of the Living Word that is life-giving for others.

Thought

The greatest word and deed is to be like Jesus.

Galatians 6:17

December 8

Stigmata

Throughout the history of Christianity, there have been some women and men who have borne the marks of Christ's suffering on their body. But we are all marked by Christ in some way.

Philip of Clairvaux, speaking of the medieval mystic Elizabeth of Spaalbeek, notes: "And they saw, and showed to other people who were there, puncture-marks of thorns round the virgin's head like a garland."[342]

It is not surprising that this should happen given Elizabeth's profound devotion to Christ. She was so spiritually united to Christ that she experienced the stigmata.

What is significant is not the stigmata, but our identification with Christ. Christ is not only someone we believe in and whose life inspires us, Christ also lives in us through the Spirit. Christ-conformity is, therefore, the heartbeat of the Christian life.

This means we carry the concerns of Christ, concerns for the reign of God, concerns for the church and its unity, mission, and renewal, concerns for the world, and concerns for family and friends. Sometimes these concerns can impact us so deeply that we may suffer spiritually and even physically.

While our concerns always call for practical engagement, a life of prayer is key to carrying the concerns of Christ.

Prayer

Lord, lead me more deeply in your concerns for our world. Amen.

Colossians 1:15–16

December 9

Creator and Savior

There have always been those who have wanted to relegate Jesus to the sidelines of life. They see him as an idealistic Galilean peasant. But in the biblical witness Christ is the Lord of history.

There are many other ways in which Jesus has been sidelined. This has happened even in the life of the church. Sometimes his divinity has been emphasized to the cost of his humanity. Sometimes his exemplary life has been emphasized to the cost of his salvific activity.

John Scottus Eriugena, however, has rightly emphasized Jesus as Savior and Creator. He writes, the Word cried out invisibly to create the world, but "cried out visibly when he came into the world in order to save it."[343]

Christ's creative activity is hidden in the mystery of faith. Christ's work of salvation was for all to see and hear. But this too had to be embraced in faith.

The importance of this double confession of Jesus as Creator and Savior lies in the fact that Jesus cannot be relegated only to the spiritual sphere. He is the Savior of the *whole* of creation. Therefore, all of creation is the sphere for Jesus' redeeming, restoring, and healing activity. The spiritual, the social, the political, the economic, and the ecological dimensions of life all need rectification, renewal, and healing. Thus, this remarkable Galilean is at the center of all of life.

Reflection

Jesus as my Savior is also the Jesus who stands at the center of every sphere of life.

John 3:17

December 10

Missional Fervor

The missional fervor of the people of God has flared up and dimmed throughout church history. In our time, particularly in the West, it urgently needs to be recovered.

It is easy for Christians to lose the excitement of their faith and become complacent. As a consequence, their love for the church becomes frayed and their passion to be witnesses for Christ is undermined.

St. Catherine of Siena is a clear exception to this scenario. She writes, with all my might I wish to draw souls "from the hands of demons." She goes on, "I would give my life for this; if I had a thousand lives."[344]

The bearers of the ancient wisdom were not only mystics, prophets, and contemplatives. They were also theologians and servants in the church. And they were also the evangelists of their time.

Mission must come from the passion of God within us. It comes from a longing for the reign of God to penetrate our world more fully. It comes from a desire to see others blessed and made whole.

This passion calls for sacrifice. It is having other people's needs in view rather than our own wants. It involves contact, availability, friendship, and service. It calls for the practice of hospitality. And it involves a life of prayer.

This fervor is nothing other than following the Great Missionary, Jesus Christ, into the world.

Prayer

Lord, set our hearts aflame once again for the needs of our world. Amen.

2 Timothy 3:16–17

December 11

The Whole People of God

One can easily gain the impression that the church is made up of clergy and laity are secondary citizens in the ecclesiastical empire. But fundamentally, we are all and only the people of God.

The church as the people of God is the mystical body of Christ. But it is this in faith and humility, not in grandeur and power. But the church is also an institutional reality. It thus has its structures, ethos, traditions, leadership, and ideologies.

It is particularly important that the structures of the church do not become self-serving, but that they serve the people in their involvement in the world.

St. John Chrysostom had this vision. He writes, as lay people "you stand continuously in the front rank, and you receive continual blows. So you need more remedies."[345] This means the maintenance of the church and its structures can never be the only focus. The nurture, encouragement, and empowerment of the people of God must be in focus. Since the laity primarily live their lives as the people of God in the world, they are most subject to temptations and therefore need special attention and care. Generally, the church fails miserably at this point. But Chrysostom is right. Therefore, more attention needs to be given to the church as the scattered people of God during the week and not only as the Sunday-gathered people of God.

Reflection

As the scattered people of God greater attention needs to be given to the supply of the necessary bread for the journey of the faith and service.

Philippians 2:12–13

December 12

Core Motivations

The idea that as long as you do good it matters little what motivates you is a misguided notion. The spring and the bubbling brook are one and the same. So are kind deeds that come from a loving heart.

St. Benedict, who profoundly shaped Western monasticism, was the father of goodness and fairness. But above all he was singularly Christo-centric and the champion of love. Do things, he wrote, "out of love for Christ." "This," he continued, "the Lord will by the Holy Spirit graciously manifest in his workmen now cleansed of vices."[346]

This central figure in Christianity, while designating love for Christ as the central motivation for our goodness, sees this motivation not as human effort but as divine gift. This is a blessing of the Spirit.

This is a most hopeful vision. Living the Christian life and doing God's good is not a human achievement as much as it is a source of inspiration unleashed within us. The grace of God is not simply to bring us *to* God in faith and repentance. It is also the power that helps us live *for* God and the neighbor.

Doing deeds of love is thus a God-inspired activity. This is the Spirit working in and through us, sowing the seeds of goodness that will flourish in their own time.

Reflection

The deepest wells within our being are wells watered by the Spirit.

1 Corinthians 2:7–8

December 13

Confronting the Powers

Powers and structures are good. But they can also become perverted. When the powers, systems, and ideologies go astray they need to be exposed and resisted.

Unfortunately, in much of the history of Christianity, the church has tended to support the political powers of the day, even when those powers were corrupted. As a consequence, instead of being a liberating force in history, the church was a complicitly oppressive institution. The Constantianization of the church aided this development.

But at the same time, there have always been powerful counter examples to this general scenario. Christians have stood up against injustice and have been willing to suffer the consequences.

One such valiant figure was St. Ambrose. He publicly rebuked the Emperor Theodosius for authorizing a massacre at Thessalonica. He had this to say, "Please listen, Your Majesty. That you have a zealous faith, I cannot deny. I am sure that you fear God. But you have a naturally hot temper."[347]

Those in power—whether that be political, economic, ideological, or ecclesiastical—must exercise their power within a framework of justice and the common good. But since the use of power is so often misused, Christians must raise their voices.

To resist the powers that are out of control is part of the Christian's calling. Since the God of the Bible is the God of justice, we too must do the work of justice.

Reflection

To challenge those in power is not an act of bravado, but one of prophetic humility.

1 John 1:9

December 14

Be Kind to Yourself

A Christian conscience must not only respond to law but also to grace. Some Christians are far too hard on themselves. They are forever repenting but know little of the generosity of God, the grace of Christ, and the freedom of the Spirit.

There are extremes that also play themselves out in the lives of Christians. One can abuse freedom and grace. One can also be too legalistic. One can neglect one's conscience. One can also have a conscience that is far too overly sensitive.

Walter Hilton, the English Christian mystic, addresses the latter problems and speaks to those who are always rummaging around in the inner cellars of their guilt. He writes, too much remorse of conscience can "weary you and distract you." This advice is plain enough. But he goes on. Ask for forgiveness, he writes, and "then leave off and spend no longer with it."[348]

This is good advice. It reflects the wideness of God's mercy. But for some to come to this good place may be more difficult than for others. Certain personalities are more perfectionist and legalistic. Such persons will need to undergo a deep transformation to come to this place of grace and freedom.

But come to it we must. It is a great tragedy to live the Christian life by re-imaging God into our unhealthy and perfectionistic tendencies. Rather, the kindness of God should pervade us. Only in this way of life is joy a possibility.

Reflection

The heartbeat of the Christian life is the joy of being forgiven.

Psalm 8:3–8

December 15

The Human Being

There are many ways in which we can understand ourselves.
All of these have ample consequences in the way we live, see
others, work, and engage our world.

Is the human being merely the product of naturalistic evolution? Is the human being simply a psychologically predetermined creature? Is the human being only a brain mechanism entity? Is the human being basically the product of one's socialization?

One could go on. There are many other options and perspectives. Who we are continues to be the subject of speculation, reflection, and research.

The medieval mystic Hildegard of Bingen has a profoundly religious perspective on the human person. She writes, "Happy soul, beautiful creature of God, you are formed in the profound depths of the wisdom of God."[349]

This view grounds the human being, not in impersonal biological forces or mere social formation, but in the wisdom and pleasure of the Creator God. This view locates us in a profound and bounteous personalism.

The idea that we have been made in love and joy places us in the sphere of well-being and shapes us for living in this way in relation to God and to others.

This view holds that we are made for joy, and as a product of God's wisdom our lives take on purpose and meaning that seeks to replicate the goodness of God in our relationships and world.

Reflection

Shaped by the love of God is much more hopeful than being the product of impersonal forces.

Matthew 5:17–18

December 16

Law and Grace

The concepts of law and grace have long plagued Christianity. The one is usually played off against the other, whereas the two should be dynamically related.

William of St. Thierry does not really help us on this matter. He overplays the distinction between law and grace. He writes, "The person who had not formerly been able to bear the precepts of the law, afterwards finds the precepts of the gospel light by reason of cooperating grace."[350]

While this sounds good in that it celebrates the power of the gospel, it is not that helpful. Law is not without grace and the gospel is not without law.

The First (Old) Testament is primarily the story of the God who liberates and heals. Its laws provide a framework for righteous living as the people of God. Thus, its story is fundamentally all about grace.

The Second (New) Testament is the story of the God who in Christ liberates and heals. Its emphasis on reconciliation and forgiveness functions within the framework of Christlikeness and godly living.

Thus, in both testaments law and grace play their part. Grace provides the freedom; law gives shape to our responsibility. Therefore, grace is the precondition and the empowering reality. Law is the execution, the outworking of a life marked by the generosity of God in Christ.

Reflection

Those who are free in Christ can live the responsibility God gives.

Ephesians 4:21–23

December 17

Being Undone

The human propensity is towards strengthening and consolidating what we are and what we have. Thus, we are inherently self-protective. But we need to be undone.

What we basically want to do is to reinforce who we are and what we have. This idea is strongly promoted in our contemporary world where we see ourselves as self-made. And we do this through self-enhancement, whether done physically, emotionally, educationally, vocationally, or spiritually.

But reinforcement is not the whole story. We also need to be renewed and re-created. And in order to be re-created we need to be undone. Our protective shell needs to be cracked. Our social masks need to be dropped. Our false self needs to be faced.

There is much that can undo us: tragedy, loss, turmoil, illness, and aging. But we have to be willing to learn the brutal lessons of such experiences. We can all too easily close the openings these circumstances have created for us.

One key way to learn is to turn from self-defense, self-pity, or bitterness to vulnerability. And in this stage of openness we may be able to see God's wounding hand in our lives.

The early church father Origen knows something of this. He writes, "I have been wounded by charity [love]."[351] To see God's re-creative activity in our difficulties opens up the possibility of being remade in love.

Reflection

To be remade in the love of God is to become the true self.

2 Corinthians 8:9–14

December 18

Sharing

We have not understood who God is unless we have understood God's great generosity. One of God's great gifts is the salvation Christ brings. And we have not fully become who we are meant to be unless generosity characterizes us.

The second-century church father Justin Martyr speaks of the changes Christ brought about in the believers of his time. He writes, "We who once took pleasure in the means of increasing our wealth and property, now bring what we have into a common fund and share with everyone in need."[352]

This is a significant indication that Christ's renewing work in us is not meant to be internal only. Christ's redemptive work is to penetrate and affect all areas of life, including the financial dimensions.

And since it is natural for us to be self-focused and to long for security, it is understandable that we want to increase our economic condition. But this should not become our primary preoccupation. Rather, we should work in order to benefit and bless others as well.

While there are many ways in which to express our generosity, some will be called to live the generosity Justin Martyr writes about. But if God is radically generous, we who seek to be like God, can hardly be different.

Thought

In generosity and service we reflect something of the image of God.

Matthew 27:15–19

December 19

God's Revelation

While the God of the biblical story is shrouded in the greatest mystery, God is also the great Revealer. God wants us to know his inexhaustible love and goodness.

Maximus the Confessor highlights God's revelation as the way in which we can see God's concern for us and the whole created order. He writes, "We do not know God from his being but from his magnificent works and his providence for beings. Through these as through mirrors we can perceive his infinite goodness and wisdom and power."[353]

We can add to this and point out that in a myriad of ways God upholds all things and works through all things in the unfolding of his goodness. But we need to see and embrace this in faith and trust.

It is, therefore, appropriate to ask: whence comes this ability to see? The answer is simple enough: it comes as a *gift*. And this gift usually comes in unexpected ways. It can come through beauty or tragedy.

Normally, we see through the lenses of rationality and the dominant values of our culture. But to see differently requires a radical disconnect. And to see in faith the gracious workings of God in human affairs requires a new set of eyes through a new inner disposition.

This can only come through some encounter with the living God, through a dream, stirrings in the depths of our being, in seeing the signs of goodness, in hearing God's Word, and being enlightened by his Spirit.

Prayer

O Lord, grant me a new way of seeing and hearing. Amen.

Mark 10:43–45

December 20

Stripped Bare

What are we? We are what we have achieved and what we possess. Thus status defines us. But what are we really? What are we when all these things are taken away?

St. Francis was the son of a rich cloth merchant. He was a young man of status and wealth. In his encounter with Christ he gave all this away. He was stripped bare.

Later St. Francis was to write, "What a person is before God, that he is and no more."[354] This profound insight calls us to a deeper reflection.

What we are before ourselves is hardly reliable. We either elevate or denigrate ourselves. And we lack self-insight. And we are often far more moved by hereditary and unconscious factors.

What we are before others has to do with our social self. This is the self based on our achievements. This is the self of human significance.

But before God, all is different. This God knows us better than we know ourselves and surprisingly loves and embraces us. Thus, what are we then before God? We are stripped bare of our false self. And we are the true self remade in the grace of Christ.

What we are and what we are to become is this new self in the love of God and the grace of Christ. In this we need to grow. This is our true destiny.

Reflection

Naked before God and not ashamed through the grace of Christ.

Luke 15:21–23

December 21

The Welcoming God

There are no limits to God's generosity when we come seeking forgiveness. And since our need for forgiveness is part of daily life, our experience of God's grace becomes a daily blessing.

Julian of Norwich knows a lot about God's generosity. She writes, God "is quick to receive us" when we come in repentance and confession. She goes on, "for we are his delight and joy, and he our salvation and our life."[355]

Daily confession does not need to come from a somber view of God. It also does not need to come from a dark view of ourselves. It may simply arise from the fact that we desire to be more fully conformed to the way of Christ.

There are also other reasons. One of the most basic is our desire to be better. We wish we could do much better in our relationships and become more thoughtful, more caring, more attentive, and more generous.

We also wish we could do more about the craziness and wounding of our world. There is so much good we could do, but we often do so little. And we feel bad about this.

Thus, our need to come to God in confession is about wrongs done and our failure to do good. This does not mean that life becomes onerous and introspective. It means, instead, that we can live in the joy of the God of bounteous grace.

Reflection

God welcomes us in our need, not in our self-sufficiency.

Psalm 8:6–8

December 22

The Human Being as Worker

We are dreamers. We are curious. We are hopeful. But we are also initiators, planners, workers. Part of our God-given task is to shape our world through human activity.

Gerard Groote—the founder of the Brethren of the Common Life, which focused on shaping the spirituality of laymen and women—wrote these simple words, "labor is necessary for the well-being of mankind."[356]

This basic statement is multi-layered. Work is good for our personal development. Even the most menial of tasks can teach us care and responsibility. But more challenging tasks can shape and mold our very being.

But work is not only for our personal development. It is also for maintaining our life and those for whom we have responsibility. Work puts food on the table.

By way of further extension, work also enables us to share with others in need. Work may leave me with excess. And some of that can be given to others who are less fortunate.

Of equal importance is the joy and responsibility that through our creative activity we can maintain and shape our social order. Through work we contribute to the common good.

Finally, work should never be seen simply in terms of economic outcomes. There is more to work than our pay. Work contributes to the social good, but also to our spiritual development. Our work is to be done to the glory of God.

Reflection

Work is a privilege and a responsibility. It builds character as well as the human community.

Galatians 5:22–25

December 23

The Holy Spirit

Third Person of the Trinity. Revealer of Christ. Life force. Renewer of the church. Source of inspiration. Giver of spiritual gifts. There is so much the Spirit is and does.

St. Bernard points us in the right direction regarding the presence and power of the Spirit. He notes, "The doctrine of the Spirit does not whet (kindle) curiosity, it enkindles Charity."[357]

That there is a lot of curiosity about the Spirit is evident in the history of the Christian church. Radical, ecstatic, and renewal movements have all claimed the inspiration of the Spirit. So have heretical groups. And so has the institutional church with its claims that it alone possesses the truth of the Spirit.

St. Bernard, however, suggests one key way in understanding that we are dealing with the Spirit is to discern the fruit the Spirit births. Love is one such fruit. There are many others.

This means we must move from speculation to fruitfulness. The way of the Spirit is not to engender conjectures but facilitate a way of life.

This way of life rooted in Christ and in community means living in a spirit of forgiveness, mutual care, generosity, peace, and service. Since it is the Spirit who brings people together and breaks down barriers, one of the fruits of the Spirit is community building.

In a divided Christendom this fruit of the Spirit should be urgently sought for.

Prayer

Come Creator Spirit, and renew the face of the church and of our world. Amen.

Philippians 2:9–11

December 24

God Source of All

Everything is not God. And God is not everything. But God not only upholds all things, and all good things come from God, but God is the very ground of all that exists.

The German mystic Meister Eckhart is adamant that God is the very ground of all being. He writes, "from God and God alone do all things have their being, one being, true being, good being."[358]

While one needs to be careful with this kind of language because it can blur the distinctions between the Creator and creation, the truth here is God can't be put away to one side or in a spiritual box. And life can't be divided up between sacred and secular.

There are five important reasons why this divide can't be maintained. First, God is the Creator of all things. Second, all humans are made in God's image. Third, all of humanity and the created order find their recovery in the redemption of Christ. Fourth, in Christ all things are held together. And finally, in God's final future heaven and earth are fully reconciled.

In this Advent season as we contemplate the coming of Christ in such humble form, it is important to remember how Jesus as the Servant of God and Son of God has been so highly exalted.

The whole world has thus been marked by the death and resurrection of Christ. All things, therefore, have been Christened.

Thought

To live in and for God in Christ is our true destiny.

Matthew 1:21

December 25

Incarnation

In this Christmas season we celebrate the mystery and bless-edness of the incarnation. Christ comes amongst us in total identification, revealing the Father, the way of the kingdom, and opening the way for the salvation and healing of all humanity.

St. Anselm cuts through all the Christmas glitter and gets to the heart of the Christmas story. He writes, "Jesus, good Lord, why did you come down from heaven [and] what did you do in the world . . . unless it was that you might save sinners."[359]

The babe is the Savior. The child is the Son of God. Joseph's carpenter son is the Lord of history. In this curious way the mystery of God's purpose for humanity is laid bare.

The Christmas season, therefore, is the time for rejoicing. It's a time of the miracle of God's presence with us. It is God's new way in the world.

This new way is not working from the outside in, but from the inside out. God does not merely come to humans, God *becomes* a human. God's way is not from above, but from below. As one of us, Christ becomes the new Adam of the new humanity healed by God's renewing presence.

In the modern world with the commercial captivity of Christmas, Christ again must be found. And we, like the shepherds of the Christmas story, must seek, find, and worship the babe who is the King.

Prayer

Lord, may I once again this Christmas prepare a place for you in my heart and life. Amen.

Matthew 6:13

December 26

Engaging the Powers

Our ancient Christian forebears not only had a profound sense of the reality of God, but also of the evil one who continues to bring chaos instead of shalom into our world.

After a period of catechesis (instruction), Christians in the ancient world underwent an elaborate initiation ceremony that included confession of faith, water baptism, prayer for Spirit baptism, anointing with oil for healing, and the casting out and rejection of the power of the evil one. These Christians had a deep sense that this spiritual enemy had to be overcome.

St. John Climacus was one such voice regarding the spiritual battle. He writes, "Strike your adversary with the name of Jesus; there is no more powerful weapon on the earth or in heaven."[360]

This does not mean one can use this name as a talisman or a magic formula. But it does mean that when one seeks to live in Christ one can pray that Christ's victory over all evil powers will be made manifest in our lives and in our world.

At the heart of Christian spirituality lies a joyful relationship with God and a strident rejection of the works of the evil one. This vision lies at the heart of the Lord's prayer and was the vision of our ancient forebears who longed to see the victory of Christ in all areas of life.

Prayer

In your name, O Lord, there is hope, healing, and rescue. Amen.

Colossians 3:5, 12

December 27

Dealing with Infection

We are not neutral. We are affected and infected with both the goodness of God and the reality of evil in our lives and world.

The first move in Christian spirituality is not growth into Christlikeness or union with God. It is rescue. It is healing. It is being set free.

St. Cyprian had this vision of rescue, of redemption. He writes, "Let the mind which the malice of the serpent had infected be purged; let all bitterness which had settled within be softened by the sweetness of Christ."[361]

It is not only bitterness that can be sown into our hearts. It may also be arrogance or lust or greed. And these things may become deeply imbedded within us. They may even have a stranglehold on our lives.

St. Cyprian suggests these things cannot just be ripped out of our lives. Rather, they need to be purged through a cleansing process. And this cleansing comes from the renewing and healing love of Christ.

That this does not occur in an instant should be rather obvious. This is a process of renewal. It is letting go of and unlearning the old, and embracing a new way of being and acting.

Thus, the heartbeat of the Christian life is the struggle towards a new life through the love of Christ.

Thought

The struggle towards goodness and light is the hope of this world.

Philippians 3:12–14

December 28

A Long Way to Go

While our ancient forebears often used the language of climbing up the ladder to be ever closer to God, they did not believe that in this life they would ever make it to the top.

St. Catherine of Genoa not only did not believe she could make it to the top, she actually believed the opposite. She writes, "From time to time I feel that I am growing only to see that I still have a long way to go."[362]

This is almost the consistent testimony of the saints we have encountered in this meditational reader. And it is the testimony of much of Christian biography throughout the ages.

The more outstanding women and men of God grew in sanctity, virtue, and service, the more they felt that they still needed to grow in the love of God. They felt that while they were in the kingdom of God, they were still far from home.

And so it is. In the various phases of our Christian journey we soon begin to recognize that it is not only our blatant sins that grieve the heart of God and hurt us and others. What we fail to do also causes grief. And the good that we do from impure motives saddens us as we see that further growth still beckons us.

But even though we have a long way to go, we can rejoice that the God of all grace continues to be our faithful companion.

Reflection

In the life of faith, the journey is the destination.

Psalm 85:8-9

December 29

The Inner Voice

While at times your best inner voice may be the voice of reason or the voice of conscience, more often the best voice is the one shaped by the gospel and empowered by the Spirit.

There are many voices within us. No wonder we are often troubled and confused. And it is hard for us to still ourselves enough to listen to the voice we most need to hear.

While we may fear that this voice will be the voice of correction— some even think it may be one of condemnation—this voice more frequently will be the voice of embrace and renewal.

St. Bernard of Clairvaux had this sense. He writes, "lift up the ears of your heart to hear this inner voice. . . . [It] is the voice of magnificence and power, rolling through the desert, revealing secrets, shaking souls free."[363]

This is the voice of the Beloved. This is the voice of the God who will not abandon us. This voice penetrates our darkness, difficulties, and barren places. This is the voice that exposes blockages. It is a voice that strips us bare. But in our nakedness, this voice heals us. It points the way for us. This voice caresses us into wellness.

Clearly, this is not our own muddled inner voice. It is not many voices. It is the one clear voice of the life-giving Spirit.

Reflection

Be still. Dare to listen. Hear the inner voice. Be not afraid. Let this voice carry you forward.

Daniel 3:24-25

December 30

God Can Make a Way

Life is refractory and it can throw up many unexpected difficulties. But we also create our own problems.

One of the Christian medieval mystics, Gertrude the Great, knew of life's general challenges and difficulties. But she also knew we can be our own worst enemy.

She writes, "Your overabundance of mercy has led me through many obstacles I have placed in the way of your love."[364]

This is a rare and moving confession. We are quick to blame others. We are slow at self-insight. Sadly, we can make a rod for our own back. And we can block the goodness God seeks to shower upon us.

But Gertrude's confession is at heart a celebration of the Hound of Heaven, of God's persistent love. This God does not pout. This God does not leave us marooned in our own stupidities. This God makes a way for us—a way of escape.

The obstacles, whatever they may be, are not taken away. We have put them there. But these need not have the final word. God can lead us *through* these difficulties.

Thus love finds a way. And we are humbled. We are chastened. We are surprised. And we are thankful, for we are saved *from* ourselves.

Reflection

See God in the midst of your difficulties.

Revelation 21:1–4

December 31

Beyond All Our Imaginings

Whenever we come to an end of something, including life itself, we are not left with understanding but only with wonder.

Things do not really come to a conclusion. Therefore, nothing can be nicely squared away. Nothing can come to final rest, for when we think all is done there are new beginnings.

So it is with all of our projects. They are never complete. They always invite renewal and reconfiguration.

And so it is with our life cycle. There are phases, but each leads to a new beginning. A life of hard work does not end. It merely invites us to live more reflectively and prayerfully.

And life itself is but a new beginning. This is the overwhelming testimony of our ancient forebears.

St. Ephraem of Syrus had this to say, "Do not let your intellect be disturbed by mere names, for Paradise has simply clothed itself in terms that are akin to you."[365]

The reality of what the new looks like is far beyond us. We can only imagine what God will yet do. We can only imagine what a whole new existence would be like.

And so we live in the hope of God's final future with new heavens and a new earth full of righteousness and the glory of God.

Reflection

Dare to imagine!

ENDNOTES

January

1. A. C. Outler (editor), *The Confessions of St. Augustine*. Mineola, NY: Dover, 2002, 89.

2. B. Ward (translator), *The Prayers and Meditations of Saint Anselm with the Proslogion*. Penguin Classics. London: Penguin, 1973, 94.

3. Quoted in B. Holt, *Thirsty for God: A Brief History of Christian Spirituality*. Minneapolis: Augsburg, 1993, 31.

4. R. B. Blakney (translator), *Meister Eckhart: A Modern Translation*. New York: Harper & Row, 1941, 34.

5. Thomas à Kempis, *The Imitation of Christ: In Four Books*. Vintage Spiritual Classics. Translated by J. N. Tylenda. New York: Vintage, 1998, 103.

6. Quoted in A. Hyma, *The Brethren of the Common Life*. Grand Rapids: Eerdmans, 1950, 29.

7. Outler (editor), *The Confessions of St. Augustine*, 88.

8. "The Epistles of Cyprian." In *The Ante-Nicene Fathers*, Vol. V, edited by A. Roberts and J. Donaldson. Edinburgh: T. & T. Clark, 1995, 287.

9. Ward (translator), *The Prayers and Meditations of Saint Anselm with the Proslogion*, 212.

10. "Clement's First Letter." In *Early Christian Fathers*, Vol. I, edited by C. C. Richardson. The Library of Christian Classics. Philadelphia: Westminster, 1953, 54.

11. Thomas à Kempis, *The Imitation of Christ*, 36.

12. Quoted in Evdokimov, *Ages of the Spiritual Life*. Crestwood, NY: St. Vladimir's Seminary Press, 1998, 137.

13. Quoted in L. S. Cunningham and K. J. Egan, *Christian Spirituality: Themes from the Tradition*. New York: Paulist, 1996, 171–72.

14. Outler (editor), *The Confessions of St. Augustine*, 172.

15. "Letters of Ignatius: Ephesians." In *Early Christian Fathers*, Vol. I, edited by C. C. Richardson. The Library of Christian Classics. Philadelphia: Westminster, 1953, 88.

16. T. Fry (editor), *The Rule of St Benedict*. Vintage Spiritual Classics. New York: Vintage, 1998, 12.

17. William of St. Thierry, *The Nature and Dignity of Love*. Cistercian Fathers Series 30. Kalamazoo, MI: Cistercian, 1981, 47.

18. Ward (translator), *The Prayers and Meditations of Saint Anselm with the Proslogion*, 224.

19. "The Teaching of the Twelve Apostles, Commonly Called the Didache." In *Early Christian Fathers*, Vol. I, edited by C. C. Richardson. The Library of Christian Classics. Philadelphia: Westminster, 1953, 173.

20. Quoted in Matthew Fox (editor), *Western Spirituality: Historical Roots, Ecumenical Routes*. Santa Fe: Bear, 1981, 174.

21. Quoted in A. Hyma, *The Brethren of the Common Life*. Grand Rapids, Eerdmans, 1950, 60.

22. Quoted in Evdokimov, *Ages of the Spiritual Life*. Crestwood, NY: St. Vladimir's Seminary Press, 1998, 195.

23. Outler (editor), *The Confessions of St. Augustine*, 286.

24. "The Theological Orations." In *Christology of the Later Fathers*, edited by E. R. Hardy. The Library of Christian Classics. Philadelphia: Westminster, 1954, 130.

25. "The Conferences of Cassian." In *Western Asceticism*, Vol. XII, translated by O. Chadwick. The Library of Christian Classics. London: SCM, 1958, 198.

26. "Address on Religious Instruction." In *Christology of the Later Fathers,* edited by E. R. Hardy. The Library of Christian Classics. Philadelphia: Westminster, 1954, 315.

27. Thomas à Kempis, *The Imitation of Christ*, 56.

28. R. B. Blakney (translator), *Meister Eckhart: A Modern Translation*, 239.

29. Helen Waddell (translator), *The Desert Fathers*. Vintage Spiritual Classics. New York: Vintage, 1998, 81.

30. T. Fry (editor), *The Rule of Saint Benedict*, 63.

31. Quoted in Simon Chan, *Spiritual Theology: A Systematic Study of the Christian Life*. Downers Grove, IL: InterVarsity, 1998, 181.

February

32. "Exposition of the Epistle to the Romans." In *A Scholastic Miscellany: Anselm to Ockham*, Vol. X, edited by E. R. Fairweather. The Library of Christian Classics. London: SCM 1956, 278.

33. *Stromateis* I.V.28. In *Documents of the Christian Church*, 2nd ed., edited by H. Bettenson. London: Oxford University Press, 1967, 6.

34. B. Ward (translator), *The Prayers and Meditations of Saint Anselm with the Proslogion*. Penguin Classics. London: Penguin, 1973, 98.

35. Helen Waddell (translator), *The Desert Fathers*. Vintage Spiritual Classics. New York: Vintage, 1998, 150.

36. A. C. Outler (editor), *The Confessions of St. Augustine*. Mineola, NY: Dover, 2002, 269.

37. "The Rule of S. Francis, 1223." In *Documents of the Christian Church*, 2nd ed., edited by H. Bettenson. London: Oxford University Press, 1967, 128.

38. "Letters of Ignatius: Ephesians." In *Early Christian Fathers*, Vol. I, edited by C. C. Richardson. The Library of Christian Classics. Philadelphia: Westminster, 1953, 92.

39. Quoted in L. S. Cunningham and K. J. Egan, *Christian Spirituality: Themes from the Tradition*. New York: Paulist, 1996, 173.

40. A. C. Outler (editor), *The Confessions of St. Augustine*. Mineola, NY: Dover, 2002, 175.

41. Thomas à Kempis, *The Imitation of Christ: In Four Books*. Vintage Spiritual Classics. Translated by J. N. Tylenda. New York: Vintage, 1998, 26

42. R. B. Blakney (translator), *Meister Eckhart: A Modern Translation*. New York: Harper & Row, 1941, 103.

43. Quoted in B. Holt, *Thirsty for God: A Brief History of Christian Spirituality*. Minneapolis: Augsburg, 1993, 64.

44. Quoted in Jean Leclercq, *The Love of Learning and the Desire for God*. New York: Fordham University Press, 1974, 284.

45. R. J. Deferrari (editor), *The Fathers of the Church*. Vol. 26: *Saint Ambrose Letters*. New York: Fathers of the Church, 1954, 401.

46. Helen Waddell (translator), *The Desert Fathers*, 155.

47. B. Ward (translator), *The Prayers and Meditations of Saint Anselm with the Proslogion*, 93

48. R. B. Blakney (translator), *Meister Eckhart: A Modern Translation*, 237

49. Thomas à Kempis, *The Imitation of Christ*, 83

50. Quoted in A Benedictine of Stanbrook, *To Any Christian: Letters from the Saints*. London: Burns & Oates, 1964, 23.

51. A. C. Outler (editor), *The Confessions of St. Augustine*, 133

52. Quoted in Jean Leclercq, *The Love of Learning and the Desire for God*. New York: Fordham University Press, 1974, 285.

53. R. J. Deferrari (editor), *The Fathers of the Church*. Vol. 26, 409.

54. Helen Waddell (translator), *The Desert Fathers*, 148.

55. Thomas à Kempis, *The Imitation of Christ*, 43.

56. A. C. Outler (editor), *The Confessions of St. Augustine*, 227.

57. R. B. Blakney (translator), *Meister Eckhart: A Modern Translation*, 57.

58. B. Ward (translator), *The Prayers and Meditations of Saint Anselm with the Proslogion*, 155.

59. Quoted in A Benedictine of Stanbrook, *To Any Christian: Letters from the Saints*, 139.

March

60. Quoted in K. Leech, *Soul Friend: A Study of Spirituality*. London: Sheldon, 1977, 38.

61. D. J. Sheerin, *The Eucharist*. Message of the Church Fathers Vol. 7. Wilmington, NC: Glazier, 1986, 149.

62. *Celebrating Common Prayer: A Version of the Daily Office SSF*. London: Continuum, 1992, 235.

63. R. B. Blakney (translator), *Meister Eckhart: A Modern Translation*. New York: Harper & Row, 1941, 245.

64. "The Letter of Ignatius to the Ephesians." In *The Apostolic Fathers in English*, 3rd ed., edited and translated by M. W. Holmes. Grand Rapids: Baker Academic, 2006, 98.

65. A. C. Outler (editor), *The Confessions of St. Augustine*. Mineola, NY: Dover, 2002, 90.

66. Helen Waddell (translator), *The Desert Fathers*. Vintage Spiritual Classics. New York: Vintage, 1998, 143.

67. J. J. O'Meara (translator), *Origen*. Ancient Christian Writers 19. New York: Newman, 1954, 125.

68. Julian of Norwich, *Revelations of Divine Love*. Translated by Clifton Wolters. London: Penguin, 1966, 99.

69. B. Ward (translator), *The Prayers and Meditations of Saint Anselm with the Proslogion*. Penguin Classics. London: Penguin, 1973, 242.

70. Quoted in K. Leech, *Soul Friend: A Study of Spirituality*, 41.

71. D. J. Sheerin, *The Eucharist*, 152.

72. Thomas à Kempis, *The Imitation of Christ: In Four Books*. Vintage Spiritual Classics. Translated by J. N. Tylenda. New York: Vintage, 1998, 163.

73. A. C. Outler (editor), *The Confessions of St. Augustine*, 206.

74. *The Apostolic Fathers in English*, 296.

75. Helen Waddell (translator), *The Desert Fathers*, 103.

76. B. Ward (translator), *The Prayers and Meditations of Saint Anselm with the Proslogion*, 219.

77. *Celebrating Common Prayer: A Version of the Daily Office SSF*, 261.

78. "The Letter of Polycarp to the Philippians." In *The Apostolic Fathers in English*, 140.

79. William of St. Thierry, *The Nature and Dignity of Love*. Kalamazoo: Cisterian, 1981, 97.

80. A. C. Outler (editor), *The Confessions of St. Augustine*, 66.

81. Quoted in A Benedictine of Stanbrook, *To Any Christian: Letters from the Saints*. London: Burns & Oates, 1964, 122.

82. Quoted in E. Underhill, *The Spiritual Life*. London: Hodder & Stoughton, 1937, 99.

83. "The Mending of Life." In *Late Medieval Mysticism*, Vol. XIII, edited by T. C. Petry. The Library of Christian Classics. London: SCM, 1957 222.

84. Quoted in Malcolm Muggeridge, *A Third Testament*. Farmington, PA: Plough, 2002, 15.

85. Quoted in D. O'Shea, *Go Down to the Potter's House: A Journey in Meditation*. Quezon City, Philippines: Claretian, 1992, 93.

86. W. Johnston. (editor), *The Cloud of Unknowing* and *The Book of Privy Counseling*. Garden City, NY: Image, 1973, 156.

87. D. J. Sheerin, *The Eucharist*, 324.

88. "First Clement." In *The Apostolic Fathers in English*, 46.

89. "On Simony, 1413." In *Advocates of Reform: From Wyclif to Erasmus*, edited by M. Spinka. The Library of Christian Classics, Vol. XIV. London: SCM, 1953, 209.

90. "Unity of the Catholic Church." In *Early Latin Theology*, edited by S. L. Greenslade. The Library of Christian Classics. Louisville: Westminster, 1957, 130.

April

91. Quoted in P. Evdokimov, *Ages of the Spiritual Life*. Crestwood, NY: St. Vladimir's Seminary Press, 1998, 130.

92. T. Fry (editor), *The Rule of St. Benedict.* Vintage Spiritual Classics. New York: Vintage, 1998, 15.

93. W. Johnston (editor), *The Cloud of Unknowing* and *The Book of Privy Counseling,* Garden City, NY: Image, 1973, 156.

94. B. Ward (translator), *The Prayers and Meditations of Saint Anselm with the Proslogion.* Penguin Classics. London: Penguin, 1973, 132.

95. "The Letter of Ignatius to the Ephesians." In *The Apostolic Father in English,* 3rd ed., edited and translated by M. W. Holmes. Grand Rapids: Baker Academic, 2006, 99.

96. Thomas à Kempis, *The Imitation of Christ: In Four Books.* Vintage Spiritual Classics. Translated by J. N. Tylenda. New York: Vintage, 1998, 63.

97. "The Blanquerna: Of the Book of the Lover and the Beloved." In *Late Medieval Mysticism,* Vol. XIII, edited by R. C. Petry. The Library of Christian Classics. London: SCM, 1957, 157.

98. Julian of Norwich, *Revelations of Divine Love.* Penguin Classics. London: Penguin, 1966, 93.

99. Quoted in J. Leclercq, *The Love of Learning and the Desire for God: A Study of Monastic Culture.* New York: Fordham University Press, 1974, 165.

100. Quoted in K. Leech, *Soul Friend: A Study of Spirituality.* London: Sheldon, 1977, 55–56.

101. A. C. Outler (editor), *The Confessions of St. Augustine.* Mineola, NY: Dover, 2002, 209.

102. Quoted in D. J. Sheerin, *The Eucharist.* Message of the Church Fathers, Vol. 7. Wilmington, NC: Glazier, 1986, 322.

103. B. Ward (translator), *The Prayers and Meditations of Saint Anselm with the Proslogion,* 193.

104. "The Letter of Ignatius to the Trallians." In *The Apostolic Fathers in English,* 3rd ed., 111.

105. Julian of Norwich, *Revelations of Divine Love,* 136–37.

106. Helen Waddell (translator), *The Desert Fathers.* Vintage Spiritual Classics. New York: Vintage, 1998, 95.

107. Quoted in A. Hyma, *The Brethren of the Common Life.* Grand Rapids: Eerdmans, 1950, 96.

108. Quoted in B. Holt, *Thirsty for God: A Brief History of Christian Spirituality.* Minneapolis: Augsburg, 1993, 42.

109. W. Johnston (editor), *The Cloud of Unknowing* and *The Book of Privy Counseling,* 155.

110. A. C. Outler (editor), *The Confessions of St. Augustine,* 279.

111. "Letter 41: The Synagogue at Callinicum." In *Early Latin Theology,* edited by S. L. Greenslade. The Library of Christian Classics. Louisville: Westminster, 1956, 247.

112. R. B. Blakney (translator), *Meister Eckhart: A Modern Translation.* New York: Harper & Row, 1941, 22.

113. Julian of Norwich, *Revelations of Divine Love,* 124–25.

114. "The Journey of the Mind to God." In *Late Medieval Mysticism,* Vol. XIII, edited by R. C. Petry. The Library of Christian Classics. London: SCM, 1957, 140–41.

115. Thomas à Kempis, *The Imitation of Christ*, 15.

116. B. Ward (translator), *The Prayers and Meditations of Saint Anselm with the Proslogion*, 197–98.

117. "Letter 108: To Eustochium." In *Early Latin Theology*, edited by S. L. Greenslade. The Library of Christian Classics. Louisville: Westminster, 1956, 350.

118. Quoted in I. Delio, *Franciscan Prayer*. Cincinnati: St. Anthony Messenger, 2004, 20.

119. W. Johnston (editor), *The Cloud of Unknowing* and *The Book of Privy Counseling*, 86.

120. "Sermons of Columbanus." In *Celtic Spirituality*, edited and translated by O. Davies. The Classics of Western Spirituality. New York: Paulist, 1999, 358.

May

121 "The Mending of Life." In *Late Medieval Mysticism*, Vol. XIII, edited by R. C. Petry. The Library of Christian Classics. London: SCM Press, 1957, 238.

122. "Letters 20 and 21: The Battle of the Basilicas." In *Early Latin Theology*, edited by S. L. Greenslade. The Library of Christian Classics. Louisville: Westminster, 1956, 214.

123. "The Breastplate of Laidcenn." In *Celtic Spirituality*, edited and translated by O. Davies. The Classics of Western Spirituality. New York: Paulist, 1999, 290–91.

124. R. B. Blakney (translator), *Meister Eckhart: A Modern Translation*. New York: Harper & Row, 1941, 157.

125. W. Johnston (editor), *The Cloud of Unknowing* and *The Book of Privy Counseling*, Garden City, NY: Image, 1973, 64.

126. Thomas à Kempis, *The Imitation of Christ: In Four Books*. Vintage Spiritual Classics. Translated by J. N. Tylenda. New York: Vintage, 1998, 90.

127. B. Ward (translator), *The Prayers and Meditations of Saint Anselm with the Proslogion*. Penguin Classics. London: Penguin, 1973, 103.

128. Quoted in P. Evdokimov, *Ages of the Spiritual Life*. Crestwood, NY: St. Vladimir's Seminary Press, 1998, 208.

129. Quoted in M. Fox (editor), *Western Spirituality: Historical Roots, Ecumenical Routes*. Santa Fe: Bear, 1981, 229.

130. "Letter 107: To Laeta." In *Early Latin Theology*, edited by S. L. Greenslade. The Library of Christian Classics. Louisville: Westminster, 1956, 332.

131. "The Rule for Monks by Columbanus." In *Celtic Spirituality*, edited and translated by O. Davies. New York: Paulist, 1999, 247.

132. Quoted in A Benedictine of Stanbrook, *To Any Christian: Letters from the Saints*, London: Burns & Oates, 1964, 118.

133. Quoted in J. Leclercq, *The Love of Learning and the Desire for God: A Study of Monastic Culture*. New York: Fordham University Press, 1974, 284.

134. A. C. Outler (editor), *The Confessions of St. Augustine*. Mineola, NY: Dover, 2002, 270.

135. Quoted in D. O'Shea, *Go Down to the Potter's House: A Journey into Meditation.* Quezon City, Philippines: Claretian, 1992, 128.

136. Quoted in T. Fry (editor), *The Rule of St. Benedict in English.* Vintage Spiritual Classics. New York: Vintage, 1998, 51.

137. B. Ward (translator), *The Prayers and Meditations of Saint Anselm With the Proslogion,* 181.

138. Thomas à Kempis, *The Imitation of Christ,* 169.

139. W. Johnston (editor), *The Cloud of Unknowing* and *The Book of Privy Counseling,* 60.

140. R. B. Blakney (translator), *Meister Eckhart: A Modern Translation,* 119.

141. Julian of Norwich, *Revelations of Divine Love.* Penguin Classics. London: Penguin, 1966, 207.

142. "On Simony." In *Advocates of Reform: From Wyclif to Erasmus,* Vol. XIV, edited by M. Spinka. The Library of Christian Classics. London: SCM, 1953, 234.

143. "The Letter of Polycarp to the Philippians,. In *The Apostolic Fathers in English,* edited and translated by M. W. Holmes. Grand Rapids: Baker Academic, 2006, 139.

144. "Unity of the Catholic Church." In *Early Latin Theology,* edited by S. L. Greenslade. The Library of Christian Classics. Louisville: Westminster, 1956, 127.

145. "The Four Hundred Chapters on Love." In *Maximus Confessor: Selected Writings,* edited and translated by G. C. Berthold. The Classics of Western Spirituality. London: SPCK, 1985, 38.

146. Quoted in T. G. Weinandy and D. A. Keating (editors), *The Theology of St. Cyril of Alexandria: A Critical Appreciation.* London: T & T Clark, 2003, 174.

147. Quoted in D. Minns, *Irenaeus.* London: Chapman, 1994, 47.

148. B. Ward (translator), *The Prayers and Meditations of Saint Anselm with the Proslogion,* 95.

149. Quoted in D. J. Sheerin, *The Eucharist.* Message of the Church Fathers, Vol. 7. Wilmington, NC: Glazier, 1986, 337-38.

150. "The Mending of Life." In *Late Medieval Mysticism,* Vol. XIII, edited by R. C. Petry. The Library of Christian Classics. London: SCM, 1957, 228.

151. Thomas à Kempis, *The Imitation of Christ,* 60.

June

152 Quoted in Rowan Williams, *Where God Happens: Discovering Christ in One Another.* Boston: New Seeds, 2005, 99.

153. John Cassian, *Conferences.* The Classics of Western Spirituality. New York: Paulist, 1995, 76.

154. "The Mind's Journey into God." In *The Essential Writings of Christian Mysticism,* edited by B. McGinn. New York: The Modern Library, 2006, 164–65.

155. "Second Clement." In *The Apostolic Fathers in English,* 3rd ed., edited and translated by M. W. Holmes. Grand Rapids: Baker Academic, 2006, 79.

156. "Revelations of Divine Love." In *Devotional Classics,* edited by R. J. Foster and J. B. Smith. San Francisco: HarperSanFrancisco, 1993, 70.

157. Quoted in I. Delio, *Franciscan Prayer*. Cincinnati: St. Anthony Messenger, 2004, 20.

158. Thomas à Kempis, *The Imitation of Christ: In Four Books*. Vintage Spiritual Classics. Translated by J. N. Tylenda. New York: Vintage, 1998, 123.

159. "The Unity of the Catholic Church." In *Early Latin Theology*, edited by S. L. Greenslade. Philadelphia: Westminster, 1956, 137.

160. "De Spiritu Sancto." In *Nicene and Post-Nicene Fathers of the Christian Church*, Vol. VIII, *St. Basil: Letters and Select Works*, edited by P. Schaff and H. Wace. Grand Rapids: Eerdmans, 1989, 15.

161. A. C. Outler (editor), *The Confessions of St. Augustine*. Mineola, NY: Dover, 2002, 66.

162. E. Griffin (editor), *Hildegard of Bingen: Selections from Her Writings*. Harper Collins Spiritual Classics. San Francisco: HarperSanFrancisco, 1990, 47.

163. B. Ward (translator), *The Prayers and Meditations of Saint Anselm with the Proslogion*. Penguin Classics. London: Penguin, 1973, 224.

164. Quoted in P. Evdokimov, *Ages of the Spiritual Life*. Crestwood, NY: St. Vladimir's Seminary Press, 1998, 190.

165. "The Letter of Ignatius to the Romans." In *The Apostolic Fathers in English*, 3rd ed., edited and translated by M. W. Holmes. Grand Rapids: Baker Academic, 2006, 113.

166. "On Loving God." In *Bernard of Clairvaux: Selected Works*, edited by E. Griffin. Harper Collins Spiritual Classics. San Francisco: HarperSanFrancisco, 2005, 79–80.

167. "The Clock of Wisdom." In *The Essential Writings of Christian Mysticism*, edited by B. McGinn. New York: The Modern Library, 2006, 236.

168. R. B. Blakney (translator), *Meister Eckhart: A Modern Translation*. New York: Harper & Row, 1941, 154.

169. A. C. Outler (editor), *The Confessions of St. Augustine*, 144.

170. Thomas à Kempis, *The Imitation of Christ*, 67.

171. "On Conversion." In *Bernard of Clairvaux: Selected Works*, edited by E. Griffin. Harper Collins Spiritual Classics. San Francisco: HarperSanFrancisco, 2005, 26.

172. B. Ward (translator), *The Prayers and Meditations of Saint Anselm with the Proslogion*, 103.

173. "Homily 10." In *The Essential Writings of Christian Mysticism*, edited by B. McGinn. New York: The Modern Library, 2006, 431.

174. "First Clement." In *The Apostolic Fathers in English*, 3rd ed., edited and translated by M. W. Holmes. Grand Rapids: Baker Academic, 2006, 43.

175. R. B. Blakney (translator), *Meister Eckhart: A Modern Translation*, 90.

176. A. C. Outler (editor), *The Confessions of St. Augustine*, 176.

177. Quoted in P. Evdokimov, *Ages of the Spiritual Life*, 77.

178. C. Roth (translator), *On the Soul and the Resurrection: St. Gregory of Nyssa*. Popular Patristic Series. Crestwood, NY: St. Vladimir's Seminary Press, 1993, 115.

179. "The Flowing Light of the Godhead." In *The Essential Writings of Christian Mysticism*, edited by B. McGinn. New York: The Modern Library, 2006, 206.

180. T. Fry (editor), *The Rule of St. Benedict in English*. Vintage Spiritual Classics. New York: Vintage, 1998, 13.

181. "Sermon 39." In *The Essential Writings of Christian Mysticism*, edited by B. McGinn. New York: The Modern Library, 2006, 106.

July

182. Clifton Wolters (translator), *Julian of Norwich: Revelations of Divine Love*. Penguin Classics. London: Penguin, 1966, 91.

183. T. X. Davis (translator), *William of St. Thierry: The Nature and Dignity of Love*. Cistercian Fathers Series 30. Kalamazoo, MI: Cistercian, 1981, 69.

184. Quoted in L. S. Cunningham and K. J. Egan, *Christian Spirituality: Themes from the Tradition*. New York: Paulist, 1996, 154.

185. H. Waddell (translator), *The Desert Fathers*. Vintage Spiritual Classics. New York: Vintage, 1998, 134.

186. W. Johnston (editor), *The Cloud of Unknowing* and *The Book of Privy Counseling*, Garden City, NY: Image, 1973, 162.

187. Quoted in I. Delio, *Franciscan Prayer*. Cincinnati: St. Anthony Messenger, 2004, 28–29.

188. "De Spiritu Sancto." In *Nicene and Post-Nicene Fathers of the Christian Church, Vol. VIII: St. Basil: Letters and Select Works*, edited by P. Schaff and H. Wace. Grand Rapids: Eerdmans, 1989, 16.

189. "Revelations of Divine Love." In *Devotional Classics*, edited by R. J. Foster and J. B. Smith. San Francisco: HarperSanFrancisco, 1993, 71.

190. L. McCauley (editor) and A. A. Stephenson (translator), *The Works of Saint Cyril of Jerusalem*, Vol. 2. The Fathers of the Church. Washington: The Catholic University of America Press, 1970, 165.

191. Quoted in D. Allen, *Spiritual Theology: The Theology of Yesterday for Spiritual Help Today*. Boston: Cowley, 1997, 82.

192. E. Griffin (editor), *Bernard of Clairvaux: Selected Works*. Harper Collins Spiritual Classics. San Francisco: HarperSanFrancisco, 2005, 110.

193. "Sermon 39." In *The Essential Writings of Christian Mysticism*, edited by B. McGinn. New York: The Modern Library, 2006, 108.

194. E. Griffin (editor), *Hildergard of Bingen: Selections from Her Writings*. Harper Collins Spiritual Classics. San Francisco: HarperSanFrancisco, 2005, 28.

195. A. C. Outler (editor), *The Confessions of St. Augustine*. Mineola, NY: Dover, 2002, 128.

196. C. Luibheid (translator), *John Cassian: Conferences*. The Classics of Western Spirituality. New York: Paulist, 1985, 106.

197. "On Idolatry." In *Early Latin Theology*, edited by S. L. Greenslade. The Library of Christian Classics. Philadelphia: Westminster, 1956, 83.

198. Quoted in P. Evdokimov, *Ages of the Spiritual Life*. Crestwood, NY: St. Vladimir's Seminary Press, 1998, 160.

199. "The Epistles of Barnabas." In *The Apostolic Fathers in English*, 3rd ed., edited and translated by M. W. Holmes. Grand Rapids: Baker Academic, 2006, 180.

200. R. B. Blakney (translator), *Meister Eckhart: A Modern Translation*. New York: Harper & Row, 1941, 88.

201. Thomas à Kempis, *The Imitation of Christ: In Four Books*. Vintage Spiritual Classics. Translated by J. N. Tylenda. New York: Vintage, 1998, 50.

202. B. Ward (translator), *The Prayers and Meditations of Saint Anselm with the Proslogion*. Penguin Classics. London: Penguin, 1973, 256.

203. "The Mending of Life." In *Late Medieval Mysticism, Vol. XIII*, edited by R. C. Petry. The Library of Christian Classics. London: SCM, 1957, 223.

204. "The Treatise on Divine Providence." In *Late Medieval Mysticism, Vol. XIII*, edited by R. C. Petry. The Library of Christian Classics. London: SCM, 1957, 275.

205. C. Wolters (translator), *Revelations of Divine Love*. Penguin Classics. London: Penguin, 1966, 188.

206. T. X. Davis (translator), *William of St. Thierry: The Nature and Dignity of Love*. Cistercian Fathers Series 30. Kalamazoo, MI: Cistercian, 1981, 100.

207. Quoted in L. S. Cunningham and K. J. Egan, *Christian Spirituality: Themes from the Tradition*, 173.

208. H. Waddell (translator), *The Desert Fathers*, 159.

209. Quoted in I. Delio, *Franciscan Prayer*, 134.

210. W. Johnston (editor), *The Cloud of Unknowing* and *The Book of Privy Counseling*, 79.

211. "The Mending of Life." In *Late Medieval Mysticism, Vol. XIII*, 222.

212. R. B. Blakney (translator), *Meister Eckhart: A Modern Translation*, 14.

August

213. B. Ward (translator), *The Prayers and Meditations of Saint Anselm with the Proslogion*, 93.

214. Thomas à Kempis, *The Imitation of Christ: In Four Books*. Vintage Spiritual Classics. Translated by J. N. Tylenda. New York: Vintage, 1998, 22.

215. "Theologia Germanica." In *Devotional Classics*, edited by R. J. Foster and J. B. Smith. San Francisco: HarperSanFrancisco, 1993, 149.

216. "Letters." In *Nicene and Post-Nicene Fathers, Vol. VIII: St. Basil: Letters and Select Works*, edited by P. . Schaff and H. Wace. Grand Rapids: Eerdmans, 1989, 110.

217. E. Griffin (editor), *Bernard of Clairvaux: Selected Works*. Harper Collins Spiritual Classics. San Francisco: HarperSanFrancisco, 2005, 121.

218. "First Lecture on the Mysteries." In *The Works of Saint Cyril of Jerusalem, Vol. II*, edited by L. McCauley and translated by A. A. Stephenson. The Fathers of the Church. Washington: The Catholic University of America Press, 1970, 155–58.

219. "The Epistle of Barnabas." In *The Apostolic Fathers in English*, 3rd ed., edited by M. W. Holmes. Grand Rapids: Baker Academic, 2006, 197.

220. A. C. Outler (editor), *The Confessions of St. Augustine*. Mineola, NY: Dover, 2002, 141.

221. Quoted in P. Evdokimov, *Ages of Spiritual Life*, Crestwood, NY: St. Vladimir's Seminary Press, 1998, 239.

222. C. Luibheid (translator), *John Cassian: Conferences*. New York: Paulist, 1985, 107.

223. "On Idolatry." In *Early Latin Theology*, edited by S. C. Greenslade. The Library of Christian Classics. Philadelphia: Westminster, 1956, 93.

224. E. Griffin (editor), *Bernard of Clairvaux: Selected Works*, 123.

225. "Dialogue with Trypho the Jew 6." In *The Essential Writings of Christian Mysticism*, edited by B. McGinn. Modern Library Classics. New York: The Modern Library, 2006, 484.

226. E. Griffen (editor), *Hildegard of Bingen: Selections from Her Writings*. Harper Collins Spiritual Classics. San Francisco: HarperSanFrancisco, 2005, 110.

227. Thomas à Kempis, *The Imitation of Christ*, 30.

228. R. A. Greer (translator), *Origen*. The Classics of Western Spirituality. London: SPCK, 1979, 49.

229. "The Sparkling Stone." In *Late Medieval Mysticism, Vol. XIII*, edited by R. C. Petry. The Library of Christian Classics. London: SCM, 1957, 301.

230. A. C. Outler (editor), *The Confessions of St. Augustine*, 173.

231. B. Ward (translator), *The Prayers and Meditations of Saint Anselm with the Proslogion*. Penguin Classics. London: Penguin, 1973, 101.

232. W. Johnston (editor), *The Cloud of Unknowing* and *The Book of Privy Counseling*, Garden City, NY: Image, 1973, 158.

233. R. B. Blakney (translator), *Meister Eckhart: A Modern Translation*. New York: Harper & Row, 1941, 15.

234. Quoted in I. Delio, *Franciscan Prayer*, Cincinnati: St. Anthony Messenger, 2004, 94.

235. H. Waddell (translator), *The Desert Fathers*. Vintage Spiritual Classics. New York: Vintage, 1998, 112.

236. Quoted in L. S. Cunningham and K. J. Egan, *Christian Spirituality: Themes from the Tradition*, New York: Paulist, 1996, 93–94.

237. T. X. Davis (translator), *William of St. Thierry: The Nature and Dignity of Love*. Cistercian Fathers Series 30. Kalamazoo: Cistercian, 1981, 56.

238. C. Wolters (translator), *Julian of Norwich: Revelations of Divine Love*. Penguin Classics. London: Penguin, 1966, 132–33.

239. C. Roth (translator), *St. Gregory of Nyssa: On the Soul and the Resurrection*. Popular Patristic Series 12. Crestwood, NY: St. Vladimir's Seminary Press, 1993, 87.

240. "The Letter of Ignatius to the Magnesians." In *The Apostolic Fathers in English*, 3rd ed., edited by M. W. Holmes. Grand Rapids: Baker Academic, 2006, 106.

241. "Letters." In *Nicene and Post-Nicene Fathers, Vol. VIII*, 110.

242. "Theologia Germanica." in *Devotional Classics*, 148.

243. "Letters." In *Early Latin Theology*, edited by S. C. Greenslade. The Library of Christian Classics. Philadelphia: Westminster, 1956, 296.

September

244. E. Griffin (editor), *Bernard of Clairvaux: Selected Works*. Harper Collins Spiritual Classics. San Francisco: HarperSanFrancisco, 2005, 139.

245. "Letter of Nicholas of Cusa to Kaspar Ayndorffer." In *The Essential Writings of Christian Mysticism*, edited by B. McGinn. New York: The Modern Library, 2006, 274.

246. E. Griffin (editor), *Hildegard of Bingen: Selected Writings*. Harper Collins Spiritual Classics. San Francisco: HarperSanFrancisco, 2005, 32.

247. Thomas à Kempis, *The Imitation of Christ: In Four Books*. Vintage Spiritual Classics. Translated by J. N. Tylenda. New York: Vintage, 1998, 113.

248. A. C. Outler (editor), *The Confessions of St. Augustine*. Mineola, NY: Dover, 2002, 252.

249. B. Ward (translator), *The Prayers and Meditations of Saint Anselm with the Proslogion*. Penguin Classics. London: Penguin, 1973, 153.

250. W. Johnston (editor), *The Cloud of Unknowing* and *The Book of Privy Counseling*, Garden City, NY: Image, 1973, 51.

251. Quoted in I. Delio, *Franciscan Prayer*. Cincinnati: St. Anthony Messenger, 2004, 130.

252. H. Waddell (translator), *The Desert Fathers*. Vintage Spiritual Classics. New York: Vintage, 1998, 68.

253. C. Roth (translator), *St. Gregory of Nyssa: On the Soul and the Resurrection* Popular Patristic Series. Crestwood, NY: St. Vladimir's Seminary Press, 1993, 27.

254. R. B. Blakney (translator), *Meister Eckhart: A Modern Translation*. New York: Harper & Row, 1941, 39.

255. Quoted in E. de Waal, *Seeking God: The Way of St. Benedict*, Collegeville, MN: Liturgical, 1984, 82.

256. "The Mending of Life." In *Late Medieval Mysticism, Vol. XIII*, edited by R. C. Petry. The Library of Christian Classics. London: SCM, 1957, 225.

257. "Letters." In *Medieval Writings on Female Spirituality*, edited by E. Spearing. Penguin Classics. New York: Penguin, 2002, 48.

258. "Treatise on the Theological Virtues." In *Nature and Grace Vol. XI: Selections from the Summa Theologica of Thomas Acquinas*, edited by A. M. Fairweather. The Library of Christian Classics. London: SCM, 1954, 219.

259. "The Sparkling Stone." In *Late Medieval Mysticism, Vol. XIII*, edited by R. C. Petry. The Library of Christian Classics. London: SCM, 1957, 302.

260. "A Treatise on Divine Providence." In *Late Medieval Mysticism, Vol XIII*, edited by R. C. Petry. The Library of Christian Classics. London: SCM, 1957, 274.

261. "The Life of St. Mary of Oignies." In *Medieval Writings on Female Spirituality*, edited by E. Spearing. Penguin Classics. New York: Penguin, 2002, 102.

262. R. B. Blakney (translator), *Meister Eckhart: A Modern Translation*. New York: Harper & Row, 1941, 144.

263. Quoted in E. de Waal, *Seeking God: The Way of St. Benedict*, 116.

264. "The Mending of Life." In *Late Medieval Mysticism, Vol XIII*, edited by R. C. Petry. The Library of Christian Classics. London: SCM, 1957, 230.

265. Quoted in K. J. Collins (editor), *Exploring Christian Spirituality: An Ecumenical Reader*. Grand Rapids: Baker, 2000, 109.

266. P. Schaff (editor), *Nicene and Post-Nicene Fathers, Vol. 9: Chrysostom: On the Priesthood, Ascetic Treatises, Select Homilies and Letters, Homilies on the Statues.* A Select Library of the Christian Church. Peabody, MA: Hendrickson, 1994, 343.

267. "Poem 17." In *Medieval Writings on Female Spirituality*, 57.

268. "The Sparkling Stone." In *Late Medieval Mysticism, Vol. XIII*, 300.

269. Quoted in E. de Waal, *Seeking God: The Way of St. Benedict*, 99.

270. "The Mending of Life." In *Late Medieval Mysticism, Vol.XIII*, 231.

271. "The Passion of Saints Perpetua and Felecity." In *Mystics, Visionaries, and Prophets*, edited by S. Madigan. Minneapolis: Fortress, 1998, 18.

272. Quoted in Paul Evdokimov, *Ages of the Spiritual Life*. Crestwood, NY: St. Vladimer's Seminary Press, 1998, 168.

273. Quoted in A. Hyma, *The Brethren of the Common Life*. Grand Rapids: Eerdmans, 1950, 56.

October

274. R. B. Blakney (translator), *Meister Eckhart: A Modern Translation*, 200.

275. "The Mirror of Love." In *The Mediaeval Mystics of England*, edited by E. Colledge. New York: Scribner's Sons, 1961, 116.

276. Quoted in I. Delio, *Franciscan Prayer*. Cincinnati: St. Anthony Messenger, 2004, 48.

277. "The Epistle of Diognetus." In *The Apostolic Fathers in English*, 3rd ed., edited and translated by M. W. Holmes. Grand Rapids: Baker Academic, 2006, 295.

278. Quoted in L. S. Cunningham and K. J. Egan, *Christian Spirituality: Themes from the Tradition*. New York: Paulist, 1996, 34.

279. "The Second Letter from Héloïse to Abelard." In *Mystics, Visionaries and Prophets*, edited by S. Madigan. Minneapolis: Fortress, 1998, 123.

280. "Patrick's Declaration of the Great Works of God." In *Celtic Spirituality*, edited and translated by O. Davies. The Classics of Western Spirituality. New York: Paulist, 1999, 82.

281. "The Dialogue." In *Devotional Classics*, edited by R. J. Foster and J. B. Smith. San Francisco: HarperSanFrancisco, 1993, 290.

282. Thomas à Kempis, *The Imitation of Christ: In Four Books*. Vintage Spiritual Classics. Translated by J. N. Tylenda. New York: Vintage, 1998, 200.

283. A. C. Outler (editor), *The Confessions of St. Augustine*. Mineola, NY: Dover, 2002, 195.

284. B. Ward (translator), *The Prayers and Meditations of Saint Anselm with the Proslogion*. Penguin Classics. London: Penguin, 1973, 193–94.

285. "The Choirs of Angels." In *Hildegard of Bingen: Selections from Her Writings*, edited by E. Griffin. Harper Collins Spiritual Classics. San Francisco: HarperSanFrancisco, 2005, 44.

286. W. Johnston (editor), *The Cloud of Unknowing* and *The Book of Privy Counseling*, Garden City, NY: Image, 1973, 101.

287. C. Luibheid (translator), *John Cassian: Conferences.* The Classics of Western Spirituality. New York: Paulist, 1985, 73.

288. "The Testament of Saint Clare." In *Francis and Clare: The Complete Works*, edited by R. J. Armstrong and translated by I. C. Brady. The Classics of Western Spirituality. New York: Paulist, 1982, 231.

289. J. B. Shaw (translator), *St. Augustine: The Enchiridion on Faith, Hope and Love.* Washington: Regnery, 1996, 14.

290. "Sermons on the Song of Songs, 83." In *The Essential Writings of Christian Mysticism*, edited by B. McGinn. New York: The Modern Library, 2006, 258.

291. C. Roth (translator), *St. Gregory of Nyssa: On the Soul and the Resurrection.* Popular Patristic Series 12. Crestwood, NY: St. Vladimir's Seminary Press, 1993, 57.

292. H. Waddell (translator), *The Desert Fathers.* Vintage Spiritual Classics. New York: Vintage, 1998, 160.

293. Thomas à Kempis, *The Imitation of Christ*, 108.

294. H. Waddell (translator), *The Desert Fathers*, 108.

295. C. Roth (translator), *St. Gregory of Nyssa: On the Soul and the Resurrection*, 110.

296. J. B. Shaw (translator), *St. Augustine: The Enchiridion on Faith, Hope and Love*, 67.

297. "The Life of St. Brigit." In *Celtic Spirituality*, edited and translated by O. Davies. The Classics of Western Spirituality. New York: Paulist, 1999, 124.

298. Quoted in L. S. Cunningham and K. J. Egan, *Christian Spirituality: Themes from the Tradition.* New York: Paulist, 1996, 184.

299. "The Shepherd of Hermas." In *The Apostolic Fathers in English.* 3rd ed., edited by M. W. Holmes. Grand Rapids: Baker Academic, 2006, 224.

300. Quoted in I. Delio, *Franciscan Prayer.* Cincinnati: St. Anthony Messenger, 2004, 91.

301. "The Mirror of Love." In *The Mediaeval Mystics*, edited by E. Colledge. New York: Scribner's Sons, 1961, 118.

302. "I Sleep and My Heart Wakes." In *The Mediaeval Mystics of England*, edited by E. Colledge. New York: Scribner's Sons, 1961, 149.

303. E. Griffin (editor), *Hildegard of Bingen: Selections from Her Writings.* Harper Collins Spiritual Classics. San Francisco: HarperSanFrancisco, 2005, 129.

304. B. Ward (translator), *The Prayers and Meditations of Saint Anselm with the Proslogion*, 241.

November

305. A. C. Outler (editor), *The Confessions of St. Augustine*, 139.

306. W. Johnston (editor), *The Cloud of Unknowing* and *The Book of Privy Counseling*, Garden City, NY: Image, 1973, 56.

307. "The Earlier Rule." In *Francis and Clare: The Complete Works*, edited by R. J. Armstrong and translated by I. C. Brady. The Classics of Western Spirituality. New York: Paulist, 1982, 115.

308. C. Luibheid (translator), *John Cassian: Conferences*. The Classics of Western Spirituality. New York: Paulist, 1985, 57.

309. "Sermon on the Song of Songs, 83." In *The Essential Writings of Christian Mysticism*, edited by B. McGinn. Modern Library Classics. New York: The Modern Library, 2006, 259.

310. "The Mirror of Simple Souls." In *Medieval Writings on Female Spirituality*, edited by E. Spearing. Penguin Classics. New York: Penguin, 2002, 141.

311. T. Fry (editor), *The Rule of St. Benedict*. Vintage Spiritual Classics. New York: Vintage, 1998, 55.

312. "Letter 14: To Heliodorus." In *Early Latin Theology*, edited by S. L. Greenslade. The Library of Christian Classics. Philadelphia: Westminster, 1956, 292.

313. J. H. Clark (editor) and R. Dorward (translator), *Walter Hilton: The Scale of Perfection*. The Classics of Western Spirituality. New York: Paulist, 1991, 78.

314. M. Atherton (translator), *Hildegard of Bingen: Selected Writings*. Penguin Classics. London: Penguin, 2001, 117.

315. Quoted in M. H. Crosby, *Finding Francis, Following Christ*. Maryknoll, NY: Orbis, 2007, 86.

316. T. X. Davis (translator), *William of St. Thierry: The Nature and Dignity of Love*. Cistercian Fathers Series 30. Kalamazoo, MI: Cistercian, 1981, 80.

317. Quoted in D. Allen, *Spiritual Theology*. Cambridge: Cowley, 1997, 154–55.

318. A. Roberts and J. Donaldson (editors), *The Ante-Nicene Fathers, Vol. V: Hippolytus, Cyprian, Caius, Novation*. Grand Rapids: Eerdmans, 1995, 423.

319. R. B. Blakney (translator), *Meister Eckhart: A Modern Translation*. New York: Harper & Row, 1941, 188.

320. Quoted in P. Evdokimov, *Ages of the Spiritual Life*. Crestwood, NY: St. Vladimir's Seminary Press, 1998, 195.

321. E. Griffen (editor), *Bernard of Clairvaux: Selected Works*. Harper Collins Spiritual Classics. San Francisco: HarperSanFrancisco, 2005, 128.

322. "Life and Teachings." In *Devotional Classics*, edited by R. J. Foster and J. B. Smith. San Francisco: HarperSanFrancisco, 1993, 213.

323. Quoted in C. Mathewes, *A Theology of Public Life*. Cambridge: Cambridge University Press, 2007, 92.

324. Quoted in B. McGinn, *The Growth of Mysticism*. The Presence of God: A History of Western Christian Mysticism, Vol. II. London: SCM, 1995, 60.

325. Quoted in A. Curtayne, *Saint Catherine of Siena*. Rockford, IL: Tan, 1980, 48.

326. Thomas à Kempis, *The Imitation of Christ: In Four Books*. Vintage Spiritual Classics. Translated by J. N. Tylenda. New York: Vintage, 1998, 59.

327. H. Waddell (translator), *The Desert Fathers*. Vintage Spiritual Classics. New York: Vintage, 1998, 128.

328. C. Roth (translator), *St. Gregory of Nyssa: On the Soul and the Resurrection*. Popular Patristic Series 30. Crestwood, NY: St. Vladimir's Seminary Press, 1993, 71.

329. J. B. Shaw (translator), *St. Augustine: The Enchiridion on Faith, Hope and Love*. Washington: Regnery, 1996, 139.

330. "Columbanus: Sermons." In *Celtic Spirituality*, edited and translated by O. Davies. New York: Paulist, 1999, 357.

331. Quoted in L. S. Cunningham and K. J. Egan, *Christian Spirituality: Themes from the Tradition*. New York: Paulist, 1996, 91.

332. "Letters of Ignatius to the Ephesians." In *The Apostolic Fathers in English*, 3rd ed., edited by M. W. Holmes. Grand Rapids: Baker Academic, 2006, 100.

333. Quoted in I. Delio, *Franciscan Prayer*. Cincinnati: St. Anthony Messenger, 2004, 150.

334. "The Mirror of Holy Church." In *The Mediaeval Mystics of England*, edited by E. Colledge. New York: Scribner's Sons, 1961, 140.

December

335. E. Griffin (editor), *Hildegard of Bingen: Selections from Her Writings*. San Francisco: HarperSanFrancisco, 2005, 127.

336. B. Ward (translator), *The Prayers and Meditations of Saint Anselm with the Proslogion*. Penguin Classics. London: Penguin, 1973, 130.

337. A. C. Outler (editor), *The Confessions of St. Augustine*. Mineola, NY: Dover, 2002, 101.

338. W. Johnston (editor), *The Cloud of Unknowing* and *The Book of Privy Counseling*, Garden City, NY: Image, 1973, 153.

339. "A Letter to the Entire Order." In *Francis and Clare: The Complete Works*, edited by R. J. Armstrong and translated by I. C. Brady. New York: Paulist, 1982, 58.

340. C. Luibheid (translator), *John Cassian: Conferences*. New York: Paulist, 1985, 164.

341. "Homily 10." In *The Essential Writings of Christian Mysticism*, edited by B. McGinn. New York: The Modern Library, 2006, 432.

342. "The Life of Elizabeth Spaalbeek." In *Medieval Writings on Female Spirituality*, edited by E. Spearing. New York: Penguin, 2002, 117.

343. Quoted in B. McGinn, *The Growth of Mysticism*. The Presence of God: A History of Western Mysticism, Vol. II. London: SCM, 1995, 108.

344. Quoted in A. Curtayne, *Saint Catherine of Siena*. Rockford, MI: Tan, 1980, 126.

345. Quoted in G. L. Sittser, *Water from a Deep Well: Spirituality from Early Martyrs to Modern Missionaries*. Downers Grove, IL: InterVarsity, 2007, 133.

346. T. Fry (editor), *The Rule of Saint Benedict*. Vintage Spiritual Classics. New York: Vintage, 1998, 20.

347. "Letter 51." In *Early Latin Theology*, edited by S. L. Greenslade. The Library of Christian Classics. Philadelphia: Westminster, 1956, 254.

348. J. H. Clark (editor) and R. Dorward (translator), *Walter Hilton: The Scale of Perfection*. New York: Paulist, 1991, 148.

349. M. Atherton (translator), *Hildegard of Bingen: Selected Writings*. London: Penguin, 2001, 55.

350. T. A. Davis (translator), *William of St. Thierry: The Nature and Dignity of Love*. Kalamazoo, MI: Cistercian, 1981, 68.

351. Quoted in B. McGinn, *The Foundations of Mysticism*. The Presence of God: A History of Western Christian Mysticism, Vol. I. New York: Crossroads, 1991, 123.

352. Quoted in G. L. Sittser, *Water from a Deep Well: Christian Spirituality from Early Martyrs to Modern Missionaries*. Downers Grove, IL: InterVarsity, 2007, 60.

353. Quoted in D. Allen, *Spiritual Theology: The Theology of Yesterday for Spiritual Help Today*. Boston: Cowley, 1997, 106.

354. Quoted in M. H. Crosby, *Finding Francis, Following Christ*. MaryKnoll, NY: Orbis, 2007, 189.

355. C. Wolters (translator), *Julian of Norwich: Revelations of Divine Love*. Penguin Classics. London: Penguin, 1996, 204.

356. Quoted in A. Hyma, *The Brethren of the Common Life*. Grand Rapids: Eerdmans, 1950, 31.

357. Quoted in J. Leclercq, *The Love of Learning and the Desire for God: A Study of Monastic Culture*. New York: Fordham University Press, 1974, 285.

358. R. B. Blakney (translator), *Meister Eckhart: A Modern Translation*. New York: Harper & Row, 1941, 278.

359. B. Ward (translator), *The Prayers and Meditations of Saint Anselm with the Proslogion*, 145–46.

360. Quoted in Paul Evdokimov, *Ages of the Spiritual Life*, Crestwood, NY: St. Vladimir's Seminary Press, 1998, 213.

361. "The Treatises of Cyprian." In *The Ante-Nicene Fathers, Vol. V: Hippolytus, Cyprian, Caius, Novation, Appendix*, edited by A. Roberts and J. Donaldson. Grand Rapids: Eerdmans, 1995, 496.

362. "Life and Teachings." In *Devotional Classics*, edited by R. J. Foster and J. B. Smith. San Francisco: HarperSanFrancisco, 1993, 212.

363. E. Griffin (editor), *Bernard of Clairvaux: Selected Works*. Harper Collins Spiritual Classics. San Francisco: HarperSanFrancisco, 2005, 5.

364. "The Herald of Divine Love." In *Mystics, Visionaries and Prophets: A Historical Anthology of Women's Spiritual Writings*, edited by S. Madigan. Minneapolis: Fortress, 1998, 153.

365. Quoted in B. Holt, *Thirsty for God: A Brief History of Christian Spirituality*. Minneapolis: Augsburg, 1993, 38.

A Brief History of Authors and Writings Cited

Abelard, Peter: 1079–1142, controversial philosopher and theologian. Alternate spelling of his name: Peter Abailard.

Anastasius II: died c.608, Patriarch of Antioch.

Athanasius: c.296–373, Bishop of Alexandria, supporter of Nicaean orthodoxy and opponent of Arianism.

Bonaventure, Giovanni di Fidanza: 1221–74, a Franciscan theologian, Minister General of the Franciscan Order and author of the famous *Life of St. Francis*.

Cassian, John: c.360–435, student of Egyptian monasticism, key articulator of monastic practices, and founder of several monasteries near Marseille.

Catherine of Genoa: 1447–1510, mystic and minister to the sick and dying.

Clement of Alexandria: c.150–c.215, one of the early theologians of the church and head of Catechetical School at Alexandria.

Cloud of Unknowing: an English mystical treatise of the fourteenth century. Author is unknown. This author also wrote *The Book of Privy Counseling*.

Desert Fathers: a movement of men and also women from the 250s to 400 A.D. who lived as hermits and later in communities in Egypt and Asia Minor to live a life of prayer.

Diadochus: dates unknown but became bishop of Photike after 451. Famous for writing a book on attaining spiritual perfection.

Didache: first or second century early church manual setting out ethics of the Christian life and church practices.

Eckhart: c.1260–1327, a German Dominican mystic. He attempted to set out an ontological understanding of God and the inexpressibility of our relationship with God.

Elizabeth of Spaalbeek: died 1266. Unmarried laywoman and mystic. Had connection with St. Bernard of Clairvaux.

Epistle of Barnabas: author unknown. Possible origin in Alexandrian Christianity between 70 and 130.

Epistle of Diognetus: written by author unknown between 150 and 225. This writing was an attempt to defend the Christian faith and therefore belongs to early Christian apologetic writing.

Erigeuna, John Scotus: c.810–c.877. Irishman. A deeply original thinker. Strong pantheistic flavor in his writings. Was head of palace school in Paris. Erigena alternative spelling.

Evagrius Ponticus: 346–399, preacher and monk and spiritual writer.

Eusebius: c.260–c.340, bishop of Caesarea, famous for his *Ecclesiastical History*.

Gertrude the Great: 1256–c.1302. German mystic and member of the monastery at Helfta. One of the first exponents of the devotion of the Sacred Heart.

Gregory the Great: c.540–604. Pope from 590. Prior to becoming Pope he sold his riches for the poor, founded many monasteries and wrote extensively on pastoral and spiritual topics.

Gregory of Nazianzus: 329–389, bishop of Nazianzus in Cappadocia and one of the famous Cappadocian Fathers known for their orthodoxy and Trinitarian theology.

Gregory of Nyssa: c.330–c.395, bishop of Nyssa and one of the Cappadocian Fathers; an outstanding early theologian and orator.

Groote, Geert de: 1340–84, founder of The Brethren of the Common Life, and a Christian mystic. He gave Christian spirituality a more life-engaging focus. His life story was written by Thomas à Kempis.

Guigo II: twelfth-century Carthusian monk and author. He is famous for his *Ladder of Monks*.

Hadewijch of Antwerp: thirteenth-century Dutch Beguine, poet, and mystic.

Héloise: 1079–1142, Peter Abelard's lover and then wife and later abbess.

Henry Suso: c.1290–1366, German Dominican mystic, preacher, and spiritual advisor.

Hildegard of Bingen: 1098–1179, Abbess of Rupertsberg, mystic, author, playwright, musician, and medico. She was an advisor to kings and popes.

Hilton, Walter: died 1396, English mystic and Augustinian canon. He articulated that faith and feeling are separated by a dark night of the soul.

Hus, John: c.1369–1415, Bohemian Reformer, priest, and later rector of the Charles University in Prague. He was burned at the stake for his reformist writings on July 6, 1415.

James of Vitry: thirteenth-century cleric and author of *Life of St. Mary of Oignies*.

Julian of Norwich: c.1342–c.1413, English mystic. Her writings focused on visions of the Passion of Christ and on the Holy Trinity.

Lull, Ramon: 1235–1315, great writer of spiritual works in Catalan, Latin, and Arabic; missionary to Asia, Armenia, and Africa; was stoned to death by a mob of Arabs in Bougie, North Africa.

Macarius: fourth century, from Alexandria and one of the Egyptian desert fathers. The Homilies ascribed to him came from elsewhere, possibly from early Syrian monasticism.

Maximus the Confessor: 580–662, he understood salvation in Christ as deification.

Nicholas of Cusa: 1401–1464, a cardinal, theologian, and mystical writer.

Origen: c.185–c.254, biblical scholar, exegete, theologian, and writer on spirituality. He was an ascetic. In 250 he was imprisoned and tortured for his faith.

Polycarp: c.69–c.155, bishop of Smyrna in Asia Minor, an important figure in the post-apostolic church. Was martyred at age eighty-eight.

Porete, Marguerite: a Beguine and mystical writer who was condemned by the church and burned at the stake in Paris some time after 1312.

Radewijns, Florentius: 1350–1400, one of the key members of The Brethren of the Common Life. Founded the Windesheim Monastery in 1387.

Rolle, Richard: c.1295–1349, English hermit and mystic. His latter years were spent at Hampole where he gave spiritual guidance to Cistercian nuns.

Ruysbroeck, Jan van: 1293–1381, Flemish mystic, founder of the *Devotio Moderna*.

Shepherd of Hermas: late first century or second century writing.

St. Ailred (Aelred): 1109–67, abbot of Rievaulx, regarded as the English St. Bernard.

A Brief History of Authors and Writings Cited

St. Ambrose: c.339–397, bishop of Milan, famous preacher and defender of Christian orthodoxy.

St. Anselm: c.1033–1109, archbishop of Canterbury, philosopher, theologian, and writer of Christian spirituality.

St. Augustine: 354–430, bishop of Hippo in North Africa and one of the great church fathers. He shaped Western Christianity. Famous for his *Confessions*.

St. Basil: c.330–379, lived for many years as a hermit and later became a bishop of the church. He was one of three Cappadocian fathers.

St. Benedict: c.480–c.550, regarded as the father of Western monasticism and famous for *The Rule of St. Benedict*.

St. Bernard: 1090–1153, Abbot of Clairvaux. He made the Cistercian Order a most influential force in Europe.

St. Brigit of Ireland: c.453–518. Irish saint. Much of her story is shrouded in the mists of history.

St. Catherine of Siena: 1347–80, a Dominican tertiary and visionary whose sanctity inspired many, including the nobility.

St. John Chrysostom: c.347–407, bishop of Constantinople, a great preacher and theologian.

St. Clare: 1194–1253, foundress of the Poor Clares. Becomes abbess of a community founded on the teaching of St. Francis.

St. Clement of Rome: c.96, bishop of Rome, early church father.

St. John Climacus: c.525–606, Abbott of Sinai, ascetic, and writer on the spiritual life.

St. Columbanus: c.540–615, Irish missionary to Gaul and founder of monastic communities.

St. Cyprian: died 258, bishop of Carthage, early church father.

St. Cyril of Alexandria: died 444, the most brilliant representative of the Alexandrian theological tradition.

St. Cyril of Jerusalem: c.315–386. His *Cathecheses* in preparing people for baptism are his chief surviving works.

St. Francis of Assisi: 1181–1226, founder of the Franciscan Order, imitator of Christ, servant to the poor and lover of nature.

St. Gregory of Nyssa: c.335–c.395, bishop of Nyssa, theologian, defender of the Nicaean doctrine of the Trinity.

St. Ignatius: c.35–c.107, bishop of Antioch, early church father.

St. Irenaeus: c.130–c.200, bishop of Lyons. He is regarded as the first great Catholic theologian.

St. Isaac the Syrian (Isaac of Nineveh): died c. 700. Ascetic writer.

St. Jerome: c.342–420, ascetic, priest, secretary to the Pope, biblical scholar, and translator of the Bible into Latin, *The Vulgate*.

St. Justin Martyr: c.100–c.165, one of the early Christian apologists who sought to give a reasoned defense of the Christian faith.

St. Maximus, the Confessor: c.580–662, monk and later abbot of the monastery at Chrysopolis. He was a prolific writer on doctrinal, exegetical, and ascetical subjects.

St. Mechthild of Magdeburg: c.1208–c.1282, a German Beguine and mystic and visionary.

St. Patrick: c.389–c.461, founder of churches and religious communities, known as the apostle to the Irish.

A Brief History of Authors and Writings Cited

St. Perpetua: died 203, an early North African martyr.

St. Edmund Rich (Edmund of Abingdon): c.1180–1240, Archbishop of Canterbury.

St. Simeon, the New Theologian: 949–1022, abbot of the Monastery of St. Mammas in Constantinople and Byzantine medieval mystic.

St. Ephraem of Syrus: c.306–373, biblical exegete and ecclesiastical writer.

St. Thomas Aquinas: 1225–74, possibly the greatest Dominican philosopher and theologian of the Middle Ages. Famous for his *Summa Theologica*.

Tauler, Johannes: c.1300–1361, disciple of Meister Eckhart and Dominican preacher. Had a profound influence on Martin Luther.

Tertullian: c.160–c.220, significant African Church Father and apologist.

Theologia Germanica: written around 1350 possibly from someone within the Friends of God renewal movement.

Theophilus: died 412, the Patriarch of Alexandria and Coptic pope.

Thomas à Kempis: c.1380–1471, belonged to the Brethren of the Common Life and a leading ascetical writer. Famous for his *The Imitation of Christ*.

William of Malmesbury: c.1095–1143, English theologian and historian who spent most of his life at the Monastery at Malmesbury.

William of St. Thierry: c.1085–c.1148, contemplative and theologian.

Author Index

Author Index

Scripture Index